Unity Essentials: Your First Steps in Game Development

Unity Game Development Series

Kameron Hussain and Frahaan Hussain

Published by Sonar Publishing, 2023.

While every precaution has been taken in the preparation of this book, the publisher assumes no responsibility for errors or omissions, or for damages resulting from the use of the information contained herein.

UNITY ESSENTIALS: YOUR FIRST STEPS IN GAME DEVELOPMENT

First edition. December 2, 2023.

Copyright © 2023 Kameron Hussain and Frahaan Hussain.

ISBN: 979-8223838135

Written by Kameron Hussain and Frahaan Hussain.

Chapter 1: Introduction to Unity and Game Development

1.1 The Evolution of Unity in Game Development

Unity has played a pivotal role in shaping the landscape of modern game development. Over the years, it has evolved from a niche game engine into a versatile and powerful platform that caters to a wide range of developers, from indie enthusiasts to AAA studios. Understanding the evolution of Unity provides valuable insights into its capabilities and why it has become a go-to choice for game development.

The Early Days

UNITY WAS FOUNDED IN 2004 by David Helgason, Joachim Ante, and Nicholas Francis as a Mac-exclusive game engine. Back then, its primary focus was on making game development accessible for indie developers and smaller teams. The engine gained early traction due to its user-friendly interface and support for a wide range of platforms.

Expanding Platform Support

AS UNITY GAINED POPULARITY, the development team expanded its focus to include more platforms, making it a cross-platform engine. This move was pivotal because it allowed developers to target various devices, including mobile, consoles, and PC, with a single codebase. This cross-platform approach greatly simplified the development process and reduced the barrier to entry for many developers.

Unity 3D

UNITY'S TRANSITION to 3D game development marked a significant milestone in its evolution. With the release of Unity 2.5 in 2009, the engine introduced comprehensive 3D capabilities, which opened the door to a wider range of game genres and experiences. Developers could now create immersive 3D worlds with ease.

Unity Asset Store

ANOTHER GAME-CHANGER was the introduction of the Unity Asset Store in 2010. This marketplace allowed developers to buy and sell assets, tools, and plugins, fostering a vibrant ecosystem around Unity. It enabled developers to accelerate their workflow by leveraging pre-made assets and components, reducing development time and costs.

Unity 5 and Graphics Enhancements

UNITY 5, RELEASED IN 2015, brought significant improvements to graphics rendering, making it even more attractive for game developers. The introduction of the Unity 5 engine featured Physically Based Shading (PBS), which improved the realism and visual quality of games. This upgrade positioned Unity as a contender in the high-end gaming market.

Unity Technologies' Growth

AS UNITY TECHNOLOGIES continued to invest in its platform, it attracted substantial funding and underwent rapid growth. Unity's user base expanded exponentially, with developers using it for not only games but also for various applications, including simulations, architectural visualization, and more.

Unity in the Present

TODAY, UNITY IS A POWERHOUSE in the game development industry. It is known for its versatility, ease of use, and robust capabilities. Developers use Unity to create games across genres, from 2D indie titles to complex 3D AAA games. The engine's continuous updates and improvements ensure that it remains at the forefront of technology, offering cutting-edge features for developers worldwide.

In conclusion, Unity's journey from its humble beginnings as a Mac-exclusive engine to its current status as a leading game development platform showcases its adaptability and commitment to empowering developers. This evolution has enabled countless creators to bring their visions to life, making Unity a cornerstone of modern game development.

1.2 Understanding the Unity Interface

THE UNITY INTERFACE is the gateway to creating your game worlds and experiences. It's crucial to familiarize yourself with its components and layout to work efficiently. In this section, we'll explore the Unity interface, breaking down its key elements and how they contribute to your game development journey.

The Unity Editor

AT THE HEART OF UNITY is the Unity Editor, the central tool for building, designing, and testing your games. When you launch Unity, you're greeted with the Editor, where you'll spend the majority of your time crafting your games. It provides a visual workspace where you can manipulate your game objects, assets, and scenes.

Main Components of the Unity Editor

1. **Scene View**: This is where you design your game world visually. You can manipulate game objects, adjust their positions, rotations, and scales, and create the layout of your scenes.

2. **Game View**: This view simulates how your game will look and behave when played. It's a real-time preview of your game, allowing you to test and iterate on your designs.

3. **Hierarchy**: The Hierarchy panel lists all the game objects in your scene. You can organize and hierarchically structure your objects here. It's also the place where you can select and manipulate objects.

4. **Project**: The Project panel holds all your project's assets, such as textures, models, scripts, and scenes. You can create folders, import assets, and manage your project's resources from here.

5. **Inspector**: The Inspector panel provides detailed information and properties of the selected game object or asset. You can adjust settings, attach components, and configure behaviors here.

6. **Console**: The Console panel is essential for debugging. It displays messages, warnings, and errors generated by your scripts and the Unity engine. It's a crucial tool for troubleshooting issues in your game.

Customizable Layout

ONE OF UNITY'S STRENGTHS is its flexibility in customizing the layout to suit your workflow. You can move, resize, and dock panels according to your preferences. This allows you to create a workspace tailored to your specific needs, whether you're focusing on 2D game development, 3D modeling, or scripting.

Keyboard Shortcuts

EFFICIENCY IN UNITY often comes down to knowing the right keyboard shortcuts. Unity provides a wide range of shortcuts for various functions, from navigating the scene to opening specific panels. Learning these shortcuts can significantly speed up your workflow. You can find a list of Unity's default shortcuts in the documentation.

Scripting Integration

UNITY'S INTERFACE SEAMLESSLY integrates with its scripting environment. You can write C# scripts directly within the Editor using the integrated MonoDevelop or Visual Studio tools. The scripts you create can be attached to game objects and used to control their behavior and interactions. This close integration simplifies the development process and allows for quick iteration.

Asset Management

UNITY'S INTERFACE ALSO includes tools for asset management. You can import, organize, and preview assets in the Project panel. Unity supports a wide range of asset types, including textures, models, audio files, and more. The ability to drag and drop assets into your scenes makes it easy to build your game worlds.

In summary, understanding the Unity interface is fundamental to effective game development. The Unity Editor, with its various panels and views, serves as your creative workspace. Customization, keyboard shortcuts, scripting integration, and asset management are key elements that empower developers to bring their game ideas to life within Unity's versatile environment.

1.3 Key Concepts in Game Design

GAME DESIGN IS A MULTIFACETED discipline that encompasses various principles and concepts essential for creating engaging and enjoyable experiences. Whether you're a beginner or an experienced developer, understanding these key concepts is crucial for crafting successful games within the Unity engine.

Player Experience

CENTRAL TO GAME DESIGN is the player experience, often referred to as player engagement or immersion. It's the emotional and psychological connection players have with a game. Successful game designers focus on creating experiences that are enjoyable, challenging, and rewarding. This involves understanding the player's motivations, desires, and reactions to different game elements.

Gameplay Mechanics

GAMEPLAY MECHANICS are the rules and systems that define how a game functions. They include movement, combat, resource management, puzzles, and more. Unity provides a framework for implementing these mechanics through scripting and component-based design. Designers must carefully balance and refine gameplay mechanics to ensure they are fun and engaging.

Game Dynamics

GAME DYNAMICS ARE THE patterns of behavior and interactions that emerge from gameplay mechanics. They dictate how players engage with the game world and with each other. For example, in a first-person shooter, the dynamic of players seeking cover, aiming, and shooting creates intense moments of gameplay. Game designers must design dynamics that lead to exciting and dynamic player experiences.

Storytelling and Narrative

STORYTELLING IS A POWERFUL tool in game design. It can provide context, emotional depth, and motivation for players. Unity offers tools for creating interactive narratives through dialogue systems, cutscenes, and scripted events. Effective storytelling in games requires a deep understanding of pacing, character development, and player agency.

Level Design

LEVEL DESIGN INVOLVES creating the physical spaces and environments in which gameplay takes place. Unity's Scene View and asset management tools are essential for level designers. Effective level design balances challenge and progression while considering player navigation and exploration.

User Interface (UI) Design

UI DESIGN IN UNITY is critical for providing players with information and interactions. Designers use Unity's UI components to create menus, HUDs, and on-screen prompts. Good UI design should be intuitive, unobtrusive, and enhance the player experience.

Game Balancing

BALANCING A GAME INVOLVES adjusting various parameters to ensure fairness and enjoyment. Unity allows designers to tweak variables like character speed, enemy difficulty, and resource availability through scripting and real-time adjustments in the Inspector.

Playtesting and Iteration

ITERATIVE DESIGN IS a fundamental concept in game development. It involves creating prototypes, playtesting with real players, and making improvements based on feedback. Unity's rapid development capabilities make it well-suited for this iterative process.

Monetization Strategies

FOR COMMERCIAL GAMES, understanding monetization strategies is crucial. Unity offers integration with ad networks, in-app purchases, and other monetization methods. Designers must balance monetization with player experience to avoid frustrating players.

Accessibility and Inclusivity

GAME DESIGNERS SHOULD prioritize accessibility to ensure that their games are enjoyable for all players, including those with disabilities. Unity provides tools for implementing accessibility features, such as adjustable text size, colorblind modes, and alternative control schemes.

In conclusion, these key concepts in game design are the foundation of creating successful games in Unity. As you delve deeper into game development, you'll find that mastering these principles and applying them effectively will lead to more engaging and enjoyable player experiences.

1.4 Overview of the Game Development Process

GAME DEVELOPMENT IS a complex and multidisciplinary process that involves various stages and tasks. Understanding the overall game development process is essential for planning and executing your projects successfully within the Unity engine. In this section, we'll provide an overview of the typical game development process, from concept to release.

Concept and Idea Generation

THE GAME DEVELOPMENT journey often begins with an idea or concept. This initial phase involves brainstorming and conceptualization. Developers, designers, and artists collaborate to define the game's core concept, genre, mechanics, and overall vision. Unity's prototyping capabilities are valuable during this phase, allowing you to quickly test and refine your ideas.

Pre-production

PRE-PRODUCTION IS THE planning phase of game development. It includes creating design documents, storyboards, and concept art. This phase also involves defining the scope of the game, setting project goals, and establishing a development timeline. Unity's project management features, asset organization, and collaborative tools help streamline pre-production tasks.

Production

THE PRODUCTION PHASE is where the bulk of game development work takes place. It involves creating assets, programming game mechanics, designing levels, and implementing features. Unity's editor, scripting capabilities, and asset management tools play a crucial role during production. Teams collaborate to build the game according to the design and specifications established in pre-production.

Playtesting and Iteration

THROUGHOUT PRODUCTION, playtesting and iteration are ongoing processes. Developers and playtesters evaluate the game's mechanics, balance, and overall experience. Feedback is collected, and necessary adjustments are made. Unity's rapid iteration capabilities, including the ability to quickly modify scenes and scripts, facilitate this process.

Quality Assurance

QUALITY ASSURANCE (QA) is a critical phase where the game is thoroughly tested for bugs, glitches, and performance issues. Unity's debugging tools and profiling features are essential for identifying and resolving issues. QA ensures that the game meets high-quality standards and is ready for release.

Optimization

OPTIMIZATION IS THE process of fine-tuning the game's performance. Developers optimize graphics, code, and assets to ensure the game runs smoothly on various platforms. Unity's performance profiling and optimization tools help identify bottlenecks and resource-intensive elements that need improvement.

Monetization and Business Model Implementation

FOR COMMERCIAL GAMES, monetization strategies are integrated during this phase. Unity offers tools for incorporating advertisements, in-app purchases, and other revenue streams. Developers must strike a balance between monetization and the player experience to achieve financial success.

Marketing and Promotion

MARKETING AND PROMOTION are essential for attracting players to your game. This phase involves creating marketing materials, trailers, press releases, and engaging with potential players on social media. Unity provides analytics tools to track user engagement and measure the effectiveness of marketing campaigns.

Distribution and Launch

UNITY OFFERS VARIOUS deployment options, allowing developers to publish their games on multiple platforms, including PC, console, mobile, and VR. The distribution phase includes preparing the game for release on platforms such as Steam, App Store, or Google Play. Developers must meet platform-specific requirements and adhere to submission guidelines.

Post-launch Support and Updates

AFTER THE GAME IS RELEASED, ongoing support and updates are crucial for maintaining player engagement. Unity's live-ops tools and analytics help developers monitor player behavior and gather feedback. Regular updates, bug fixes, and new content keep the game fresh and appealing to the player base.

Community Engagement

BUILDING AND ENGAGING with a player community is essential for long-term success. Unity provides features for creating forums, community hubs, and player feedback channels. Engaging with players, addressing their concerns, and listening to their suggestions can foster a dedicated player community.

In summary, the game development process is a structured journey that encompasses concept generation, pre-production, production, playtesting, QA, optimization, monetization, marketing, distribution, post-launch support, and community engagement. Unity's versatile tools and features support developers at every stage of this process, making it a valuable platform for game development.

1.5 Setting Up Your First Unity Project

GETTING STARTED WITH Unity requires setting up your first project. In this section, we'll walk you through the steps to create a new Unity project, explore the project structure, and familiarize you with the basic elements you'll encounter.

Installing Unity

BEFORE YOU CAN CREATE a Unity project, you need to install the Unity Editor on your computer. Unity offers both free and paid versions, with the free version providing extensive capabilities for most game development needs.

1. Visit the Unity website (https://unity.com/).
2. Download the Unity Hub, which is a management tool for Unity projects.
3. Install Unity Hub and sign in with your Unity ID or create one if you don't have an account.

4. Once signed in, go to the "Installs" section and choose a Unity version to install. Unity Hub allows you to install and manage multiple Unity versions.

Creating a New Project

ONCE UNITY IS INSTALLED, you can start by creating a new project.

1. Open Unity Hub.
2. Click the "New" button to create a new project.
3. Choose a template or select "3D" or "2D" depending on the type of game you want to create.
4. Provide a name and location for your project's folder.
5. Configure other project settings like the render pipeline and template. You can leave most settings at their default values for now.

Unity Interface Overview

AFTER CREATING YOUR project, you'll be greeted with the Unity Editor interface. Let's briefly overview some of the key elements:

- **Scene View**: This is where you design your game world visually. You can navigate, place objects, and set up your scenes here.

- **Game View**: It shows a real-time preview of your game, allowing you to see how it will appear to players.

- **Hierarchy**: The Hierarchy panel displays a list of all the objects in your current scene. You can select and organize objects here.

- **Project**: The Project panel contains all your project assets, including textures, models, scripts, and scenes. You can organize assets into folders and import new ones here.

- **Inspector**: The Inspector panel displays the properties and components of the currently selected object in the Hierarchy or Project panel. You can modify object properties and attach scripts here.

- **Toolbar**: The Toolbar at the top provides quick access to common functions like saving, playing, and switching between 2D and 3D modes.

Creating and Manipulating Game Objects

IN UNITY, GAME ELEMENTS are represented as game objects. You can create game objects in various ways:

1. Right-click in the Hierarchy panel and choose "Create Empty" to create an empty game object.
2. Right-click and select other predefined game objects like cubes, spheres, or lights.
3. Import 3D models or assets from external software or Unity's Asset Store.

You can manipulate game objects in the Scene View by selecting and dragging them. The Inspector panel allows you to modify their properties, add components, and attach scripts.

Saving Your Project

UNITY AUTOMATICALLY saves your project as you work, but it's a good practice to save manually, especially before making significant changes. To save your project:

1. Click "File" in the menu.
2. Select "Save" or "Save As" to specify a new location or name for your project if needed.

Building and Running Your Project

TO TEST AND RUN YOUR project:

1. Click the "File" menu.
2. Choose "Build Settings."
3. Select your target platform (e.g., PC, Mac, Android, iOS).
4. Click "Build" to generate an executable or deployable file.
5. Run the generated file to play your game.

Getting Started with Scripting

UNITY USES C# FOR SCRIPTING. You can create and attach scripts to game objects to control their behavior. To create a script:

1. In the Project panel, right-click and select "Create > C# Script."
2. Give your script a name and double-click it to open it in your chosen code editor (e.g., Visual Studio or Visual Studio Code).

Unity provides a range of scripting functions and APIs to interact with game objects and the engine. You can use these to implement game mechanics, controls, and interactions.

In conclusion, setting up your first Unity project is the initial step on your game development journey. It involves installing Unity, creating a new project, understanding the Unity interface, creating and manipulating game objects, saving your project, and getting started with scripting. As you progress, you'll delve deeper into these aspects and explore more advanced features to bring your game ideas to life.

Chapter 2: Exploring Basic Unity Operations

2.1 Navigating the Unity Editor

Navigating the Unity Editor is a fundamental skill for game developers. In this section, we will explore the key aspects of navigating the Unity Editor, which is your primary workspace for creating, editing, and managing Unity projects.

The Unity Interface

UPON OPENING THE UNITY Editor, you will be greeted with a user-friendly interface. Let's take a closer look at its main components:

1. **Scene View**: The Scene View is where you design and edit your game world visually. You can manipulate objects, adjust their positions, rotations, and scales, and create the layout of your scenes. You can also switch between 2D and 3D views depending on your project's needs.
2. **Game View**: The Game View provides a real-time preview of how your game will appear and behave when played. It's a crucial tool for testing and iterating on your game's visuals and interactions.
3. **Hierarchy**: The Hierarchy panel lists all the game objects present in the current scene. You can organize these objects hierarchically, making it easier to manage complex scenes. You can also select and manipulate objects directly from the Hierarchy.

4. **Project**: The Project panel stores all your project's assets, including scripts, textures, models, audio files, and scenes. You can organize your assets into folders and create new assets or import existing ones from external sources.

5. **Inspector**: The Inspector panel provides detailed information and properties of the selected game object or asset. You can use it to adjust settings, attach components, and configure behaviors. The Inspector is where you fine-tune the attributes of your game elements.

6. **Toolbar**: The Toolbar at the top of the Unity Editor provides quick access to various functions, including saving your project, playing the game, pausing, and other common tasks. It's a handy way to control your workflow.

Navigating the Scene View

THE SCENE VIEW IS WHERE you'll spend much of your time designing your game. Here are some essential navigation controls and tips:

• **Orbit**: Hold down the right mouse button and drag to orbit around the selected object or the center of the scene.

• **Pan**: Hold down the middle mouse button or the Alt key while dragging with the left mouse button to pan the view.

• **Zoom**: Use the scroll wheel to zoom in and out of the scene view. You can also use the scroll wheel while holding down the Alt key for more precise zooming.

• **Framing**: To focus on a specific object or area, select it in the Hierarchy panel and press the "F" key. Unity will frame the selected object, centering it in the view.

- **Orthographic/Perspective**: You can toggle between orthographic (2D) and perspective (3D) views using the buttons at the top of the Scene View. This is useful when working on 2D or 3D projects.

Saving Your Scene

UNITY AUTOMATICALLY saves your scenes as you work. However, it's essential to manually save your scene when you reach a significant milestone or before making major changes. To save your scene:

1. Click "File" in the menu.
2. Select "Save Scene" or "Save Scene As" to specify a new name or location for your scene if needed.

Navigating the Unity Editor and mastering the Scene View is crucial for effective game development. It's where you'll create and manipulate the elements that make up your game world. As you become more familiar with Unity's interface and navigation controls, you'll gain confidence in bringing your game ideas to life.

2.2 Working with Game Objects and Components

IN UNITY, GAME OBJECTS are the building blocks of your scenes, and components define their behavior and appearance. Understanding how to work with game objects and components is essential for creating interactive and visually appealing games. In this section, we'll delve into the basics of creating, managing, and customizing game objects and their components.

Creating Game Objects

CREATING A GAME OBJECT in Unity is a straightforward process. Here's how you can do it:

1. **Hierarchy Panel**: In the Hierarchy panel, right-click and select "Create Empty" to create an empty game object. This is often used as a parent for other objects or as a placeholder in your scene.
2. **Predefined Game Objects**: Unity provides a range of predefined game objects you can add to your scene, such as cubes, spheres, lights, cameras, and more. Right-click in the Hierarchy panel, choose "3D Object" or "2D Object," and select the desired object type.
3. **Import Assets**: You can also create game objects by importing 3D models, textures, or other assets. These imported assets are automatically converted into game objects.

Transform Component

EVERY GAME OBJECT IN Unity has a Transform component by default. The Transform component defines the object's position, rotation, and scale in the scene. Here are some important properties of the Transform component:

• **Position**: Specifies the object's position in the scene as X, Y, and Z coordinates.

• **Rotation**: Determines the object's orientation in degrees along the X, Y, and Z axes.

• **Scale**: Sets the object's size along the X, Y, and Z axes, allowing you to resize objects.

Adding Components

COMPONENTS ARE SCRIPTS and other assets that provide functionality to game objects. You can add components to a game object to make it interactive, give it physical properties, render it with materials, and more. Here's how to add components:

1. **Inspector Panel**: Select a game object in the Hierarchy panel, and in the Inspector panel, click the "Add Component" button. You can then search for and select the desired component to attach it to the game object.

2. **Context Menu**: Right-click on a game object in the Hierarchy panel, hover over "3D Object" or "2D Object," and you'll see a list of components you can add. Selecting one will attach it to the object.

3. **Scripts**: If you have a custom script, you can attach it to a game object by dragging and dropping the script file from the Project panel onto the game object in the Hierarchy or Scene view.

Customizing Components

AFTER ADDING A COMPONENT to a game object, you can customize its properties in the Inspector panel. For example, if you add a Rigidbody component to a game object, you can adjust parameters like mass, drag, and gravity scale. If you attach a script, you can edit the script's variables and parameters in the Inspector.

Parenting and Hierarchical Structure

GAME OBJECTS CAN BE organized hierarchically in Unity. You can make a game object the child of another by dragging it onto the parent object in the Hierarchy panel. This hierarchical structure is useful for grouping objects and controlling their transformations as a unit. When you move, rotate, or scale a parent object, its children will also be affected.

Scripting and Interactions

COMPONENTS CAN BE SCRIPTED to provide custom behavior to game objects. You can write scripts in C# and attach them to game objects. These scripts can respond to user input, trigger events, update the game state, and perform various actions to make your game interactive.

For example, you can write a script that makes a character move when the player presses the arrow keys or that plays a sound when the player interacts with an object.

```csharp
using UnityEngine;

public class MoveCharacter : MonoBehaviour

{

public float speed = 5f;

void Update()

{

float horizontalInput = Input.GetAxis("Horizontal");

float verticalInput = Input.GetAxis("Vertical");

Vector3 movement = new Vector3(horizontalInput, 0f, verticalInput) * speed * Time.deltaTime;

transform.Translate(movement);

}
```

}

In this script, we move the game object based on user input.

Understanding how to work with game objects and components is essential for creating dynamic and interactive Unity scenes. By mastering these fundamentals, you'll have the foundation to build complex gameplay mechanics and intricate game worlds.

2.3 Introduction to Unity's Asset Store

UNITY'S ASSET STORE is a valuable resource for game developers, providing a vast library of assets, tools, and services to enhance your game development projects. In this section, we'll introduce you to the Unity Asset Store, its benefits, and how to use it effectively in your Unity projects.

What is the Unity Asset Store?

THE UNITY ASSET STORE is an online marketplace integrated directly into the Unity Editor. It offers a wide variety of assets and resources to help game developers in various aspects of game creation, including 3D models, 2D sprites, animations, scripts, shaders, audio clips, and more. These assets can significantly accelerate your development process, whether you're a solo developer or part of a team.

Benefits of Using the Unity Asset Store

1. Time Savings:

- Access to ready-made assets can save you significant development time.

- Avoid reinventing the wheel by using existing solutions for common tasks.

2. High-Quality Assets:

- Many assets on the store are created by professional artists, developers, and studios, ensuring high quality.

- User reviews and ratings help you identify the best assets.

3. Asset Diversity:

- Find assets for various genres, styles, and project needs, from realistic to stylized, 2D to 3D, and more.

- Discover assets for different platforms and technologies.

4. Community Support:

- Join a community of developers who share their knowledge and creations.

- Learn from other developers' assets and code.

5. Collaboration:

- Collaborate with other developers by using their assets in your projects or contributing your creations to the store.

Accessing the Unity Asset Store

TO ACCESS THE UNITY Asset Store:

1. Open Unity Editor.
2. In the top menu, click on "Window" and select "Asset Store."

This will open the Asset Store window within Unity.

Navigating the Asset Store

THE ASSET STORE WINDOW allows you to browse, search, and download assets. Here are some key features:

1. Search Bar:

- Use the search bar to find specific assets or browse by category.

2. Categories:

- Assets are organized into categories such as 3D models, 2D sprites, scripts, audio, and more.

3. Asset Details:

- Click on an asset to view its details, including a description, screenshots, reviews, and related assets.

4. Downloading Assets:

- To download an asset, click the "Download" button on the asset's page. Unity will automatically import the asset into your project.

5. My Assets:

- Under "My Assets," you can manage the assets you've downloaded, update them, and import them into your scenes.

Importing Assets into Your Project

ONCE YOU'VE DOWNLOADED an asset from the Unity Asset Store, it's automatically imported into your Unity project. You can find it in the Project panel under the "Assets" folder. From there, you can drag and drop assets into your scenes, use them in scripts, or customize them as needed.

Purchasing Assets

WHILE THERE ARE MANY free assets available on the Asset Store, premium assets may require a purchase. To purchase an asset:

1. Click the "Buy" button on the asset's page.
2. Follow the prompts to complete the purchase, which may involve creating a Unity ID if you haven't already.

Once purchased, the asset will be available in your "My Assets" section for download and use in your projects.

Asset Licensing

PAY ATTENTION TO THE licensing terms of assets you download, especially if you plan to use them in commercial projects. Some assets may have specific usage restrictions or require attribution. Always review and adhere to the asset's license terms.

The Unity Asset Store is a valuable tool for game developers, offering a wide range of assets and resources to enhance your Unity projects. By leveraging the Asset Store effectively, you can save time, access high-quality assets, and enhance the quality and efficiency of your game development endeavors.

2.4 Basic Scripting in C

UNITY USES C# AS ITS primary programming language for scripting game behavior. In this section, we'll introduce you to the basics of C# scripting in Unity, including creating scripts, attaching them to game objects, and writing simple code to control game behavior.

Creating a New Script

TO CREATE A NEW C# script in Unity:

1. In the Unity Editor, go to the "Assets" menu.
2. Select "Create" and then "C# Script."
3. Give your script a name, and Unity will create the script file in your project's "Assets" folder.

Attaching Scripts to Game Objects

SCRIPTS DEFINE THE behavior of game objects in Unity. To attach a script to a game object:

1. Select the game object you want to attach the script to in the Hierarchy panel or Scene view.
2. In the Inspector panel, click the "Add Component" button.
3. Type the name of the script you created in the search bar and select it.

The script is now attached to the selected game object, and you can edit it by double-clicking on the script file in the Project panel.

Understanding the MonoBehaviour Class

IN UNITY, SCRIPTS THAT control game objects inherit from the MonoBehaviour class. This class provides various methods that Unity calls automatically at specific points during a game object's lifecycle. You can override these methods to add custom functionality to your game objects.

Here are some commonly used MonoBehaviour methods:

- Start(): Called once when the script is initialized, typically used for setup.

- Update(): Called every frame and is often used for regular updates, such as player input processing and object movement.

- FixedUpdate(): Called at fixed time intervals and is suitable for physics-related calculations.

- LateUpdate(): Called after all Update() methods, useful for camera or procedural animation adjustments.

- OnCollisionEnter(): Called when a collision occurs with another object.

- OnTriggerEnter(): Called when a trigger event is triggered by another object.

Writing Your First Script

LET'S CREATE A SIMPLE script to understand the basics of C# scripting in Unity. This script will make a game object rotate continuously when the game starts.

```csharp
using UnityEngine;

public class SimpleRotation : MonoBehaviour
{
    public float rotationSpeed = 30f;

    void Start()
    {
        // This code runs when the game starts.
    }

    void Update()
    {
        // Rotate the game object continuously.
        transform.Rotate(Vector3.up * rotationSpeed * Time.deltaTime);
    }
```

```
}
```

In this script:

- We declare a public variable rotationSpeed to control the rotation speed of the game object.

- In the Update() method, we continuously rotate the game object around its Y-axis using transform.Rotate().

Accessing Components

YOU CAN ACCESS AND modify other components attached to the same game object using the GetComponent method. For example, you can access a Rigidbody component and change its properties:

```
Rigidbody rb = GetComponent<Rigidbody>();
```

```
rb.velocity = new Vector3(1f, 0f, 0f);
```

Debugging with Debug.Log()

TO DEBUG YOUR SCRIPTS and inspect variable values, you can use Debug.Log() to print messages to the Unity console:

```
void Start()

{

Debug.Log("Script initialized.");
}

void Update()

{
```

```
float currentRotation = transform.rotation.eulerAngles.y;

Debug.Log("Current Rotation: " + currentRotation);

}
```

These messages can help you understand the flow of your script and diagnose issues.

C# scripting is a fundamental skill in Unity game development. By creating and attaching scripts to game objects, you can control their behavior, create interactions, and bring your game ideas to life. As you become more proficient in scripting, you'll be able to develop complex game mechanics and systems.

2.5 Scene Management and Organization

EFFECTIVE SCENE MANAGEMENT and organization are crucial aspects of Unity game development. In this section, we'll explore how to create, manage, and optimize scenes to build cohesive and engaging game experiences.

What is a Scene?

IN UNITY, A SCENE IS a container that holds all the game objects, assets, and settings for a particular part of your game. Scenes allow you to divide your game into different levels, menus, or segments, making it easier to work on and manage specific parts of your project.

Creating and Saving Scenes

TO CREATE A NEW SCENE in Unity:

1.   Click on "File" in the menu.

2. Select "New Scene."
3. You can also use the keyboard shortcut Ctrl + N (Windows) or Command + N (Mac) to create a new scene quickly.

After creating a scene, you should save it:

1. Click on "File" in the menu.
2. Select "Save Scene."
3. Choose a location and provide a name for the scene.

Switching Between Scenes

YOU CAN SWITCH BETWEEN different scenes in Unity to work on various parts of your project. To switch between scenes:

1. Click on "File" in the menu.
2. Select "Open Scene."
3. Choose the scene you want to open from the list.

Scene Hierarchy

THE HIERARCHY PANEL displays a list of all the game objects in the current scene. It helps you organize and manage the elements in your scene. You can create parent-child relationships between game objects to represent their hierarchical structure. This is useful for organizing complex scenes and managing transformations.

Scene View

THE SCENE VIEW IS WHERE you visually design your scenes. You can place, move, rotate, and scale game objects in this view. Scene View also allows you to set up cameras, lights, and visual effects. It's essential for creating the visual layout of your game.

Building Scenes for Gameplay

WHEN BUILDING SCENES for gameplay, consider the following:

1. Level Design:

- Plan the layout and challenges of your levels.

- Use the Scene View to create and arrange obstacles, enemies, and interactive elements.

2. Lighting and Environment:

- Set up lighting to create the desired mood and atmosphere.

- Add environmental details like terrain, trees, and props.

3. Cameras:

- Configure cameras to provide the player with the best perspective.

- Use multiple cameras for different gameplay scenarios.

4. Scripting:

- Attach scripts to game objects to control behavior and interactions.

- Write code to manage game progression, character movement, and AI behavior.

5. Testing:

- Regularly playtest your scenes to ensure they are fun, balanced, and free of bugs.

- Adjust and iterate based on player feedback.

Scene Optimization

OPTIMIZING YOUR SCENES is essential for maintaining good performance in your game. Here are some optimization techniques:

1. Occlusion Culling:

- Use occlusion culling to hide objects that are not visible to the camera, reducing rendering overhead.

2. Level of Detail (LOD):

- Implement LOD systems for complex models to reduce the number of polygons rendered at a distance.

3. Scene Batching:

- Combine static objects into batches to reduce draw calls and improve rendering performance.

4. Asset Optimization:

- Compress textures and models to reduce memory usage.

- Remove unused assets from your project to reduce build size.

5. Scene Organization:

- Keep scenes organized by using proper naming conventions and hierarchy structures.

- Use layers and tags to categorize game objects for easier management.

Loading and Unloading Scenes

IN UNITY, YOU CAN LOAD and unload scenes dynamically to create seamless transitions between levels or game sections. You can use the following code to load a new scene:

```csharp
using UnityEngine;

using UnityEngine.SceneManagement;

public class SceneLoader : MonoBehaviour

{

public void LoadNextScene()

{

int currentSceneIndex = SceneManager.GetActiveScene().buildIndex;

SceneManager.LoadScene(currentSceneIndex + 1);

}

}
```

This script loads the next scene in the build index when called.

```csharp
SceneManager.LoadScene("SceneName");
```

You can also load scenes by name, where "SceneName" is the name of the scene you want to load.

Managing scenes effectively is essential for creating organized, performant, and engaging games in Unity. By understanding how scenes work and optimizing their content, you can create a smooth and immersive player experience as you progress in your game development journey.

Chapter 3: 3D Modeling and Environment Design

3.1 Basics of 3D Modeling in Unity

3D modeling is a fundamental skill in game development, allowing you to create realistic or stylized game environments, characters, and objects. In Unity, you can work with 3D models to build immersive game worlds. In this section, we'll explore the basics of 3D modeling in Unity, including creating, importing, and manipulating 3D models.

Understanding 3D Models

IN UNITY, A 3D MODEL is a digital representation of an object or character in three-dimensional space. These models are created using specialized software known as 3D modeling software. The most common file formats for 3D models in Unity are FBX, OBJ, and DAE (Collada).

Creating 3D Models

WHILE UNITY IS NOT a 3D modeling software, it provides some basic modeling tools that allow you to create simple shapes and objects within the editor. You can create primitive shapes like cubes, spheres, and cylinders using the "GameObject" menu:

1. Go to "GameObject" in the menu.
2. Select "3D Object" and choose the desired shape.

These primitive objects can serve as placeholders or be combined to create more complex structures. However, for detailed 3D modeling, it's recommended to use dedicated modeling software like Blender, Maya, or 3ds Max.

Importing 3D Models

TO IMPORT 3D MODELS into Unity:

1. Place the 3D model file (e.g., .FBX) in your project's "Assets" folder or a subfolder.
2. Unity will automatically import the model and associated textures.

After importing, the 3D model appears in the Project panel, and you can drag it into your scene.

Manipulating 3D Models

IN UNITY'S SCENE VIEW, you can select and manipulate 3D models using the Transform tools. Here are some common operations:

- **Move**: Click and drag the arrows on the model to move it along the X, Y, or Z axis.

- **Rotate**: Click and drag the circles around the model to rotate it.

- **Scale**: Click and drag the cubes at the edges of the model to resize it.

You can also adjust the position, rotation, and scale values in the Inspector panel to precisely control the model's transformation.

Materials and Textures

3D MODELS CAN APPEAR visually appealing with the use of materials and textures. Materials define the visual properties of a model, such as its color, shininess, and transparency. Textures are images applied to a model's surface to add details like patterns or wear and tear.

To create and apply materials in Unity:

1. Select the 3D model in the Hierarchy or Scene view.
2. In the Inspector panel, click "Add Component" and search for "Material." Create a new material.
3. Adjust the material's properties, such as color and texture, by selecting it in the Project panel and making changes in the Inspector.

Rigging and Animation

FOR ANIMATED 3D CHARACTERS or objects, rigging is essential. Rigging involves adding a skeleton or bone structure to the model, allowing it to be animated. In Unity, you can create and manage animations through the Animation window. Unity also supports retargeting animations between different models.

Creating 3D models and integrating them into your Unity project is a foundational step in game development. Whether you're building a realistic world or a stylized environment, understanding the basics of 3D modeling and Unity's tools will help you bring your game's visuals to life.

3.2 Creating Realistic Game Environments

CREATING REALISTIC game environments in Unity is a complex and rewarding task that involves various aspects such as modeling, texturing, lighting, and optimization. Realistic environments can immerse players in your game and enhance the overall gaming experience. In this section, we'll delve into the key principles and techniques for crafting realistic game environments.

Planning and Conceptualization

BEFORE YOU START CREATING a realistic game environment, it's crucial to plan and conceptualize your vision. Consider the following:

- **Theme and Style**: Define the theme and style of your environment, whether it's a futuristic city, a medieval castle, or a natural landscape. Understanding the visual direction is essential.

- **Reference and Research**: Gather reference images, videos, and materials related to your environment. Research real-world locations or artistic inspirations to guide your design.

- **Layout and Flow**: Plan the layout of your environment. Consider how players will navigate through it, where key points of interest will be, and how the environment serves your game's narrative or gameplay.

Terrain Design

FOR OUTDOOR ENVIRONMENTS or landscapes, Unity offers a Terrain system that allows you to create detailed and realistic terrain features like mountains, hills, valleys, and rivers. You can sculpt the terrain, paint textures, and add foliage for a lifelike appearance.

The Terrain system also supports the use of heightmaps and splatmaps, which enable you to control elevation and texture distribution across the terrain. You can import custom heightmaps and texture maps to achieve specific terrain designs.

Modeling and Asset Integration

TO POPULATE YOUR ENVIRONMENT with 3D models, you can use assets from the Unity Asset Store or create custom models in external 3D modeling software. Ensure that models are optimized for performance by using efficient polygon counts and appropriate LOD (Level of Detail) models.

Unity's Prefab system allows you to create reusable game objects with predefined components and settings. You can create prefabs for trees, rocks, buildings, and other objects to quickly populate your environment.

Texture Mapping and Materials

REALISTIC ENVIRONMENTS rely heavily on high-quality textures and materials. Unity's Material system allows you to create materials that simulate various surfaces, including metal, wood, stone, and more. You can also use Physically Based Rendering (PBR) shaders to achieve realistic lighting and reflections.

To enhance realism, consider using normal maps, specular maps, and occlusion maps in your materials. These maps add fine details and interact with lighting to create convincing surfaces.

Lighting and Shadows

LIGHTING PLAYS A PIVOTAL role in creating a realistic environment. Unity's lighting system allows you to use both real-time and baked lighting techniques. Real-time lighting is dynamic and responds to changes in the game world, while baked lighting is precomputed and offers better performance.

To achieve realism, pay attention to the following lighting aspects:

- **Directional Lighting**: Use directional lights to simulate sunlight or moonlight. Adjust the color and intensity to match the time of day.

- **Point and Spot Lights**: Use point and spot lights for localized light sources like lamps or torches.

- **Global Illumination**: Enable global illumination for realistic indirect lighting and accurate reflections.

- **Light Probes**: Use light probes to capture lighting information in dynamic environments.

- **Shadows**: Configure shadow settings to cast realistic shadows from objects and characters.

Particle Systems and Visual Effects

PARTICLE SYSTEMS CAN add dynamic and immersive elements to your environment. You can use particle systems for effects like rain, fire, smoke, and sparks. Unity provides a robust Particle System component that allows you to customize particle behavior, size, color, and emission patterns.

Visual effects, such as post-processing effects, bloom, and color grading, can also enhance the realism of your game environment. Unity's Post-Processing Stack makes it easy to apply cinematic effects to your camera.

Optimization and Performance

WHILE CREATING A REALISTIC environment, it's essential to optimize performance to ensure smooth gameplay. Here are some optimization tips:

- **Level of Detail (LOD)**: Implement LOD models for distant objects to reduce polygon count.

- **Occlusion Culling**: Use occlusion culling to hide objects that are not visible to the camera.

- **Texture Compression**: Compress textures to reduce memory usage.

- **Baking**: Bake lighting and reflection probes for improved performance.

Iteration and Testing

CREATING A REALISTIC environment is an iterative process. Continuously test your environment, gather feedback, and make improvements. Test how the environment performs on various hardware configurations to ensure a broad audience can enjoy your game.

Crafting realistic game environments in Unity requires a combination of artistic skills, technical knowledge, and attention to detail. By following these principles and techniques, you can create immersive and visually stunning game worlds that captivate players.

3.3 Lighting and Texturing Techniques

LIGHTING AND TEXTURING are crucial elements in creating immersive and visually appealing game environments in Unity. Properly implementing lighting and texturing techniques can transform a bland environment into a realistic and engaging world. In this section, we'll explore various lighting and texturing techniques you can use in Unity to enhance the visual quality of your game environments.

Lighting Techniques

1. Real-time Lighting:

- Unity provides real-time lighting solutions that simulate the interaction of light with objects in your scene. Real-time lights can cast dynamic shadows and affect the environment in real-time, enhancing realism.

- Point lights, spotlights, and directional lights are common real-time light sources. Directional lights are often used to simulate sunlight, while point and spotlights are used for localized lighting effects.

- To use real-time lighting, you need to consider its impact on performance, especially in scenes with many dynamic objects and lights.

2. Baked Lighting:

- Baked lighting is precomputed and is suitable for scenes with static or mostly static objects. It can significantly improve performance because Unity calculates lighting and shadows offline.

• To use baked lighting, you need to mark objects as static and set up lighting probes and lightmaps. You can bake lighting using the Unity Editor's Lighting window.

• Baked lighting is ideal for architectural visualization, static environments, and scenes with a fixed time of day.

3. Global Illumination (GI):

• Global Illumination simulates how light bounces off surfaces and affects the overall lighting in a scene. Unity's Progressive Lightmapper is an advanced GI solution that provides high-quality global illumination effects.

• GI enhances realism by considering indirect lighting, reflections, and color bleeding. It's particularly useful for achieving realistic and believable lighting scenarios.

• However, GI calculations can be computationally expensive, so use it judiciously in your scenes.

4. HDRP and URP:

• Unity offers two rendering pipelines: High Definition Render Pipeline (HDRP) and Universal Render Pipeline (URP). HDRP is designed for high-end graphics and realism, while URP is optimized for performance and supports a wide range of platforms.

• HDRP features advanced rendering techniques like ray tracing, volumetric lighting, and improved post-processing effects, making it ideal for creating highly detailed and visually stunning environments.

• URP is more lightweight but still provides excellent visual quality. It's suitable for a broader range of projects, including mobile and VR/AR applications.

Texturing Techniques

1. PBR Texturing:

• Physically Based Rendering (PBR) is a texturing technique that simulates how materials interact with light in the real world. PBR materials are defined by attributes such as albedo (diffuse color), metallic, roughness, and normal maps.

• Unity's Standard Shader and HDRP's Lit Shader support PBR materials, making it easy to create realistic surfaces.

• Ensure that your textures are calibrated to match PBR workflows for consistent and physically accurate results.

2. Texture Mapping:

• Proper texture mapping is essential for realistic environments. UV mapping ensures that textures are applied correctly to 3D models. You can use 3D modeling software or Unity's UV mapping tools to create UV layouts.

- Pay attention to texture resolution and quality. High-resolution textures can make your environment more detailed, but be mindful of memory usage.

3. *Normal and Bump Maps:*

- Normal maps and bump maps add surface details to objects without increasing their geometry. They simulate bumps, creases, and imperfections on surfaces, enhancing the perception of depth and realism.

- Unity supports both normal maps and bump maps. Normal maps are RGB-encoded, while bump maps are grayscale.

4. *Parallax Mapping:*

- Parallax mapping is an advanced technique that gives the illusion of depth by displacing pixels based on height information in a texture. This technique can make surfaces like brick walls and cobblestones appear three-dimensional.

- Unity provides shaders that support parallax mapping for enhanced realism.

5. *Detail Textures:*

- Detail textures are used to add small-scale surface details that break up the monotony of large, flat surfaces. They can represent dirt, stains, or fine patterns.

- Unity's Standard Shader and HDRP's Lit Shader allow you to blend detail textures with base textures for added realism.

6. Texture Tiling and Blending:

- Properly tiling and blending textures is crucial for seamless transitions between different surfaces. Unity's Terrain system, for instance, allows you to blend textures based on height or slope.

- Use alpha masks to control the blending of textures, ensuring a smooth and natural transition.

7. Shader Graphs:

- Unity's Shader Graph enables you to create custom shaders and effects without writing code. You can use Shader Graph to experiment with unique texturing and shading techniques.

- Shader Graph allows for the creation of visually stunning and customized materials for your environment.

INCORPORATING ADVANCED lighting and texturing techniques into your Unity environments can elevate the visual quality of your game and immerse players in a more realistic and captivating world. Experiment with different techniques and shaders to achieve the desired visual effects for your specific project.

3.4 Implementing Skyboxes and Weather Effects

SKYBOXES AND WEATHER effects are essential elements in creating immersive game environments that can transport players to different worlds and atmospheres. In this section, we'll explore how to implement skyboxes and weather effects in Unity to enhance the ambiance and realism of your game environments.

Skyboxes

A SKYBOX IS A TEXTURED cube that surrounds your entire scene, creating the illusion of a distant sky or horizon. Unity allows you to use skyboxes to set the mood, time of day, or location of your game environment. Here's how you can implement skyboxes in Unity:

1. Skybox Materials:

- Unity uses Skybox Materials to render the sky. You can create a new Skybox Material by right-clicking in the Project panel, selecting "Create," and then choosing "Material." Set the Shader of the material to "Skybox/Procedural" or "Skybox/Cubemap."

- Procedural skyboxes are generated in real-time based on parameters like sun intensity, fog, and cloudiness. Cubemap skyboxes use a 6-sided cube texture to define the sky's appearance.

2. Assigning Skybox Material:

• To assign a Skybox Material to your scene, go to the "Window" menu, select "Rendering," and choose "Lighting." In the Lighting window, navigate to the "Scene" tab and find the "Skybox Material" section. Drag your Skybox Material into the "Skybox Material" field.

3. Customizing Skyboxes:

• Unity provides options to customize skyboxes further. For procedural skyboxes, you can adjust parameters like sun size, sun latitude, and atmosphere thickness to achieve different looks and times of day.

• Cubemap skyboxes allow you to use panoramic images as sky textures. You can create or import custom cubemaps to represent various sky conditions.

4. Dynamic Skyboxes:

• To create dynamic day-night cycles or weather effects, you can animate the Skybox Material's properties over time. For example, you can change the color of the sky, sun position, and cloud cover to simulate different weather conditions.

Weather Effects

WEATHER EFFECTS ADD realism and variety to your game environments. Here are some common weather effects and how to implement them in Unity:

1. *Rain:*

- Rain can be achieved by creating particle systems that spawn raindrops. Unity's Particle System component allows you to customize raindrop appearance, density, and movement.

- You can control when the rain starts and stops using scripting. Adjust the particle system's emission rate to simulate rainfall intensity.

2. *Snow:*

- Snow is similar to rain but with different particle properties. You can create snowfall by using a particle system and modifying its settings to create snowflakes.

- Implementing accumulation of snow on objects requires additional scripting to detect surfaces and gradually build up snow layers.

3. *Fog:*

- Fog is a great way to create a mysterious or atmospheric feel in your environment. Unity's built-in fog system allows you to control fog density and color.

- You can animate fog settings to create dynamic scenes where fog thickens or disperses over time.

4. Lightning and Thunder:

- Lightning and thunder effects can add drama to your game's weather. Create lightning bolts as particle systems or by animating the intensity of point lights.

- To synchronize lightning with thunder, you can use audio cues or visual effects.

5. Wind:

- Wind affects objects like trees, flags, and grass. You can use Unity's Wind Zone component to simulate wind forces on objects.

- Animate objects' movement and deformation in response to wind to make your environment feel dynamic and alive.

6. Dynamic Weather Systems:

- To create realistic weather systems that transition naturally, you can use Unity's scripting capabilities. Implement weather patterns that change over time, affecting skybox, lighting, and weather effects.

- Consider using state machines or timeline animations to manage weather transitions and variations.

Performance Considerations

IMPLEMENTING WEATHER effects can impact performance, particularly on lower-end devices. To maintain good performance:

- Use LOD (Level of Detail) models for objects affected by weather.

- Optimize particle systems for efficiency.

- Limit the range and intensity of weather effects based on the player's proximity to them.

- Profile and test your game to ensure it runs smoothly on your target platforms.

By incorporating skyboxes and weather effects into your Unity game environments, you can create diverse and immersive worlds that engage players and enhance their overall gaming experience. Experiment with different settings, textures, and animations to achieve the desired atmospheric effects for your game.

3.5 Advanced Terrain Editing Tools

TERRAIN EDITING IS a critical aspect of creating realistic and detailed game environments in Unity. Terrain provides the foundation for outdoor scenes, landscapes, and natural settings. In this section, we'll explore advanced terrain editing tools and techniques available in Unity to help you create complex and dynamic terrains for your games.

Terrain Layers

UNITY'S TERRAIN SYSTEM allows you to work with multiple terrain layers. Terrain layers are used to define the materials and textures that cover the terrain's surface. This enables you to create diverse landscapes with different ground types, such as grass, dirt, sand, or snow. Here's how you can work with terrain layers:

1. **Creating Terrain Layers:**

– To create terrain layers, go to the Terrain settings by selecting your terrain object and clicking on the "Paint Texture" button in the Inspector.

– In the "Terrain Layers" section, you can add and configure new layers. Each layer can have its own texture, normal map, and other properties.

1. **Painting Terrain Layers:**

– After adding terrain layers, you can use the Terrain Paint Brush to paint different textures onto your terrain. This allows you to blend multiple textures seamlessly.

1. **Splatmaps:**

– Splatmaps are grayscale textures that control the blending of terrain layers. You can create custom splatmaps in external image editing software or use Unity's terrain tools to paint them directly on the terrain.

1. **Detail Layers:**

– Detail layers are used to add small-scale features to the terrain, such as grass, rocks, or debris. You can define different types of detail objects and place them using brushes or rules.

Heightmap Editing

THE HEIGHTMAP IS A crucial component of terrain editing, as it defines the elevation and shape of the terrain. Unity provides various tools for advanced heightmap editing:

1. **Terrain Sculpting**:

– Unity offers sculpting tools that allow you to raise, lower, flatten, and smooth the terrain's heightmap. These tools help you shape the terrain according to your design.

1. **Importing Heightmaps**:

– You can import custom heightmaps created in external software to quickly generate terrains with specific shapes and features.

1. **Noise Generation**:

– Unity's Terrain Noise tool lets you add random noise to the terrain's heightmap. This is useful for creating natural variations and roughness in the terrain.

1. **Erosion and Smoothing**:

– Erosion and smoothing tools simulate natural processes like erosion and sediment deposition. They can create realistic terrain features over time.

Vegetation and Trees

ADDING VEGETATION AND trees to your terrain is essential for creating lush and realistic outdoor environments. Unity provides tools for managing vegetation:

1. **Tree Creator:**

   – Unity's Tree Creator allows you to create custom trees by assembling tree components like branches and leaves. You can adjust the tree's parameters to create a wide variety of tree types.

1. **SpeedTree Integration:**

   – Unity has integrated SpeedTree, a powerful tool for creating highly detailed and realistic trees. SpeedTree assets can be imported and customized for your game.

1. **Grass and Detail Objects:**

   – Unity's terrain system supports the placement of grass and detail objects. You can define different types of grass and details and control their density and placement on the terrain.

Advanced Terrain Features

UNITY OFFERS ADVANCED terrain features that enhance the realism and interactivity of your game environments:

1. **Terrain LOD (Level of Detail):**

– Implementing LOD for your terrain ensures that distant parts of the terrain use lower-polygon models, improving performance while maintaining visual quality.

1. **Realistic Water:**

– Unity's water system allows you to create realistic water bodies like lakes, rivers, and oceans. You can control water properties such as transparency, reflection, and waves.

1. **Terrain Texturing and Shading:**

– To achieve advanced visual effects, you can use custom shaders and materials on your terrain. This enables features like tessellation, parallax mapping, and advanced shading techniques.

1. **Procedural Terrain Generation:**

– For large open-world games, procedural terrain generation techniques can be used to create vast and diverse landscapes without hand-crafting every detail.

1. **Terrain Data Export and Import:**

– Unity allows you to export terrain heightmaps, splatmaps, and other data. This data can be edited externally and re-imported into Unity for further refinement.

Advanced terrain editing in Unity opens up a wide range of possibilities for creating diverse and realistic game environments. By mastering these tools and techniques, you can design terrains that capture the essence of your game world, from sprawling landscapes to intricate natural settings.

Chapter 4: Character Design and Animation

4.1 Designing Game Characters in Unity

Designing game characters in Unity is a creative and essential aspect of game development. Characters are the interactive entities that players control or encounter within your game world, and their design greatly influences gameplay, storytelling, and player engagement. In this section, we'll explore the key principles and considerations for designing game characters in Unity.

Character Concept and Visual Design

1. Character Concept:

- Start by defining the concept and role of your game character. What is their backstory, personality, and motivation? Understanding these aspects helps shape the character's design.

- Consider the character's role in the game. Are they the protagonist, antagonist, or a non-playable character (NPC)? Each role may require different design elements.

2. Visual Design:

- Character design encompasses the character's appearance, including their visual style, clothing, accessories, and distinguishing features.

• Create concept art or sketches to explore various design options. Pay attention to silhouettes, proportions, and color schemes to make the character visually appealing.

3. Unity's Sprite Renderer:

• For 2D games, Unity's Sprite Renderer component is commonly used to display character sprites. Import character sprite sheets and configure the Sprite Renderer component to display the appropriate sprite animations.

• Unity's 2D animation system allows you to create and manage character animations easily.

Rigging and Animation

1. Rigging:

• Rigging is the process of creating a skeleton or armature for your character. The skeleton consists of bones that define the character's structure and movement.

• Use Unity's 2D or 3D rigging tools, depending on your game's style, to create a rig for your character. Ensure that bones are appropriately placed and weighted.

2. Animation State Machines:

• Unity provides Animation State Machines to control character animations. Define animation states such as idle, walk, run, jump, and attack. Create transitions between these states to control character behavior.

● Blend trees can be used to smoothly transition between animations based on character input or in-game events.

3. Character Animation:

● Animate your character using Unity's Animation window or Animator component. Use keyframes to define animations for various actions and movements.

● Consider secondary animations for added realism, such as hair movement, cloth physics, or facial expressions.

Character Controllers

1. Player Controller:

● For player-controlled characters, implement a character controller script that handles input and movement. Unity's Input system can be used to capture player input.

● Implement logic for character movement, jumping, and interacting with the game world. Unity's Rigidbody component is often used for physics-based character movement.

2. NPC Behavior:

● Non-playable characters (NPCs) require behavior scripts to define their actions and responses. Create AI scripts that determine NPC movement, decision-making, and interactions with the player.

- Implement pathfinding algorithms if NPCs need to navigate complex environments.

Facial Animation and Lip Syncing

1. Facial Animation:

- For characters with facial expressions and emotions, use Unity's blend shapes (morph targets) or bone-based facial rigs to create facial animations.

- Blend shape animations can be controlled by scripts based on character emotions or dialogue.

2. Lip Syncing:

- Implement lip syncing for characters that have spoken dialogue. Unity's Timeline or third-party solutions can synchronize lip movements with audio dialogue.

- Use phoneme or viseme animations to achieve accurate lip syncing.

Adding Interactivity with NPCs

1. Dialogue Systems:

- To create interactive conversations with NPCs, design a dialogue system. Dialogue trees or scripting can be used to define branching dialogues and choices.

- Implement UI elements to display dialogue options and character responses.

2. *Quests and Objectives:*

- NPCs often provide quests or objectives in games. Create systems for quest tracking, completion, and rewards.

- Design NPC behaviors that react to quest progress and player decisions.

CHARACTER DESIGN AND animation are integral to the storytelling and gameplay experience in Unity games. By following these principles and leveraging Unity's tools, you can bring your game characters to life, making them engaging and memorable for players.

4.2 Rigging and Animating Characters

RIGGING AND ANIMATING characters in Unity is a crucial step in bringing your game characters to life. Rigging involves creating a skeletal structure for characters, while animation involves defining how characters move and interact with their environment. In this section, we'll explore the process of rigging and animating characters in Unity.

Rigging Characters

1. *Skeleton Creation:*

- Rigging begins with the creation of a character's skeleton or armature. The skeleton consists of bones that represent the character's joints and structure.

- In Unity, you can use the **Rigging** package to create 2D or 3D character skeletons. This package provides tools for generating humanoid or generic rigs.

2. Bone Hierarchy:

- Arrange the bones in a hierarchy that matches the character's anatomy. For example, a humanoid character's hierarchy typically includes bones for the head, neck, arms, legs, and so on.

- Ensure proper bone orientation and alignment to make animations behave realistically.

3. Weight Painting:

- Weight painting assigns influence to each bone over the character's mesh. Each vertex of the character's mesh is associated with one or more bones, and weight painting determines how much each bone affects a vertex.

- Use Unity's **Weight Painting** tools to adjust the influence of bones on the mesh. Achieve smooth deformations by painting weights accurately.

4. Constraints and IK:

- Unity offers constraints and inverse kinematics (IK) solutions to simplify complex character animations. Constraints can limit bone rotations, while IK allows you to control the end-effector of a bone chain, such as a character's hand or foot.

• Implement constraints and IK to achieve specific character behaviors, like locking an elbow joint or making the character's hand reach for an object.

Animating Characters

1. Animation Clips:

• Character animations are defined using animation clips. An animation clip contains keyframes that specify the character's pose and movement at different points in time.

• Create animation clips for various character actions, such as walking, running, jumping, and attacking.

2. Animation Window:

• Unity's **Animation Window** is a powerful tool for creating and editing animations. You can use it to keyframe bone transforms, adjust timing, and preview animations in real-time.

• Set up animation curves to control interpolation between keyframes, achieving smooth transitions.

3. Blend Trees:

• Blend trees are used to blend between multiple animations based on parameter values. They are particularly useful for characters that have different movement speeds or actions.

• Create blend trees in the **Animator Controller** to smoothly transition between animations as character behavior changes.

4. Animation Events:

• Animation events are points in an animation timeline where you can trigger scripts or functions. Use animation events to synchronize character actions with in-game events or interactions.

• Define animation events in the Animation Window and handle them in your scripts.

State Machines and Transitions

1. Animator Controller:

• The **Animator Controller** is a visual tool for defining character animation states and transitions. States represent different character behaviors, while transitions define how the character switches between states.

• Organize your character's animations into a state machine within the Animator Controller.

2. Parameters:

• Parameters in the Animator Controller allow you to control transitions and behaviors. Common parameters include bools for character states (e.g., "isWalking," "isJumping"), floats for animation blend values, and triggers for one-time events.

- Modify parameters in your scripts to control character animations dynamically.

Animation Best Practices

1. Looping Animations:

- Looping animations, like character idle or walking animations, should be designed to seamlessly loop. Pay attention to the first and last frames to avoid noticeable transitions.

2. Root Motion:

- For more realistic character movement, consider enabling root motion. Root motion moves the character's entire body based on animation, including translation.

3. Performance Optimization:

- Optimize character animations for performance by using the **Animation Compression** settings. Reduce unnecessary keyframes and use lower-quality settings when possible.

4. Testing and Tweaking:

- Regularly test character animations in the Unity Editor and make adjustments as needed. Pay attention to clipping issues, unintended deformations, and unnatural movements.

RIGGING AND ANIMATING characters in Unity requires a combination of artistic and technical skills. By following these guidelines and leveraging Unity's animation tools, you can create lifelike and engaging character animations that enhance your game's immersion and storytelling.

4.3 Implementing Character Controllers

IMPLEMENTING CHARACTER controllers in Unity is essential for enabling player interaction and movement within the game world. Character controllers handle input, physics, and collisions to make characters respond to player commands and navigate the environment. In this section, we'll explore the process of implementing character controllers for both player-controlled characters and non-playable characters (NPCs).

Player Character Controller

1. Input Handling:

- To control a player character, begin by handling input. Unity's **Input** system allows you to capture player input from various devices such as keyboards, gamepads, and touchscreens.

- Create input scripts that read input values (e.g., horizontal and vertical axes) and store them for character movement.

// SAMPLE INPUT HANDLING for player movement

float horizontalInput = Input.GetAxis("Horizontal");

float verticalInput = Input.GetAxis("Vertical");

2. *Character Movement:*

- Use a character controller component or Unity's **Rigidbody** component to handle character movement. Rigidbody provides physics-based movement, while a character controller offers more precise control over character interactions.

- Apply forces or set velocity based on input to move the character.

```
// SAMPLE CHARACTER MOVEMENT using Rigidbody

Vector3 moveDirection = new Vector3(horizontalInput, 0, verticalInput).normalized;

rigidbody.velocity = moveDirection * speed;
```

3. *Jumping:*

- Implement jumping by detecting jump input and applying an upward force. Ensure that the character is grounded before allowing jumps to prevent mid-air jumps.

```
// SAMPLE CHARACTER JUMPING using Rigidbody

if (isGrounded && Input.GetButtonDown("Jump")) {

rigidbody.AddForce(Vector3.up * jumpForce, ForceMode.Impulse);

}
```

4. Collision Handling:

- Character controllers or Rigidbody components automatically handle collisions with the environment. Implement collision detection and response to prevent characters from passing through objects.

- You can use Unity's layers and collision matrices to control which objects interact with characters.

// SAMPLE COLLISION HANDLING with OnCollisionEnter

```
void OnCollisionEnter(Collision collision) {
// Check collision and respond accordingly
}
```

NPC Character Controller

1. AI Behavior:

- Non-playable characters (NPCs) require AI behavior scripts to control their actions and responses. Create AI scripts that determine NPC movement, decision-making, and interactions with the player.

- Implement state machines, behavior trees, or finite state machines (FSM) to define NPC behaviors.

// SAMPLE AI BEHAVIOR with FSM

```
public class NPCStateMachine : MonoBehaviour {

private enum NPCState { Idle, Patrol, Chase, Attack };
```

```csharp
private NPCState currentState;

void Update() {

// Update AI behavior based on the current state

switch (currentState) {

case NPCState.Idle:

// Handle idle behavior

break;

case NPCState.Patrol:

// Handle patrol behavior

break;

case NPCState.Chase:

// Handle chase behavior

break;

case NPCState.Attack:

// Handle attack behavior

break;

}

}

}
```

2. *Pathfinding:*

- Implement pathfinding algorithms to enable NPCs to navigate complex environments. Unity's **NavMesh** system provides built-in pathfinding capabilities.

- Set up NavMesh agents and define NavMesh areas to control where NPCs can move.

```csharp
// SAMPLE PATHFINDING using NavMesh

using UnityEngine;

using UnityEngine.AI;

public class NPCPathfinding : MonoBehaviour {

public Transform target;

private NavMeshAgent agent;

void Start() {

agent = GetComponent<NavMeshAgent>();

}

void Update() {

agent.SetDestination(target.position);

}

}
```

3. Interaction:

- Define interaction systems for NPCs to respond to player actions. This includes dialogues, quests, and reactions to player proximity.

- Create systems for triggering dialogues and quest events when the player interacts with an NPC.

// SAMPLE NPC INTERACTION script

```
public class NPCInteraction : MonoBehaviour {

public Dialogue dialogue;

public void Interact() {

// Trigger dialogue or quest event

DialogueManager.StartDialogue(dialogue);

}

}
```

Implementing character controllers in Unity is a fundamental aspect of game development, enabling characters to move, interact, and respond to player input. By following these guidelines and using Unity's built-in components and scripting capabilities, you can create dynamic and engaging character controllers for both player characters and NPCs in your game.

4.4 Facial Animation and Lip Syncing Techniques

FACIAL ANIMATION AND lip syncing play a significant role in enhancing the expressiveness and realism of characters in Unity games. These techniques bring characters to life by synchronizing facial movements with speech and emotions. In this section, we'll explore the principles and methods for implementing facial animation and lip syncing in Unity.

Facial Rigging

1. Blend Shapes (Morph Targets):

- Blend shapes are a common method for animating facial expressions in Unity. They involve creating a set of predefined facial poses (morph targets) and blending between them to achieve different expressions.

- Use Unity's **Skinned Mesh Renderer** component to set up blend shapes for your character's face.

2. Bone-Based Facial Rig:

- For more complex facial animations, consider a bone-based facial rig. This involves adding bones to the character's face to control different parts, such as the eyes, eyebrows, and mouth.

- Create a bone hierarchy that mimics the movement of facial features and use constraints to limit bone rotations.

Animation and Emotions

1. Keyframe Animation:

• Animate facial expressions using keyframes in Unity's Animation Window. Keyframes define the position, rotation, and scale of blend shapes or bone transformations at different points in time.

• Use the Animation Window to create emotion-specific animations, such as smiling, frowning, or raising eyebrows.

2. Emotion Controllers:

• Implement emotion controllers that allow you to switch between predefined facial expressions or emotions at runtime. This enables characters to react to in-game events or dialogue.

```csharp
// SAMPLE EMOTION CONTROLLER script

public class EmotionController : MonoBehaviour {

public SkinnedMeshRenderer faceRenderer;

public AnimationClip smileAnimation;

public AnimationClip frownAnimation;

public void Smile() {

faceRenderer.SetBlendShapeWeight(0, 100);

}
```

public void Frown() {

faceRenderer.SetBlendShapeWeight(1, 100);

}

}

Lip Syncing

1. Phoneme Animation:

- Lip syncing involves matching character lip movements with spoken dialogue. Create a set of phoneme animations that represent different mouth shapes for speech sounds like "A," "E," "O," etc.

- Blend between phoneme animations based on the character's spoken lines.

2. Text-to-Speech (TTS):

- Utilize text-to-speech libraries or services to convert written dialogue into spoken audio. You can then synchronize character lip syncing with the generated audio.

- Popular TTS solutions include Google Text-to-Speech and Microsoft Azure Cognitive Services.

Tools and Plugins

1. Asset Store Solutions:

- Explore Unity Asset Store for facial animation and lip syncing solutions. Many third-party plugins and assets are available to streamline the process.

- Look for plugins that offer automatic lip syncing based on audio input.

2. Face Tracking Hardware:

- For VR or AR experiences, consider using face-tracking hardware devices like depth-sensing cameras or facial motion capture rigs. These devices can capture facial movements in real-time for more immersive character interactions.

Animation Best Practices

1. Realism and Exaggeration:

- Balance realism with exaggeration in facial animations. Slight exaggerations can make characters more expressive and visually appealing.

2. Smooth Transitions:

- Ensure smooth transitions between different facial expressions and lip sync animations. Use animation curves to control the interpolation between keyframes.

3. Performance Optimization:

- Optimize facial animations for performance by using animation compression and LOD settings. Minimize the number of blend shapes or bones used for animations when possible.

4. Testing and Tweaking:

- Continuously test and fine-tune facial animations to ensure they match character dialogue and emotions. Pay attention to syncing issues, such as delays or inaccuracies.

FACIAL ANIMATION AND lip syncing are essential for creating characters that convey emotions and engage players on a deeper level. By following these techniques and exploring available tools and plugins, you can achieve realistic and expressive character animations in Unity games.

4.5 Adding Interactivity with NPCs

ADDING INTERACTIVITY with non-playable characters (NPCs) is a crucial aspect of game development that enhances the player's immersion and creates dynamic gameplay experiences. NPCs can provide quests, engage in dialogues, react to the player's actions, and contribute to the overall storytelling of the game. In this section, we'll explore the methods and techniques for implementing interactivity with NPCs in Unity.

Dialogue Systems

1. Dialogue Trees:

• Implement dialogue systems that use tree structures to create branching conversations. Each node in the tree represents a dialogue option or character response.

• Design dialogue trees that allow players to make choices that impact the story or character relationships.

```
// SAMPLE DIALOGUE TREE structure

public class DialogueNode {

public string text;

public List<DialogueOption> options;

}

public class DialogueOption {

public string text;

public DialogueNode nextNode;

}
```

2. Dialogue Triggers:

• Place triggers in the game world that initiate dialogues when the player interacts with them. These triggers can be associated with specific NPCs or objects.

```
// SAMPLE DIALOGUE TRIGGER script
```

```csharp
public class DialogueTrigger : MonoBehaviour {

public Dialogue dialogue;

public void Interact() {

DialogueManager.StartDialogue(dialogue);

}

}
```

Quest Systems

1. Quest Tracking:

- Implement quest systems to track the player's progress in completing quests. Create data structures to represent quests, objectives, and rewards.

```csharp
// SAMPLE QUEST AND OBJECTIVE classes

public class Quest {

public string title;

public List<QuestObjective> objectives;

public int experienceReward;

}

public class QuestObjective {

public string description;

public bool isComplete;
```

```
}
```

2. Quest Givers:

- Design NPCs that act as quest givers. These NPCs offer quests to the player and provide information about quest objectives.

- Use quest markers or journal systems to help players keep track of their active quests.

NPC Behavior

1. Finite State Machines (FSM):

- Implement FSM or behavior tree systems to control NPC actions and reactions. Define states for behaviors like idle, patrol, follow, attack, and more.

```
// SAMPLE NPC FSM

public class NPCStateMachine : MonoBehaviour {

private enum NPCState { Idle, Patrol, Follow, Attack };

private NPCState currentState;

void Update() {
// Update NPC behavior based on the current state

switch (currentState) {

case NPCState.Idle:
// Handle idle behavior
```

```
break;

case NPCState.Patrol:

// Handle patrol behavior

break;

case NPCState.Follow:

// Handle follow behavior

break;

case NPCState.Attack:

// Handle attack behavior

break;

}

}

}
```

2. Dynamic Responses:

- NPCs should dynamically respond to the player's actions and decisions. Implement systems that change NPC behavior based on player choices and events in the game world.

- Use variables or flags to store information about the player's interactions with NPCs and the game world.

Reactive NPCs

1. Reacting to Player Choices:

- Create NPCs that remember and react to the player's choices and decisions. This can influence the game's branching narrative and character relationships.

2. Affinity Systems:

- Implement affinity or reputation systems that track the player's relationship with NPCs and factions. Positive interactions can lead to benefits, while negative interactions may result in consequences.

```
// SAMPLE AFFINITY SYSTEM

public class AffinitySystem : MonoBehaviour {

public Dictionary<string, int> affinityLevels;

}
```

Adding interactivity with NPCs is a dynamic and creative process that enhances the depth of storytelling and gameplay in Unity games. By implementing dialogue systems, quest systems, defining NPC behavior, and creating reactive NPCs, you can create memorable and immersive interactions between players and the game world's inhabitants.

Chapter 5: Scripting Fundamentals

5.1 Introduction to C# for Unity

Scripting is a fundamental part of game development, and in Unity, the primary programming language used for scripting is C#. C# is a versatile and powerful language that allows you to create complex game logic, control game objects, and interact with various Unity components. In this section, we'll introduce you to the basics of C# scripting for Unity.

Writing Your First C# Script

1. Creating a C# Script:

- To create a new C# script in Unity, go to the **Assets** menu, select **Create**, and choose **C# Script**. Give your script a meaningful name, and Unity will create a .cs file in your project.

2. Opening the Script:

- Double-click on the script to open it in your preferred code editor, such as Visual Studio or Visual Studio Code, which are well-integrated with Unity.

3. Basic Structure:

- A typical C# script in Unity begins with a class declaration. Unity scripts should derive from the

MonoBehaviour class, which allows you to interact with
GameObjects and Unity's update cycle.

USING UnityEngine;

public class MyScript : MonoBehaviour {

// *Your code goes here*

}

Variables, Types, and Data Structures

1. Variables:

- Variables are used to store and manage data in your
scripts. In C#, you need to declare a variable with a
specific data type before using it.

INT SCORE = 100;

float speed = 5.0f;

string playerName = "John";

2. Data Types:

- C# supports various data types, including integers (int),
floating-point numbers (float), strings (string), booleans
(bool), and more.

INT HEALTH = 100;

float distance = 10.5f;

string playerName = "Alice";

```
bool isGameOver = false;
```

3. Arrays and Lists:

- Arrays and lists allow you to store collections of data. Arrays have a fixed size, while lists can dynamically grow.

```
INT[] SCORES = new int[] { 10, 20, 30 };
```

```
List<string> playerNames = new List<string>() { "Alice", "Bob", "Charlie" };
```

Control Structures and Loops

1. Conditional Statements (if-else):

- Conditional statements let you make decisions in your code. For example, you can use if to check a condition and execute different code blocks based on the result.

```
INT SCORE = 80;

if (score >= 90) {

Debug.Log("Excellent!");

} else if (score >= 70) {

Debug.Log("Good job!");

} else {

Debug.Log("Keep practicing.");

}
```

2. Loops (for, while):

- Loops allow you to repeat a set of instructions. The for loop is used when you know the number of iterations, while the while loop is used when the condition is true.

```
FOR (int i = 0; i < 5; i++) {

Debug.Log("Iteration " + i);

}

int countdown = 3;

while (countdown > 0) {

Debug.Log("Countdown: " + countdown);

countdown—;

}
```

Functions and Methods in Unity Scripts

1. Functions and Methods:

- Functions are blocks of code that perform a specific task. In C#, methods are functions defined within a class.

```
VOID START() {

// Code here runs once at the start of the script's execution.

}

void Update() {
```

// Code here runs once per frame.

```
}
```

2. Unity Callbacks:

- Unity provides specific methods that are automatically called at different points in the game's lifecycle. For example, Start() is called when an object is initialized, and Update() is called every frame.

```
VOID START() {
```

```
Debug.Log("Object initialized.");
```

```
}
```

```
void Update() {
```

// Code that runs every frame.

```
}
```

Debugging and Error Handling

1. Debugging with Debug:

- The Debug class in Unity is essential for debugging your scripts. You can use Debug.Log() to print messages to the console, helping you track and diagnose issues.

```
INT HEALTH = 0;
```

```
Debug.Log("Health: " + health);
```

2. Exception Handling:

- In C#, you can use try-catch blocks to handle exceptions and prevent your game from crashing when errors occur.

```csharp
TRY {

// Code that might throw an exception

} catch (Exception ex) {

Debug.LogError("An error occurred: " + ex.Message);

}
```

These fundamentals of C# scripting are essential for building interactive and dynamic gameplay in Unity. As you become more familiar with C# and Unity's scripting environment, you'll be able to create complex behaviors and systems for your games.

5.2 Variables, Types, and Data Structures

VARIABLES, DATA TYPES, and data structures are fundamental concepts in programming, and they play a crucial role in C# scripting for Unity game development. In this section, we'll dive deeper into these concepts to help you understand how they are used in Unity scripting.

Variables

VARIABLES ARE LIKE containers that store data that your script can use and manipulate. In C#, you need to declare a variable before you can use it, specifying its type and an optional initial value. Here are some common variable types:

1. int (Integer):

- Integers are used to store whole numbers, such as player scores or item counts.

INT PLAYERSCORE = 100;

2. float (Floating-Point Number):

- Floats are used to store decimal numbers, such as player health or position coordinates.

FLOAT PLAYERHEALTH = 75.5f;

3. string (Text):

- Strings are used to store text data, such as player names or dialogue lines.

STRING PLAYERNAME = "Alice";

4. bool (Boolean):

- Booleans can have two values: true or false. They are used for conditions and switches.

BOOL ISGAMEOVER = **false**;

Data Types

C# PROVIDES SEVERAL data types to work with different kinds of data. Here are some commonly used data types:

1. Arrays:

- Arrays are collections of values of the same type. They have a fixed size when declared.

INT[] SCORES = **new** int[5]; // *Array of 5 integers*

scores[0] = 10;

scores[1] = 20;

2. Lists:

- Lists are dynamic arrays that can grow or shrink in size as needed.

LIST<STRING> PLAYERNAMES = **new** List<string>(); // *List of strings*

playerNames.Add("Alice");

playerNames.Add("Bob");

3. Enums (Enumerations):

- Enums define a set of named constant values, which can represent states or options.

PUBLIC ENUM GameDifficulty {

Easy,

Medium,

Hard

```
}
```

GameDifficulty difficulty = GameDifficulty.Medium;

4. Structures (structs):

- Structures are similar to classes but are value types. They are useful for creating custom data types.

PUBLIC STRUCT Point {

public int x;

public int y;

}

Point playerPosition;

playerPosition.x = 10;

playerPosition.y = 5;

Constants and Read-Only Variables

IN ADDITION TO REGULAR variables, you can also define constants and read-only variables:

1. Constants:

- Constants are values that cannot be changed after they are defined. They are declared using the const keyword.

CONST FLOAT GRAVITY = 9.81f;

2. Read-Only Variables:

- Read-only variables can only be assigned a value in their declaration or constructor and cannot be changed afterward.

READONLY string playerName;

playerName = "Alice";

Type Conversion

TYPE CONVERSION IS the process of changing a variable's data type. You may need to convert data types when performing operations or assigning values. C# provides two types of type conversion:

1. Implicit Conversion:

- Implicit conversion happens automatically when there is no data loss, such as converting an int to a float.

INT SCORE = 100;

float scoreFloat = score; // *Implicit conversion*

2. Explicit Conversion (Casting):

- Explicit conversion requires casting, and it may result in data loss or errors if not done carefully.

FLOAT TEMPERATURE = 32.5f;

int temperatureInt = (int)temperature; // *Explicit conversion (casting)*

Understanding variables, data types, and type conversion is fundamental for writing effective Unity scripts. These concepts provide the foundation for managing and manipulating data in your game logic.

5.3 Control Structures and Loops

CONTROL STRUCTURES and loops are essential tools in C# scripting for Unity, allowing you to make decisions, control the flow of your code, and repeat actions. In this section, we'll explore the different control structures and loops available in C# and how they can be applied in Unity game development.

Conditional Statements

CONDITIONAL STATEMENTS are used to execute different code blocks based on specific conditions. The primary conditional statement in C# is the if-else statement:

1. if-else Statement:

THE if-else statement evaluates a condition and executes one block of code if the condition is true and another block if it's false.

int playerHealth = 80;

if (playerHealth > 0) {

Debug.Log("Player is alive.");

} **else** {

```
Debug.Log("Player is dead.");

}
```

You can also use the else if clause to test additional conditions when the initial condition is false:

```
int score = 75;

if (score >= 90) {

Debug.Log("Excellent!");

} else if (score >= 70) {

Debug.Log("Good job!");

} else {

Debug.Log("Keep practicing.");

}
```

Loops

LOOPS ALLOW YOU TO repeat a block of code multiple times, making them useful for tasks that need to be performed iteratively.

2. for Loop:

THE for loop is used when you know the number of iterations in advance. It consists of an initialization, a condition, and an update statement:

```
for (int i = 0; i < 5; i++) {

Debug.Log("Iteration " + i);
```

```
}
```

In this example, the loop initializes i to 0, executes the code block while i is less than 5, and increments i by 1 in each iteration.

3. *while Loop:*

THE while loop is used when the number of iterations is not known in advance, and it continues as long as a condition is true:

```
int countdown = 3;

while (countdown > 0) {

Debug.Log("Countdown: " + countdown);

countdown—;

}
```

In this example, the loop continues as long as countdown is greater than 0. It decrements countdown in each iteration.

Control Statements

CONTROL STATEMENTS allow you to change the flow of control in your code. Some commonly used control statements are:

4. *break Statement:*

THE break statement is used to exit a loop prematurely, typically based on a condition:

```
for (int i = 0; i < 10; i++) {

if (i == 5) {
```

```
break; // Exit the loop when i equals 5

}

Debug.Log("Iteration " + i);

}
```

5. *continue Statement:*

THE continue statement is used to skip the current iteration and move to the next iteration of a loop:

```
for (int i = 0; i < 5; i++) {

if (i == 2) {

continue; // Skip iteration when i equals 2

}

Debug.Log("Iteration " + i);

}
```

Switch Statement

THE switch statement is used to select one of many code blocks to execute, based on the value of an expression. It's a more concise way to handle multiple conditional cases:

```
int day = 3;

switch (day) {

case 1:

Debug.Log("Monday");
```

```
break;

case 2:

Debug.Log("Tuesday");

break;

case 3:

Debug.Log("Wednesday");

break;

default:

Debug.Log("Other day");

break;

}
```

The switch statement checks the value of day and executes the corresponding code block.

Control structures and loops are essential for creating dynamic and responsive gameplay in Unity. By using these constructs, you can control the flow of your code and create complex interactions and behaviors in your games.

5.4 Functions and Methods in Unity Scripts

FUNCTIONS, ALSO KNOWN as methods in object-oriented programming, are blocks of code that perform specific tasks or operations. They are a fundamental part of C# scripting in Unity and are used to encapsulate logic, organize code, and promote reusability. In this section, we'll explore functions and methods in Unity scripts.

Defining Functions

1. Function Signature:

A FUNCTION IN C# IS defined by its signature, which includes the following components:

- Access Modifier: Specifies the visibility of the function.

- Return Type: Defines the type of value the function returns, or void if it doesn't return a value.

- Name: The unique name of the function.

- Parameters: Input values that the function can use.

Here's a basic function signature:

```
public int CalculateSum(int a, int b) {

// Function body

int sum = a + b;

return sum;

}
```

In this example:

- public is the access modifier, indicating that the function is accessible from other parts of the code.

- int is the return type, specifying that the function returns an integer value.

- CalculateSum is the function name.

- (int a, int b) are the parameters, indicating that the function expects two integer values as input.

2. Function Body:

THE FUNCTION BODY CONTAINS the code that gets executed when the function is called. It includes statements and expressions that perform specific actions or calculations.

```
public void GreetPlayer(string playerName) {

Debug.Log("Hello, " + playerName + "!");

}
```

In this example, the function GreetPlayer takes a string parameter playerName and logs a greeting message using Debug.Log().

Function Invocation

TO EXECUTE A FUNCTION, you need to invoke or call it. Function invocation involves specifying the function name and providing the required arguments (if any) based on the function's parameter list.

3. Calling Functions:

YOU CAN CALL A FUNCTION by its name and pass the required arguments:

```
int result = CalculateSum(5, 3); // Calling the CalculateSum function

GreetPlayer("Alice"); // Calling the GreetPlayer function
```

In the first line, the CalculateSum function is called with arguments 5 and 3, and it returns the result, which is stored in the result variable. In the second line, the GreetPlayer function is called with the argument "Alice".

Unity Callbacks

UNITY PROVIDES A SET of predefined functions, often referred to as Unity callbacks, that are automatically called at specific points in the game's lifecycle. These callbacks are essential for controlling GameObject behavior, responding to events, and implementing game logic.

4. Start() and Update():

TWO OF THE MOST COMMONLY used Unity callbacks are Start() and Update():

void Start() {

// Code here runs once at the start of the script's execution.

}

void Update() {

// Code here runs once per frame.

}

- Start() is called when the GameObject is initialized.

- Update() is called every frame, allowing you to implement continuous actions or checks.

5. *Other Unity Callbacks:*

UNITY OFFERS VARIOUS other callbacks, such as Awake(), OnEnable(), OnDisable(), and more, which you can use to handle specific events during the GameObject's lifecycle.

```
void Awake() {

// Called when the script instance is initialized.

}

void OnEnable() {

// Called when the GameObject is set to active.

}

void OnDisable() {

// Called when the GameObject is deactivated.

}
```

These Unity callbacks provide precise control over your GameObjects and allow you to respond to various events in your game.

Modular Programming

FUNCTIONS ENABLE MODULAR programming by breaking down complex tasks into smaller, manageable units. This approach promotes code organization, reusability, and maintainability, making it easier to collaborate on larger game projects and troubleshoot issues.

```
// Function to move a GameObject forward by a specified distance
```

```csharp
public void MoveForward(Transform objectTransform, float distance) {

Vector3 newPosition = objectTransform.position + objectTransform.forward * distance;

objectTransform.position = newPosition;

}

void Update() {

// Move the player GameObject forward by 1 unit each frame

MoveForward(playerTransform, 1.0f);

}
```

In this example, the MoveForward function is responsible for moving a GameObject forward. By encapsulating this behavior in a function, you can reuse it for multiple GameObjects and easily maintain consistent movement logic.

Understanding how to define and use functions is a critical skill for Unity developers. Functions help you structure your code, create reusable components, and implement complex game behaviors effectively.

5.5 Debugging and Error Handling

DEBUGGING IS AN ESSENTIAL skill for game developers, as it helps identify and resolve issues in your code. Unity provides tools and techniques to debug your scripts effectively, allowing you to find and fix errors. In this section, we'll explore debugging techniques and error handling in Unity.

Debugging with Debug

THE Debug class in Unity is a valuable tool for printing messages to the console, which can help you track the execution of your scripts and diagnose issues.

1. Logging Messages:

THE MOST BASIC DEBUGGING technique is to use Debug.Log() to print messages to the console:

int health = 100;

Debug.Log("Player health: " + health);

This line of code logs the player's health to the console, making it easier to monitor variables and values during runtime.

2. Logging Variables:

YOU CAN LOG THE VALUES of variables to check if they are correct:

int score = 75;

Debug.Log("Current score: " + score);

This helps you verify that variables hold the expected values.

3. Conditional Logging:

YOU CAN LOG MESSAGES conditionally using if statements to control when messages are printed:

int lives = 3;

```
if (lives <= 0) {

Debug.LogError("Game over!");

} else {

Debug.Log("Player has " + lives + " lives.");

}
```

In this example, an error message is logged when the player's lives reach zero or below.

Breakpoints and Stepping

UNITY ALSO PROVIDES the ability to set breakpoints and step through your code during runtime to inspect variables and control the execution flow.

4. Setting Breakpoints:

YOU CAN SET BREAKPOINTS by clicking in the left margin of your code editor (e.g., Visual Studio) next to the line number. When the breakpoint is hit during debugging, the code execution pauses, allowing you to inspect variables and step through the code.

5. Stepping:

WHILE DEBUGGING, YOU can step through your code one line at a time using the following commands:

- **Step Over**: Proceed to the next line of code.

- **Step Into**: Enter a function or method being called.

- **Step Out**: Exit the current function or method.

Stepping helps you trace the flow of your code and identify the source of issues.

Exception Handling

IN ADDITION TO DEBUGGING, error handling is crucial for gracefully handling unexpected issues that might cause your game to crash.

6. *try-catch Blocks:*

THE try-catch block is used to catch and handle exceptions, preventing your game from crashing when errors occur:

```
try {

// Code that might throw an exception

} catch (Exception ex) {

Debug.LogError("An error occurred: " + ex.Message);

}
```

In this example, if an exception occurs within the try block, it's caught in the catch block, and an error message is logged.

7. *Throwing Exceptions:*

YOU CAN ALSO THROW custom exceptions to signal specific error conditions in your code:

```
int playerHealth = -10;

if (playerHealth < 0) {
```

```
throw    new    ArgumentOutOfRangeException("playerHealth",
"Health cannot be negative.");
```

```
}
```

By throwing exceptions, you can provide meaningful error messages and handle exceptional cases more effectively.

Debugging Tools

UNITY OFFERS A RANGE of debugging tools and features, including:

- **Inspector**: You can inspect and modify variables in real-time using the Inspector window.

- **Console**: The Console window displays log messages, warnings, and errors.

- **Profiler**: The Profiler window helps analyze performance and identify bottlenecks.

- **Debug Draw**: You can use Gizmos and Debug.DrawLine to visualize data in the Scene view.

Debugging and error handling are integral parts of game development. They help ensure the stability and quality of your games by identifying and resolving issues during development and testing. By mastering these techniques and tools, you can create more robust and reliable Unity games.

Chapter 6: Physics and Collisions

Section 6.1: Understanding Unity's Physics Engine

In this section, we'll delve into the fundamental aspects of Unity's built-in physics engine, which is crucial for creating realistic and interactive game worlds. Understanding how Unity handles physics can greatly enhance your ability to develop engaging gameplay experiences.

Physics in Unity

PHYSICS IN UNITY REFERS to the simulation of real-world physical interactions within the virtual environment of your game. This includes how objects move, collide, and react to forces like gravity and user input. Unity's physics engine provides a robust framework for handling these interactions.

Rigidbody Component

THE Rigidbody component is central to Unity's physics simulation. It's used to make GameObjects behave physically in the game world. When you attach a Rigidbody component to an object, Unity calculates its motion based on forces and collisions. You can control its mass, drag, and other physical properties through script or the Inspector.

```
using UnityEngine;

public class MyPhysicsObject : MonoBehaviour
```

```
{

private Rigidbody rb;

void Start()

{

// Get the Rigidbody component attached to this GameObject

rb = GetComponent<Rigidbody>();

// Apply a force to the object

rb.AddForce(Vector3.forward * 10.0f, ForceMode.Impulse);

}

}
```

In the example above, we access the Rigidbody component of a GameObject and apply an impulse force to it.

Colliders

COLLIDERS ARE COMPONENTS used to define the shape of GameObjects for collision detection. Unity provides various types of colliders like BoxCollider, SphereCollider, and CapsuleCollider. These colliders allow you to create precise collision boundaries for your objects.

```
using UnityEngine;

public class CollisionHandler : MonoBehaviour

{

void OnCollisionEnter(Collision collision)
```

```csharp
{
    // Detect collision with another object
    if (collision.gameObject.CompareTag("Obstacle"))
    {
        Debug.Log("Collision with obstacle!");
    }
}
}
```

In the code snippet above, we use the OnCollisionEnter method to detect when a collision occurs with an object tagged as "Obstacle."

Physics Layers

UNITY USES LAYERS TO help manage and filter collision interactions between objects. By assigning objects to specific layers and configuring collision matrix settings, you can control which objects can collide with each other.

Physics Materials

PHYSICS MATERIALS ARE used to fine-tune how objects interact when they collide. You can adjust parameters like friction and bounciness to make surfaces behave as desired. For instance, you can create a slippery ice surface or a bouncy trampoline by adjusting the physics material properties.

```csharp
using UnityEngine;

public class BouncyPlatform : MonoBehaviour
```

```csharp
{

private PhysicMaterial bouncyMaterial;

void Start()

{

// Create a physics material with high bounciness

bouncyMaterial = new PhysicMaterial();

bouncyMaterial.bounciness = 0.8f;

// Apply the physics material to the collider

GetComponent<Collider>().material = bouncyMaterial;

}

}
```

In this example, we create a bouncy platform using a custom physics material with high bounciness.

Constraints and Joints

UNITY PROVIDES JOINT components like HingeJoint and SpringJoint that allow you to simulate complex interactions between objects. Constraints and joints can be used to create realistic behaviors, such as swinging doors, suspension systems, or ragdoll physics for characters.

Understanding Unity's physics engine and its various components is essential for creating dynamic and interactive game worlds. Experimenting with these features and combining them with your gameplay mechanics can lead to exciting and engaging player experiences. In the next sections, we'll explore more advanced aspects of physics and collisions in Unity, including rigidbody movement, collision detection, and advanced simulations.

Section 6.2: Working with Rigidbodies and Colliders

IN THIS SECTION, WE will delve deeper into working with Unity's rigidbodies and colliders. Rigidbodies and colliders are essential components for creating realistic physics-based interactions in your games.

Rigidbody Movement

UNITY'S Rigidbody component allows you to simulate the physics of an object, including its movement and interaction with forces. To make an object move using a Rigidbody, you can apply forces or directly manipulate its velocity.

```
using UnityEngine;

public class RigidbodyMovement : MonoBehaviour

{

private Rigidbody rb;

public float moveSpeed = 5.0f;

void Start()

{

rb = GetComponent<Rigidbody>();

}
```

```csharp
void Update()
{
float horizontalInput = Input.GetAxis("Horizontal");

float verticalInput = Input.GetAxis("Vertical");

Vector3 movement = new Vector3(horizontalInput, 0.0f, verticalInput);

rb.velocity = movement * moveSpeed;
}
}
```

In this script, we use Input.GetAxis to get player input for movement and set the Rigidbody's velocity based on the input, allowing the object to move in response to player commands.

Rigidbody Rotation

YOU CAN ALSO CONTROL the rotation of an object with a Rigidbody. For example, to make an object rotate when the player presses certain keys, you can modify the angular velocity.

```csharp
using UnityEngine;

public class RigidbodyRotation : MonoBehaviour
{
private Rigidbody rb;

public float rotationSpeed = 100.0f;

void Start()
```

```csharp
{

rb = GetComponent<Rigidbody>();

}

void Update()

{

float rotationInput = Input.GetAxis("Rotation");

Vector3 rotation = new Vector3(0.0f, rotationInput, 0.0f);

rb.angularVelocity = rotation * rotationSpeed;

}

}
```

This script allows the object to rotate around its vertical axis in response to player input.

Rigidbody Constraints

UNITY'S Rigidbody also provides the option to constrain its movement along certain axes. This can be useful for creating objects that move only in specific directions, such as a platform that moves horizontally.

```csharp
using UnityEngine;

public class RigidbodyConstraints : MonoBehaviour

{

private Rigidbody rb;

void Start()
```

```
{

rb = GetComponent<Rigidbody>();

rb.constraints = RigidbodyConstraints.FreezePositionY;

}

}
```

In this example, we freeze the object's position along the Y-axis, allowing it to move only in the horizontal plane.

Collision Detection Modes

UNITY PROVIDES DIFFERENT collision detection modes for Rigidbody components. These modes determine how and when collisions are detected. The available modes include:

- Discrete: Collisions are checked at fixed intervals.

- Continuous: Continuous collision detection is used to prevent fast-moving objects from passing through others.

- Continuous Dynamic: Similar to continuous, but only for objects with non-kinematic rigidbodies.

You can choose the collision detection mode that best fits your game's requirements in the Rigidbody settings.

Interpolation and Extrapolation

UNITY ALSO OFFERS INTERPOLATION and extrapolation settings for Rigidbody components. These settings can help smooth out the visual appearance of rigidbody movement, especially in networked games.

Interpolation helps smooth the positions of objects, while extrapolation can predict where an object will be in the future based on its current state.

```csharp
using UnityEngine;

public class RigidbodyInterpolation : MonoBehaviour

{

private Rigidbody rb;

void Start()

{

rb = GetComponent<Rigidbody>();

rb.interpolation = RigidbodyInterpolation.Interpolate;

rb.extrapolate = RigidbodyExtrapolation.Interpolate;

}

}
```

In this script, we set the interpolation and extrapolation modes for a Rigidbody.

Understanding how to work with rigidbodies and colliders in Unity is crucial for creating dynamic and interactive environments. These components enable you to simulate realistic physics-based interactions, making your games more engaging and immersive. In the next sections, we will explore collision detection and response, as well as advanced physics simulations and optimizations.

Section 6.3: Implementing Realistic

Movements and Forces

IN THIS SECTION, WE will dive into the techniques for implementing realistic movements and forces in Unity using the Rigidbody component. Realistic movement and physics are crucial for creating immersive gaming experiences.

Applying Forces

UNITY'S RIGIDBODY COMPONENT allows you to apply forces to objects to make them move realistically. Forces can be applied in different directions and magnitudes to achieve desired movements. Here's an example of applying a force to simulate a jump:

```
using UnityEngine;

public class JumpingCharacter : MonoBehaviour

{

private Rigidbody rb;

public float jumpForce = 5.0f;

void Start()

{

rb = GetComponent<Rigidbody>();

}

void Update()

{

if (Input.GetKeyDown(KeyCode.Space))
```

```csharp
{

rb.AddForce(Vector3.up * jumpForce, ForceMode.Impulse);

}

}

}
```

In this script, we use rb.AddForce to apply an upward force to the object when the Space key is pressed, simulating a jump.

Gravitational Force

UNITY'S PHYSICS ENGINE includes a built-in gravitational force that can be enabled for Rigidbody objects. The gravitational force is automatically applied downward, and you can adjust its strength through the Physics settings in Unity. Rigidbody objects will respond to this gravitational force without any additional scripting.

Applying Torque

IN ADDITION TO LINEAR forces, you can also apply torque to rotate Rigidbody objects. This is useful for simulating spinning or rolling motion. Here's an example of applying torque to create a spinning object:

```csharp
using UnityEngine;

public class SpinningObject : MonoBehaviour

{

private Rigidbody rb;
```

```csharp
public float torqueForce = 10.0f;

void Start()

{

rb = GetComponent<Rigidbody>();

}

void Update()

{

if (Input.GetKeyDown(KeyCode.T))

{

rb.AddTorque(Vector3.up * torqueForce, ForceMode.Impulse);

}

}

}
```

In this script, we apply torque in the upward direction when a specific key (T) is pressed, causing the object to spin around its vertical axis.

Drag and Angular Drag

RIGIDBODY OBJECTS CAN also experience resistance to motion through drag and angular drag. Drag simulates air resistance for linear movement, while angular drag simulates rotational resistance. You can adjust these values to control how quickly an object slows down or stops moving.

```csharp
using UnityEngine;

public class DragExample : MonoBehaviour

{

private Rigidbody rb;

public float linearDrag = 0.2f;

public float angularDrag = 0.5f;

void Start()

{

rb = GetComponent<Rigidbody>();

rb.drag = linearDrag;

rb.angularDrag = angularDrag;

}

}
```

In this script, we set the linear and angular drag values for a Rigidbody object.

Custom Forces and Movement

FOR MORE COMPLEX MOVEMENT behaviors, you can implement custom force calculations in FixedUpdate. For example, you might create a custom script to simulate rocket propulsion:

```csharp
using UnityEngine;

public class RocketPropulsion : MonoBehaviour
```

```csharp
{

private Rigidbody rb;

public float thrustForce = 10.0f;

void Start()

{

rb = GetComponent<Rigidbody>();

}

void FixedUpdate()

{

if (Input.GetKey(KeyCode.W))

{

rb.AddForce(transform.forward * thrustForce, ForceMode.Force);

}

}

}
```

In this example, we apply a forward force when the W key is held down, simulating rocket propulsion.

Understanding how to apply forces, torques, and manage drag is essential for creating realistic movements in your Unity games. These techniques allow you to achieve lifelike motion for objects and characters, enhancing the overall player experience. In the upcoming sections, we will explore collision detection and response, advanced physics simulations, and optimization strategies to further enhance your game's physics.

Section 6.4: Collision Detection and Response

IN THIS SECTION, WE'LL delve into collision detection and response in Unity, an essential aspect of creating realistic and interactive game physics. Collision detection involves identifying when objects come into contact, while response involves how objects react when they collide.

Unity's Collision Detection System

UNITY EMPLOYS A ROBUST collision detection system that automatically detects collisions between GameObjects equipped with colliders. Colliders are the components responsible for defining the shape of objects for collision calculations. Unity provides various types of colliders, including BoxCollider, SphereCollider, CapsuleCollider, and more.

```csharp
using UnityEngine;

public class CollisionExample : MonoBehaviour

{

void OnCollisionEnter(Collision collision)

{

// Called when this object collides with another object

Debug.Log("Collision detected with: " + collision.gameObject.name);
```

```
}

}
```

In the example above, the OnCollisionEnter method is used to detect when the GameObject this script is attached to collides with another GameObject. You can customize the behavior that occurs when a collision happens.

Collision Layers and Matrix

UNITY'S COLLISION SYSTEM allows you to organize objects into collision layers and define collision matrix settings to control which layers can interact with each other. This is essential for selectively enabling or disabling collision detection between specific types of objects.

```csharp
using UnityEngine;

public class CollisionLayers : MonoBehaviour
{
    void Start()
    {
        // Ignore collisions between the "Player" layer and the "Enemies" layer
        Physics.IgnoreLayerCollision(LayerMask.NameToLayer("Player"),
        LayerMask.NameToLayer("Enemies"));
    }
}
```

In this script, we use Physics.IgnoreLayerCollision to prevent collisions between GameObjects on the "Player" layer and the "Enemies" layer.

Trigger Colliders

IN ADDITION TO STANDARD colliders, Unity also provides trigger colliders. Trigger colliders do not physically block objects but are used to detect when objects pass through a specific area.

```
using UnityEngine;

public class TriggerExample : MonoBehaviour

{

void OnTriggerEnter(Collider other)

{

// Called when another object enters the trigger collider

Debug.Log("Trigger entered by: " + other.gameObject.name);

}

}
```

In the code snippet above, the OnTriggerEnter method is called when another object enters the trigger collider attached to the GameObject.

Rigidbody and Collision Detection Modes

WHEN USING RIGIDBODY components, you can set collision detection modes to control how Unity detects collisions. Unity offers three modes: Discrete, Continuous, and Continuous Dynamic.

- **Discrete**: Collisions are checked at fixed intervals.

- **Continuous**: Continuous collision detection is used to prevent fast-moving objects from passing through others.

- **Continuous Dynamic**: Similar to continuous, but only for objects with non-kinematic rigidbodies.

Selecting the appropriate collision detection mode depends on the specific requirements of your game and the type of physics behavior you want to achieve.

Collision Response

UNITY PROVIDES SEVERAL ways to handle collision response, including physics-based reactions, custom scripting, and event-driven responses. You can use forces, impulses, or custom calculations to determine how objects react when they collide.

```csharp
using UnityEngine;

public class CollisionResponse : MonoBehaviour
{

private Rigidbody rb;

public float forceMultiplier = 10.0f;

void Start()
{

rb = GetComponent<Rigidbody>();
```

```
}

void OnCollisionEnter(Collision collision)

{

// Apply a force in the opposite direction of the collision

Vector3 forceDirection = -collision.contacts[0].normal;

rb.AddForce(forceDirection * forceMultiplier, ForceMode.Impulse);

}

}
```

In this script, we apply an impulse force to the Rigidbody in the opposite direction of the collision normal when a collision occurs.

Understanding collision detection and response is essential for creating dynamic and interactive game physics. Properly configuring colliders, layers, and response behaviors can lead to realistic and engaging gameplay experiences. In the upcoming sections, we will explore advanced physics simulations, such as raycasting, and optimization strategies to improve collision performance in your Unity games.

Section 6.5: Advanced Physics Simulations

IN THIS SECTION, WE'LL explore advanced physics simulations in Unity that go beyond basic rigidbody interactions. These techniques allow you to create more complex and dynamic behaviors in your games.

Raycasting

RAYCASTING IS A POWERFUL technique used for various purposes, including detecting objects in a specific direction, aiming, and even implementing vision for AI characters. Unity provides functions like Physics.Raycast and Physics.RaycastAll to perform raycasts.

```csharp
using UnityEngine;

public class RaycastExample : MonoBehaviour

{

void Update()

{

// Cast a ray from the object's position forward

Ray ray = new Ray(transform.position, transform.forward);

RaycastHit hit;

if (Physics.Raycast(ray, out hit, Mathf.Infinity))

{

// Check if the ray hit an object

Debug.Log("Hit: " + hit.collider.gameObject.name);

}

}

}
```

In this script, a ray is cast forward from the object's position, and if it hits any object, information about the hit is logged.

Physics Materials and Friction

UNITY'S PHYSICS MATERIALS allow you to control how objects interact when they collide. You can adjust properties like friction and bounciness to fine-tune the behavior of colliding objects.

```csharp
using UnityEngine;

public class FrictionExample : MonoBehaviour

{

private Rigidbody rb;

void Start()

{

rb = GetComponent<Rigidbody>();

// Set a custom physics material with low friction

PhysicMaterial customMaterial = new PhysicMaterial();

customMaterial.staticFriction = 0.2f;

customMaterial.dynamicFriction = 0.2f;

// Assign the custom material to the collider

GetComponent<Collider>().material = customMaterial;

}

}
```

In this script, we create a custom physics material with low friction and assign it to the object's collider, affecting how it interacts with other objects.

Joints and Constraints

UNITY PROVIDES A VARIETY of joint components, such as HingeJoint, FixedJoint, and SpringJoint, to simulate complex interactions between objects. These joints allow you to create mechanisms, hinges, and other realistic connections between GameObjects.

```csharp
using UnityEngine;

public class HingeJointExample : MonoBehaviour
{
    public Transform connectedObject;

    private HingeJoint hinge;

    void Start()
    {
        hinge = GetComponent<HingeJoint>();

        hinge.connectedBody = connectedObject.GetComponent<Rigidbody>();
    }
}
```

In this example, we create a hinge joint between two objects, allowing one object to rotate around the other.

Cloth Simulation

UNITY'S CLOTH SIMULATION is a physics-based system for simulating fabric, ropes, and other flexible materials. You can create cloth objects using the Cloth component and control their behavior through settings like wind and gravity.

```csharp
using UnityEngine;

public class ClothSimulation : MonoBehaviour

{

public Transform windZone;

private Cloth clothComponent;

void Start()

{

clothComponent = GetComponent<Cloth>();

}

void Update()

{

// Apply wind force to the cloth

clothComponent.externalAcceleration = windZone.forward * 5.0f;

}

}
```

In this script, we apply wind force to a cloth object, causing it to react realistically to the wind direction.

Soft Body Simulation

SOFT BODY SIMULATION is used to create deformable objects like jelly or soft cushions. While Unity's built-in physics system primarily deals with rigidbodies, you can find third-party assets and plugins that enable soft body simulations in Unity.

These advanced physics techniques add depth and realism to your game's interactions and can be crucial for creating unique gameplay experiences. Understanding how to use raycasting, physics materials, joints, and even third-party assets for soft body simulations can greatly expand your game development possibilities. In the upcoming sections, we will explore optimization strategies and best practices for handling complex physics simulations in Unity.

Chapter 7: Audio and Sound Effects

Section 7.1: Integrating Audio in Unity Games

In this section, we'll delve into the integration of audio and sound effects in Unity games. Audio is a vital component of game development, enhancing immersion and creating a more engaging player experience. Unity provides a robust audio system that allows you to work with both 2D and 3D audio, as well as manage sound effects, background music, and more.

Audio Sources

IN UNITY, AUDIO IS controlled using Audio Sources. An Audio Source represents a sound emitter in your scene and can be attached to GameObjects. You can configure various properties of an Audio Source, such as the audio clip it plays, volume, pitch, and spatial settings.

Here's a basic example of how to set up an Audio Source and play a sound effect:

```
using UnityEngine;

public class AudioManager : MonoBehaviour

{

public AudioClip soundEffect;

private AudioSource audioSource;
```

```
void Start()

{

audioSource = GetComponent<AudioSource>();

audioSource.clip = soundEffect;

}

void Update()

{

if (Input.GetKeyDown(KeyCode.Space))

{

audioSource.Play();

}

}
```

In this script, we attach an Audio Source to a GameObject and assign an AudioClip to it. When the Space key is pressed, the audio is played.

3D Audio and Spatial Sound

UNITY'S AUDIO SYSTEM supports 3D audio, allowing sounds to be perceived as coming from specific positions in the game world. This adds depth and realism to the auditory experience, especially in virtual reality or augmented reality applications.

To enable 3D audio, you can adjust the spatial blend property of an Audio Source. A value of 0 represents 2D audio (no spatialization), while a value of 1 represents full 3D spatialization.

```csharp
using UnityEngine;

public class SpatialAudio : MonoBehaviour
{

private AudioSource audioSource;

void Start()
{

audioSource = GetComponent<AudioSource>();

audioSource.spatialBlend = 1.0f; // Enable 3D spatialization

}

}
```

In this example, we set the spatial blend to 1, enabling full 3D audio.

Audio Mixing and Mastering

UNITY PROVIDES A BUILT-in Audio Mixer that allows you to control the mixing and mastering of audio in your game. You can create complex audio hierarchies, apply effects, and control volume levels. Audio Mixers are especially useful for managing background music, sound effects, and dialogue independently.

```csharp
using UnityEngine;

using UnityEngine.Audio;
```

```csharp
public class AudioMixing : MonoBehaviour

{

public AudioMixer audioMixer;

public string mixerGroup;

void Start()

{

audioMixer.SetFloat(mixerGroup + "Volume", 0.0f); // Set the volume for a specific group

}

}
```

In this script, we adjust the volume of a specific mixer group in the Audio Mixer.

Dynamic Audio Scripting

YOU CAN ALSO CONTROL audio elements dynamically through scripting. This allows you to trigger sounds, change their properties, and create dynamic audio experiences in response to gameplay events.

```csharp
using UnityEngine;

public class DynamicAudio : MonoBehaviour

{

private AudioSource audioSource;

public float pitchRange = 0.2f;
```

```
void Start()

{

audioSource = GetComponent<AudioSource>();

}

void Update()

{

if (Input.GetKeyDown(KeyCode.Space))

{

// Play the audio with a random pitch variation

audioSource.pitch  =  1.0f  +  Random.Range(-pitchRange,
pitchRange);

audioSource.Play();

}

}

}
```

In this example, we change the pitch of the audio randomly each time the Space key is pressed, creating variety in the sound.

Audio Events and Triggers

YOU CAN SET UP AUDIO events and triggers to synchronize audio with specific gameplay events. For example, you might play a sound effect when a character takes damage or when a new level is loaded.

Unity's Animation Events or scripting can be used to trigger audio playback at specific moments in your game.

```
using UnityEngine;

public class AudioEventTrigger : MonoBehaviour

{

public AudioClip soundEffect;

private AudioSource audioSource;

void Start()

{

audioSource = GetComponent<AudioSource>();

}

public void PlaySoundEffect()

{

audioSource.clip = soundEffect;

audioSource.Play();

}

}
```

In this script, the PlaySoundEffect method is called to play a sound effect when an event triggers it.

Integrating audio effectively in your Unity games enhances immersion and creates a more enjoyable player experience. Whether it's spatial sound for realism or dynamic audio scripting for interactivity, Unity's audio system offers a wide range of possibilities. In the upcoming sections, we will explore sound effects, background music, 3D audio techniques, and dynamic audio scripting in more detail, allowing you to create rich and engaging auditory experiences for your players.

Section 7.2: Sound Effects and Background Music

IN THIS SECTION, WE'LL delve into the world of sound effects and background music in Unity game development. Sound effects and music play a significant role in shaping the atmosphere and enhancing the overall player experience. Unity provides tools and techniques to incorporate both sound effects and background music seamlessly into your games.

Sound Effects

SOUND EFFECTS ARE SHORT audio clips that are used to convey various in-game events and actions. These can include footsteps, gunfire, explosions, button clicks, and more. Unity allows you to trigger sound effects in response to specific events or actions within your game.

To use sound effects, you typically attach an AudioSource component to a GameObject and assign an audio clip to it. You can then play the sound effect programmatically when the event occurs.

```
using UnityEngine;

public class SoundEffectPlayer : MonoBehaviour
{
    public AudioClip soundEffect;
```

```
private AudioSource audioSource;

void Start()

{

audioSource = GetComponent<AudioSource>();

audioSource.clip = soundEffect;

}

// Function to play the sound effect

public void PlaySoundEffect()

{

audioSource.Play();

}

}
```

In the example above, we attach an AudioSource component to a GameObject, assign an audio clip (soundEffect) to it, and create a function (PlaySoundEffect) to play the sound effect.

Background Music

BACKGROUND MUSIC SETS the tone and mood of your game. It can be a looping musical track that plays continuously throughout the game or changes dynamically based on the gameplay situation. Unity allows you to manage background music using AudioSource components and provides features for seamless music transitions.

```
using UnityEngine;
```

```csharp
public class BackgroundMusicController : MonoBehaviour

{

public AudioClip[] musicTracks;

private AudioSource audioSource;

private int currentTrackIndex = 0;

void Start()

{

audioSource = GetComponent<AudioSource>();

audioSource.loop = true;

PlayNextTrack();

}

// Function to play the next music track

public void PlayNextTrack()

{

audioSource.clip = musicTracks[currentTrackIndex];

audioSource.Play();

currentTrackIndex = (currentTrackIndex + 1) % musicTracks.Length;

}

}
```

In this script, we create a BackgroundMusicController that allows you to loop through a list of music tracks and play them one after another.

Crossfading and Transitions

SMOOTH TRANSITIONS between music tracks can greatly enhance the player experience. Unity provides the ability to crossfade between audio clips, allowing you to create seamless transitions when switching between different pieces of background music.

```
using UnityEngine;

public class MusicTransition : MonoBehaviour

{

public AudioSource audioSource1;

public AudioSource audioSource2;

public float crossfadeDuration = 1.0f;

// Function to crossfade between two audio sources

public void Crossfade()

{

StartCoroutine(CrossfadeCoroutine());

}

private IEnumerator CrossfadeCoroutine()

{
```

```csharp
float timer = 0.0f;

float initialVolume1 = audioSource1.volume;

float initialVolume2 = audioSource2.volume;

while (timer < crossfadeDuration)

{

float t = timer / crossfadeDuration;

audioSource1.volume = Mathf.Lerp(initialVolume1, 0.0f, t);

audioSource2.volume = Mathf.Lerp(initialVolume2, 1.0f, t);

timer += Time.deltaTime;

yield return null;

}

audioSource1.Stop();

}

}
```

In this script, we create a MusicTransition class that performs a crossfade between two AudioSource components over a specified duration.

Dynamic Music

DYNAMIC MUSIC SYSTEMS adapt to the gameplay situation, creating a more immersive experience. You can use scripts and triggers to change the background music based on in-game events, such as combat, exploration, or dramatic moments.

```csharp
using UnityEngine;

public class DynamicMusicManager : MonoBehaviour

{

public AudioClip explorationMusic;

public AudioClip combatMusic;

private AudioSource audioSource;

void Start()

{

audioSource = GetComponent<AudioSource>();

PlayExplorationMusic();

}

// Function to switch to exploration music

public void PlayExplorationMusic()

{

audioSource.clip = explorationMusic;

audioSource.Play();

}

// Function to switch to combat music

public void PlayCombatMusic()

{
```

```
audioSource.clip = combatMusic;

audioSource.Play();

    }

}
```

In this example, we create a DynamicMusicManager that allows you to switch between exploration and combat music based on gameplay events.

Integrating sound effects and background music effectively in your Unity games can elevate the player experience and immerse players in your game world. Whether it's triggering sound effects for in-game actions or creating dynamic and adaptive background music, Unity's audio system provides the tools to enhance the auditory aspect of your games. In the upcoming sections, we will explore 3D audio, spatial sound techniques, audio mixing, and more advanced audio scripting to further refine your game's auditory experience.

Section 7.3: 3D Audio and Spatial Sound Techniques

IN THIS SECTION, WE will explore 3D audio and spatial sound techniques in Unity. Spatial audio allows you to create a more immersive experience by simulating sound sources in a three-dimensional space. This means that sounds can appear to come from different directions and distances, enhancing the realism of your game's audio.

Understanding 3D Audio

3D AUDIO SIMULATES how sound behaves in the real world. It takes into account the position and orientation of the listener (usually the player), as well as the position of sound sources. Unity's 3D audio system calculates how a sound should be heard based on these factors, providing a sense of direction, distance, and movement for sound sources.

To work with 3D audio in Unity, you can use the AudioSource component and configure its spatialization properties. Here's a basic example of how to enable 3D audio:

```csharp
using UnityEngine;

public class SpatialAudioExample : MonoBehaviour

{

public AudioClip soundEffect;

private AudioSource audioSource;

void Start()

{

audioSource = GetComponent<AudioSource>();

audioSource.spatialize = true; // Enable 3D spatialization

audioSource.spatialBlend = 1.0f; // Full 3D spatialization

audioSource.clip = soundEffect;

}

void Update()

{
```

```
// Set the position of the audio source to follow an object (e.g., a moving character)

audioSource.transform.position = transform.position;

}

}
```

In this script, we enable 3D spatialization for the AudioSource and set its spatial blend to 1 for full 3D audio.

Positioning Sound Sources

TO MAKE SOUND SOURCES appear as if they are coming from specific directions, you can position the AudioSource accordingly. You can also change the position dynamically to simulate sound sources that move in the game world.

```
using UnityEngine;

public class MovingSoundSource : MonoBehaviour

{

public AudioClip soundEffect;

private AudioSource audioSource;

void Start()

{

audioSource = GetComponent<AudioSource>();

audioSource.spatialize = true;

audioSource.spatialBlend = 1.0f;
```

```csharp
    audioSource.clip = soundEffect;

}

void Update()

{

    // Move the audio source position to follow the object

    audioSource.transform.position = transform.position;

}

}
```

In this example, the AudioSource position follows the position of the object it is attached to, creating the illusion of a sound source moving with the object.

Attenuation and Distance Effects

IN THE REAL WORLD, sound becomes quieter as you move away from the source. Unity's 3D audio system simulates this effect through attenuation. You can control how sound attenuates over distance by adjusting the AudioSource properties.

```csharp
using UnityEngine;

public class DistanceAttenuation : MonoBehaviour

{

public AudioClip soundEffect;

private AudioSource audioSource;

void Start()
```

```
{

audioSource = GetComponent<AudioSource>();

audioSource.spatialize = true;

audioSource.spatialBlend = 1.0f;

audioSource.clip = soundEffect;

}

void Update()

{

// Set the maximum distance at which the sound is audible

audioSource.maxDistance = 10.0f;

}

}
```

In this script, we set the maxDistance property of the AudioSource to control when the sound becomes inaudible due to distance.

Doppler Effect

THE DOPPLER EFFECT simulates the change in frequency (pitch) of a sound as it moves relative to an observer. Unity's 3D audio system automatically applies the Doppler effect when you have a moving AudioSource and listener.

You don't need to write additional code to enable the Doppler effect in Unity; it is handled by the audio system.

Sound Occlusion and Obstruction

IN REAL-WORLD ENVIRONMENTS, objects can block or partially obstruct sound. Unity's audio system can simulate sound occlusion and obstruction to enhance realism.

To achieve this, you can use the Raycast method to check if there are any objects blocking the sound path between the AudioSource and the listener. If an obstruction is detected, you can adjust the sound properties accordingly to simulate muffled or partially blocked audio.

```csharp
using UnityEngine;

public class SoundObstruction : MonoBehaviour

{

public AudioClip soundEffect;

private AudioSource audioSource;

void Start()

{

audioSource = GetComponent<AudioSource>();

audioSource.spatialize = true;

audioSource.spatialBlend = 1.0f;

audioSource.clip = soundEffect;

}

void Update()
```

```
{
    // Check for obstructions and adjust audio properties accordingly
    RaycastHit hit;
    if (Physics.Raycast(transform.position, listenerTransform.position - transform.position, out hit, maxDistance))
    {
        // Adjust audio properties based on the obstruction
        audioSource.volume = 0.5f;
    }
    else
    {
        // No obstruction, reset audio properties
        audioSource.volume = 1.0f;
    }
}
```

In this script, we use raycasting to detect obstructions and adjust the AudioSource properties accordingly.

Unity's 3D audio and spatial sound techniques allow you to create more immersive and realistic auditory experiences in your games. Whether you're simulating sound sources in 3D space, handling attenuation and distance effects, or implementing sound occlusion and obstruction, Unity's audio system provides the tools to enhance the audio aspect of your game. In the upcoming sections, we will explore audio mixing, audio scripting, and advanced audio features to further refine your game's auditory experience.

Section 7.4: Audio Mixing and Mastering

IN THIS SECTION, WE will dive into audio mixing and mastering in Unity. Audio mixing is the process of adjusting the levels and properties of individual audio sources to create a balanced and immersive audio experience in your game. Mastering, on the other hand, is the final step in audio production, where you polish and optimize the audio before it's integrated into your game.

Unity's Audio Mixer

UNITY PROVIDES AN AUDIO Mixer asset that allows you to control and manipulate audio in real-time. You can create complex audio hierarchies, apply effects, control volume levels, and manage the balance between different audio sources, such as background music, sound effects, and voiceovers.

To get started with audio mixing, follow these steps:

1. Create an Audio Mixer asset in your Unity project by right-clicking in the Project panel and selecting "Create > Audio Mixer."
2. Attach the Audio Mixer to an Audio Listener in your scene. You can do this by selecting the Audio Listener component in the Inspector and assigning the Audio Mixer asset to the "Output" field.
3. Create Audio Mixer Groups within the Audio Mixer. These groups act as submixes for different types of audio

sources (e.g., background music, sound effects).

4. Assign individual audio sources to the appropriate Audio Mixer Group. You can do this by selecting the AudioSource component and setting the "Output" field to the desired group.

5. Use the Audio Mixer to control volume, apply effects, and create audio snapshots for different game scenarios.

Here's an example of adjusting the volume of an Audio Mixer Group in code:

```csharp
using UnityEngine;

using UnityEngine.Audio;

public class AudioMixingExample : MonoBehaviour

{

public AudioMixer audioMixer;

public void SetBackgroundMusicVolume(float volume)

{

audioMixer.SetFloat("BackgroundMusicVolume", volume);

}

}
```

In this script, we access an Audio Mixer named audioMixer and adjust the volume of a group named "BackgroundMusicVolume."

Creating Audio Snapshots

AUDIO SNAPSHOTS ARE presets that store the state of an Audio Mixer at a particular moment. You can use them to transition between different audio settings smoothly. For example, you can create snapshots for different game scenarios, such as combat, exploration, and cutscenes.

To create an audio snapshot, follow these steps:

1. Select the Audio Mixer in the Unity Inspector.
2. In the Audio Mixer window, click the "Snapshot" button to create a new snapshot.
3. Adjust the properties of the Audio Mixer (e.g., volume levels, effect parameters) to match the desired state.
4. Rename the snapshot to describe the scenario it represents (e.g., "Combat Snapshot").

To transition between snapshots, you can use code like this:

```csharp
using UnityEngine;

using UnityEngine.Audio;

public class AudioSnapshotTransition : MonoBehaviour

{

public AudioMixerSnapshot combatSnapshot;

public AudioMixerSnapshot explorationSnapshot;

public void TransitionToCombatSnapshot()

{
```

combatSnapshot.TransitionTo(1.0f); *// 1.0f represents the transition time*

```
}

public void TransitionToExplorationSnapshot()

{

explorationSnapshot.TransitionTo(1.0f);

}

}
```

In this script, we have two audio snapshots, combatSnapshot and explorationSnapshot. The TransitionTo method is used to smoothly transition from one snapshot to another.

Applying Effects and EQ

UNITY'S AUDIO MIXER allows you to apply various audio effects and equalization (EQ) to individual audio sources or groups. You can add effects like reverb, echo, and chorus to create specific auditory atmospheres. Additionally, you can use EQ to adjust the frequency balance, enhancing the overall sound quality.

To add an effect to an Audio Mixer Group, follow these steps:

1. Select the Audio Mixer in the Unity Inspector.
2. In the Audio Mixer window, select the desired group.
3. In the Group Effects section, click the "+" button to add an effect.
4. Configure the parameters of the effect as needed.

Here's an example of how to add a reverb effect to an Audio Mixer Group:

```
using UnityEngine;

using UnityEngine.Audio;

public class AddReverbEffect : MonoBehaviour

{

public AudioMixer audioMixer;

public AudioMixerGroup reverbGroup;

public AudioReverbPreset reverbPreset;

public void ApplyReverbEffect()

{

audioMixer.SetFloat("ReverbWetMix", 100.0f);

audioMixer.SetFloat("ReverbDryMix", -100.0f);

reverbGroup.audioMixer.SetFloat("ReverbPreset",
(float)reverbPreset);

}

}
```

In this script, we access an Audio Mixer named audioMixer, adjust the reverb wet and dry mix, and apply a reverb preset to the specified group.

Mastering and Optimization

BEFORE INTEGRATING audio into your game, it's essential to master and optimize the audio assets. This involves tasks such as:

- Normalizing audio levels to ensure consistent volume.

- Removing noise and unwanted artifacts.

- Compressing and encoding audio in appropriate formats (e.g., Ogg Vorbis, MP3) to minimize file size while maintaining quality.

- Setting appropriate sample rates and bit depths for your target platform.

Mastering and optimizing audio assets can significantly improve performance and reduce the storage footprint of your game.

Unity's audio system, combined with audio mixing and mastering techniques, provides the tools you need to create a rich and immersive auditory experience for your players. Whether you're adjusting volume levels, applying effects, creating audio snapshots, or optimizing audio assets, effective audio management is crucial for delivering a polished and engaging game. In the upcoming sections, we will explore dynamic audio scripting, event-driven audio, and advanced audio features to further enhance your game's auditory experience.

Section 7.5: Dynamic Audio Scripting

IN THIS SECTION, WE will explore dynamic audio scripting in Unity, which allows you to control audio elements programmatically in response to gameplay events and interactions. Dynamic audio scripting gives you the flexibility to create immersive audio experiences that respond to player actions, providing a more engaging gameplay environment.

Dynamic Sound Effects

ONE COMMON USE OF DYNAMIC audio scripting is to trigger sound effects in response to in-game events. For example, you might play a gunshot sound when a player fires a weapon or a footstep sound as a character walks.

```csharp
using UnityEngine;

public class DynamicSoundEffects : MonoBehaviour

{

public AudioClip gunshotSound;

private AudioSource audioSource;

void Start()

{

audioSource = GetComponent<AudioSource>();

}

public void PlayGunshotSound()

{

audioSource.PlayOneShot(gunshotSound);

}

}
```

In this example, we have an AudioSource component attached to a GameObject, and we play the gunshot sound effect using the PlayOneShot method when the PlayGunshotSound function is called.

Footstep Sounds

IMPLEMENTING FOOTSTEP sounds is a common scenario in many games. You can create a system that plays different footstep sounds based on the character's movement speed or the type of surface they are walking on.

```csharp
using UnityEngine;

public class FootstepSounds : MonoBehaviour
{

public AudioClip[] footstepSounds;

private AudioSource audioSource;

void Start()
{

audioSource = GetComponent<AudioSource>();

}

public void PlayFootstepSound()
{

// Randomly select a footstep sound from the array
int randomIndex = Random.Range(0, footstepSounds.Length);
```

```
AudioClip footstepSound = footstepSounds[randomIndex];

// Play the selected footstep sound

audioSource.PlayOneShot(footstepSound);

}

}
```

In this script, we have an array of footstep sounds, and when the PlayFootstepSound function is called, a random sound is selected and played.

Dynamic Music Transitions

DYNAMIC AUDIO SCRIPTING also enables you to create seamless transitions between different music tracks in response to changing gameplay situations. For example, you might switch to intense combat music when a battle begins and transition back to calm exploration music when the battle ends.

```
using UnityEngine;

using UnityEngine.Audio;

public class MusicManager : MonoBehaviour

{

public AudioMixerSnapshot explorationSnapshot;

public AudioMixerSnapshot combatSnapshot;

public void SwitchToExplorationMusic()

{
```

```
explorationSnapshot.TransitionTo(1.0f);

}

public void SwitchToCombatMusic()

{

combatSnapshot.TransitionTo(1.0f);

}

}
```

In this script, we have two audio snapshots, explorationSnapshot and combatSnapshot, which we transition to when switching between exploration and combat music.

Interactive Soundscapes

YOU CAN USE DYNAMIC audio scripting to create interactive soundscapes that respond to the player's actions and the game's state. For example, you might adjust the volume and intensity of environmental sounds based on the time of day, weather conditions, or the player's location within the game world.

```
using UnityEngine;

public class InteractiveSoundscape : MonoBehaviour

{

public AudioSource ambientSound;

public Light dayNightCycle;

void Update()
```

```
{

    // Adjust the ambient sound based on the time of day

    float intensity = Mathf.Clamp01(dayNightCycle.intensity);

    ambientSound.volume = intensity;

}

}
```

In this example, we adjust the volume of an ambient sound based on the intensity of the day-night cycle light, creating a dynamic soundscape that responds to the time of day.

Implementing Sound Triggers

SOUND TRIGGERS ARE regions or events within the game world that, when entered or activated, trigger specific audio responses. This can include triggering the sound of a door opening when a player interacts with it or playing a sound when a character enters a specific area.

```
using UnityEngine;

public class SoundTrigger : MonoBehaviour
{

    public AudioClip soundEffect;

    private AudioSource audioSource;

    void Start()
    {
```

```
audioSource = GetComponent<AudioSource>();

audioSource.clip = soundEffect;

}

void OnTriggerEnter(Collider other)

{

if (other.CompareTag("Player"))

{

audioSource.Play();

}

}

}
```

In this script, we play a sound effect when a GameObject with a collider tagged as "Player" enters the trigger zone.

Dynamic audio scripting opens up a wide range of possibilities for creating immersive and responsive audio experiences in your Unity games. Whether you're triggering sound effects, implementing interactive soundscapes, managing music transitions, or using sound triggers, the ability to control audio elements through scripting adds depth and realism to your game's auditory environment. In the upcoming sections, we will explore more advanced audio features, including 3D audio, spatial sound, and advanced audio effects, to further enhance your game's audio quality and immersion.

Chapter 8: User Interface and HUD Design

Section 8.1: Designing User Interfaces in Unity

User interfaces (UI) are a critical component of any game, as they provide players with essential information and controls. In this section, we'll explore the fundamentals of designing user interfaces in Unity, including creating menus, buttons, and sliders, and implementing HUDs (Heads-Up Displays) to enhance the player's experience.

Canvas and UI Elements

UNITY'S UI SYSTEM REVOLVES around the concept of a Canvas, which serves as a container for UI elements. To create a Canvas, go to "GameObject > UI > Canvas" in the Unity Editor. Once you have a Canvas, you can add UI elements such as Text, Image, Button, and Slider to it.

UI elements are added as child GameObjects of the Canvas and are rendered on the screen based on their position within the Canvas hierarchy. You can adjust their properties, such as size, position, color, and text content, in the Inspector.

```
using UnityEngine;

using UnityEngine.UI;

public class UIManager : MonoBehaviour
```

```csharp
{
public Text scoreText;

public Button startButton;

private int score = 0;

void Start()

{

// Add a listener to the button's click event

startButton.onClick.AddListener(StartGame);

}

void StartGame()

{

// Start the game and hide the UI elements

startButton.gameObject.SetActive(false);

scoreText.gameObject.SetActive(true);

}

void Update()

{

// Update the score text

scoreText.text = "Score: " + score;

}
```

```
}
```

In this script, we have references to a Text element (scoreText) and a Button element (startButton) that are part of the UI. We add a listener to the button's click event so that when it's clicked, we can start the game by hiding the button and displaying the score text. The score text is updated in the Update method.

Anchors and Layouts

UI ELEMENTS ARE OFTEN designed to adapt to different screen sizes and resolutions. Unity provides anchoring and layout options to ensure that your UI elements are positioned correctly and scale appropriately on various devices.

- Anchors determine how UI elements are anchored to the edges of the Canvas or their parent elements. You can set anchors to ensure that an element maintains its relative position and size when the screen resolution changes.

- Layout components like Horizontal Layout Group and Vertical Layout Group help you arrange UI elements automatically. For instance, you can create a list of buttons that expands or contracts based on the available space.

Event System and Interactivity

TO MAKE UI ELEMENTS interactive, you need to use Unity's Event System. This system manages input events like clicks and touches and routes them to the appropriate UI elements. Ensure that you have an Event System GameObject in your scene to handle UI interactions.

```
using UnityEngine;
```

```csharp
using UnityEngine.UI;

public class ButtonClickHandler : MonoBehaviour

{

public Text resultText;

public void OnButtonClick()

{

resultText.text = "Button Clicked!";

}

}
```

In this example, we have a Button element with a ButtonClickHandler script attached. When the button is clicked, the OnButtonClick method is invoked, and it updates the resultText to display "Button Clicked!".

HUD Design

HEADS-UP DISPLAYS (HUDs) are essential for displaying critical in-game information without obstructing the gameplay view. Unity's UI system allows you to create HUDs that show player health, ammunition, mini-maps, and more.

```csharp
using UnityEngine;

using UnityEngine.UI;

public class HUDManager : MonoBehaviour

{
```

```csharp
public Slider healthSlider;

public Text ammoText;

public Image minimap;

// Update the HUD elements based on game data

public void UpdateHUD(int health, int ammo)

{

healthSlider.value = health;

ammoText.text = "Ammo: " + ammo;

}

}
```

In this script, we have references to a Slider (for health), a Text (for ammo), and an Image (for the minimap). The UpdateHUD method allows you to update these elements based on the game's data.

Designing user interfaces in Unity is a crucial aspect of creating a polished and user-friendly game. Whether you're designing main menus, in-game UI, or HUDs, understanding Unity's UI system, anchors, layouts, and interactivity is essential. In the following sections, we'll delve deeper into creating menus, buttons, sliders, scripting UI elements, and implementing best practices for UI/UX in games.

Section 8.2: Creating Menus, Buttons, and Sliders

IN THIS SECTION, WE will explore the creation of menus, buttons, and sliders in Unity's user interface (UI) system. Menus provide an essential component of game navigation and interaction, while buttons and sliders are commonly used to allow players to make choices and adjust settings.

Creating Menus

UNITY ALLOWS YOU TO design menus using the Canvas and UI elements we discussed earlier. Menus typically include options such as starting a new game, loading saved games, accessing settings, and exiting the game.

To create a menu in Unity:

1. Create a new Canvas GameObject by right-clicking in the Hierarchy panel and selecting "UI > Canvas."
2. Add UI elements like buttons and text to the Canvas to represent menu options.
3. Customize the appearance and layout of menu elements using the Inspector.
4. Implement functionality for menu options by attaching scripts to UI elements. For example, you can create a script that starts the game when the "Start" button is clicked.

```
using UnityEngine;

using UnityEngine.SceneManagement;

public class MainMenu : MonoBehaviour

{
```

```csharp
public void StartGame()

{

// Load the game scene

SceneManager.LoadScene("GameScene");

}

public void ExitGame()

{

// Quit the application (works in standalone builds)

Application.Quit();

}

}
```

In this example, the StartGame method loads the "GameScene," while the ExitGame method quits the application. Attach this script to the appropriate UI elements in the menu.

Buttons for Interactivity

BUTTONS ARE ESSENTIAL for providing interaction in your game's UI. Unity's UI system includes a Button component that can trigger actions when clicked.

To create a button:

1. Add a Button element to your Canvas.
2. Customize the button's appearance and text in the Inspector.
3. Attach a script to the button to define its behavior when

clicked.

```csharp
using UnityEngine;

using UnityEngine.UI;

public class ButtonClickHandler : MonoBehaviour

{

public Text resultText;

public void OnButtonClick()

{

resultText.text = "Button Clicked!";

}

}
```

In this script, the OnButtonClick method updates a Text element (resultText) to display "Button Clicked!" when the button is clicked. Assign the Text element and this script to your button in the Inspector.

Sliders for Adjustments

SLIDERS ARE OFTEN USED to allow players to adjust settings or values within the game. Unity's UI system provides a Slider component that can be used for this purpose.

To create a slider:

1. Add a Slider element to your Canvas.
2. Customize the slider's appearance, range, and initial value

in the Inspector.

3. Attach a script to the slider to respond to value changes.

```csharp
using UnityEngine;

using UnityEngine.UI;

public class SliderHandler : MonoBehaviour

{

public Text valueText;

public void OnSliderValueChanged(float value)

{

valueText.text = "Value: " + value.ToString("F2");

}

}
```

In this script, the OnSliderValueChanged method updates a Text element (valueText) to display the current slider value with two decimal places when the slider's value changes. Attach the Text element and this script to your slider in the Inspector.

Menus, buttons, and sliders are fundamental elements of game UI that provide players with essential interaction and customization options. By creating and customizing these UI components and adding functionality through scripts, you can enhance the user experience and make your game more engaging. In the next section, we'll delve into implementing Heads-Up Displays (HUDs) for in-game information display and continue to explore best practices for UI/UX in games.

Section 8.3: Implementing Heads-Up Displays (HUDs)

IN THIS SECTION, WE will explore the implementation of Heads-Up Displays (HUDs) in Unity. HUDs are an integral part of many games, providing players with real-time information and feedback while maintaining their immersion in the game world. We'll discuss various elements commonly found in HUDs and how to create them in Unity.

HUD Elements

HEADS-UP DISPLAYS TYPICALLY contain elements such as health bars, ammunition counters, mini-maps, and objective markers. These elements convey critical information to the player without the need for separate menus or screens.

Health Bars

HEALTH BARS ARE A COMMON HUD element used to display a player's or character's remaining health or vitality. To create a health bar in Unity, you can use the Slider UI component. Set the Slider's minimum and maximum values to represent the minimum and maximum health values, and update its value in code as the character's health changes.

```
using UnityEngine;

using UnityEngine.UI;

public class HealthBar : MonoBehaviour

{

public Slider healthSlider;
```

```csharp
private int maxHealth = 100;

private int currentHealth = 100;

void Start()

{

// Initialize the health slider

healthSlider.minValue = 0;

healthSlider.maxValue = maxHealth;

healthSlider.value = currentHealth;

}

public void UpdateHealth(int newHealth)

{

currentHealth = Mathf.Clamp(newHealth, 0, maxHealth);

healthSlider.value = currentHealth;

}

}
```

In this script, the UpdateHealth method is used to update the health value on the slider, ensuring that it remains within the valid range.

Ammunition Counters

AMMUNITION COUNTERS are essential for games involving weapons or inventory systems. You can display ammunition counts using Text UI elements in Unity. Create a Text element, and then update its text content as the player's ammunition changes.

```csharp
using UnityEngine;

using UnityEngine.UI;

public class AmmoCounter : MonoBehaviour

{

public Text ammoText;

private int currentAmmo = 30;

void Start()

{

// Initialize the ammo counter

UpdateAmmoText();

}

public void UpdateAmmo(int newAmmo)

{

currentAmmo = Mathf.Max(newAmmo, 0);

UpdateAmmoText();

}

void UpdateAmmoText()

{

ammoText.text = "Ammo: " + currentAmmo;
```

```
}

}
```

Here, the UpdateAmmo method updates the current ammunition count, ensuring it remains non-negative, and the UpdateAmmoText method updates the Text element.

Mini-Maps

MINI-MAPS PROVIDE PLAYERS with a simplified view of the game world, highlighting their position and important locations. Implementing mini-maps in Unity often involves creating a secondary camera that captures the relevant part of the game world and displaying it on a UI Raw Image.

```csharp
using UnityEngine;

using UnityEngine.UI;

public class MiniMap : MonoBehaviour

{

public RawImage miniMapImage;

public Transform playerTransform;

public Camera miniMapCamera;

void LateUpdate()

{

// Update the mini-map's position to follow the player
```

```csharp
Vector2                positionOnMap                =
miniMapCamera.WorldToViewportPoint(playerTransform.position);

miniMapImage.rectTransform.anchoredPosition = new Vector2(

positionOnMap.x * miniMapImage.rectTransform.sizeDelta.x,

positionOnMap.y * miniMapImage.rectTransform.sizeDelta.y

);

}

}
```

In this script, the LateUpdate method continuously adjusts the position of the mini-map image to follow the player's position on the mini-map.

Objective Markers

OBJECTIVE MARKERS ARE often used in open-world games to guide players towards missions or objectives. They are typically represented as icons on the screen that point in the direction of the objective. Implementing objective markers involves determining the position of the objective in the game world, converting it to screen space, and displaying the marker accordingly.

```csharp
using UnityEngine;

using UnityEngine.UI;

public class ObjectiveMarker : MonoBehaviour

{

public Image markerImage;
```

```csharp
public Transform objectiveTransform;

public Camera mainCamera;

void Update()

{

// Calculate the position of the objective in screen space

Vector3 screenPosition = mainCamera.WorldToScreenPoint(objectiveTransform.position);

// Update the position of the marker image

markerImage.rectTransform.position = screenPosition;

}

}
```

In this script, the Update method calculates the screen position of the objective and updates the marker's position accordingly.

Designing HUD Layout

CREATING AN EFFECTIVE HUD layout is crucial for a good user experience. Consider factors like the placement of HUD elements, their size, and their visual style. Ensure that the HUD doesn't obstruct the player's view of the game world and that it provides relevant information at a glance.

Unity's UI system allows you to easily arrange and customize HUD elements by adjusting their anchors, sizes, and positions within the Canvas.

Implementing HUDs in Unity requires a combination of UI elements, scripting, and positioning to create a seamless and informative user experience. Whether you're displaying health bars, ammunition counters, mini-maps, or objective markers, designing and implementing effective HUDs enhances player engagement and immersion in your game. In the next section, we'll dive into scripting UI elements to make them interactive and responsive to player actions.

Section 8.4: Scripting UI Elements

IN THIS SECTION, WE'LL explore how to script user interface (UI) elements in Unity. Scripting UI elements allows you to add interactivity and functionality to buttons, sliders, text fields, and other UI components, making them responsive to player actions and enhancing the overall user experience.

UI Element References

BEFORE YOU CAN SCRIPT UI elements, you need to obtain references to them in your scripts. In Unity, you can use the public keyword to expose UI elements as serialized fields in your script, allowing you to drag and drop UI components from the Unity Editor.

```csharp
using UnityEngine;

using UnityEngine.UI;

public class UIScript : MonoBehaviour

{

public Text scoreText;
```

```
public Button startButton;

public Slider volumeSlider;

// Add references to other UI elements as needed

// Rest of your script

}
```

In this example, we have references to a Text element (scoreText), a Button element (startButton), and a Slider element (volumeSlider). These references can be assigned in the Unity Editor.

Button Click Events

ADDING FUNCTIONALITY to a button's click event is a common use case for scripting UI elements. You can attach a script to a button and define a method that is called when the button is clicked. Unity's UI system makes it easy to wire up these events in the Inspector.

```
using UnityEngine;

using UnityEngine.UI;

public class ButtonClickHandler : MonoBehaviour

{

public Text resultText;

public void OnButtonClick()

{

resultText.text = "Button Clicked!";
```

```
}

}
```

In this script, we have a method OnButtonClick that updates a Text element (resultText) to display "Button Clicked!" when the button is clicked. To set up the button click event, attach this script to the button GameObject and use the dropdown in the button's OnClick event section in the Inspector to select the GameObject and method to call.

Slider Value Change Events

SLIDERS ARE OFTEN USED for adjusting settings such as volume, brightness, or character attributes. You can script sliders to respond to value changes and update the game accordingly.

```csharp
using UnityEngine;

using UnityEngine.UI;

public class SliderHandler : MonoBehaviour

{

public Text valueText;

public void OnSliderValueChanged(float value)

{

valueText.text = "Value: " + value.ToString("F2");

}

}
```

In this example, the OnSliderValueChanged method updates a Text element (valueText) to display the current slider value with two decimal places whenever the slider's value changes. To set this up, attach this script to the slider GameObject and use the OnValueChanged event in the Inspector to link it to the method.

Input Fields for User Input

INPUT FIELDS ARE USED when you need to collect textual input from the player, such as their name or a password. You can script input fields to retrieve and process the input.

using UnityEngine;

using UnityEngine.UI;

public class InputFieldHandler : MonoBehaviour

{

public InputField nameInputField;

public Text resultText;

public void OnSubmit()

{

string playerName = nameInputField.text;

resultText.text = "Hello, " + playerName + "!";

}

}

In this script, the OnSubmit method retrieves the text entered in an InputField (nameInputField) and displays a greeting message using a Text element (resultText). To set this up, attach this script to the input field GameObject and use the OnEndEdit event in the Inspector to link it to the method.

Text Updates and Dynamic UI

YOU CAN ALSO SCRIPT Text elements to dynamically update their content during gameplay. For example, you might use Text elements to display player scores, mission objectives, or in-game notifications.

```csharp
using UnityEngine;

using UnityEngine.UI;

public class ScoreDisplay : MonoBehaviour

{

public Text scoreText;

private int score = 0;

public void UpdateScore(int points)

{

score += points;

scoreText.text = "Score: " + score;

}

}
```

In this script, the UpdateScore method takes a parameter (points) and updates the Text element (scoreText) with the current score. This can be useful for displaying dynamic information to the player.

Scripting UI elements in Unity opens up endless possibilities for creating interactive and dynamic user interfaces. By linking UI components to scripts, you can respond to player actions, provide feedback, and enhance the overall gameplay experience. In the next section, we'll explore best practices for UI/UX in games to ensure that your user interfaces are intuitive, user-friendly, and visually appealing.

Section 8.5: Best Practices for UI/UX in Games

CREATING A SEAMLESS and enjoyable user interface (UI) and user experience (UX) is crucial in game development. In this section, we'll explore some best practices for designing UI/UX in games using Unity. These practices will help you create interfaces that are intuitive, user-friendly, and visually appealing.

1. Consistency

CONSISTENCY IN DESIGN is key to a good UI/UX. Maintain a consistent style, color scheme, and layout throughout your game. This helps players navigate your game with ease and creates a cohesive and professional look.

2. User-Centered Design

ALWAYS DESIGN YOUR UI with the user in mind. Consider the player's perspective and needs. Test your UI with real players to gather feedback and make improvements based on their experiences.

3. Clarity and Simplicity

KEEP YOUR UI ELEMENTS clear and simple. Avoid clutter and excessive visual noise. Use concise and easily understandable language for labels and instructions. Less is often more when it comes to UI design.

4. Responsiveness

ENSURE THAT YOUR UI elements respond promptly to user actions. Buttons should provide feedback when clicked, and sliders should smoothly update values. A responsive UI enhances the feeling of control and immersion.

5. Accessibility

MAKE YOUR GAME ACCESSIBLE to a wide range of players. Provide options for adjusting text size, color schemes, and audio settings. Ensure that players with disabilities can enjoy your game with features like screen readers and keyboard controls.

6. Mobile Optimization

IF YOU'RE DEVELOPING for mobile platforms, prioritize mobile-friendly UI/UX. Design for touch input and consider various screen sizes and resolutions. Test your game on different devices to ensure a consistent experience.

7. Visual Hierarchy

USE VISUAL HIERARCHY to guide the player's attention to important UI elements. Larger fonts, contrasting colors, and positioning can help emphasize critical information. Important buttons or options should stand out.

8. Feedback and Animation

PROVIDE FEEDBACK TO confirm user actions. For example, when a button is pressed, it should visually depress to indicate that it's been clicked. Use subtle animations to enhance the user experience, but avoid excessive or distracting animations.

9. Load Times and Performance

MINIMIZE LOADING TIMES for your UI elements and optimize performance. Slow-loading menus or laggy UI can frustrate players. Use asynchronous loading and efficient asset management.

10. Testing and Iteration

REGULARLY TEST YOUR UI with different players and gather feedback. Iteratively refine your UI based on user testing results. What may seem intuitive to you might not be the same for others.

11. Contextual Help

PROVIDE CONTEXTUAL help and tooltips when necessary, especially for complex systems or menus. Tooltips can clarify the purpose of buttons, icons, or unfamiliar terms.

12. Localization

IF YOUR GAME IS INTENDED for a global audience, consider localization. Translate text and provide support for different languages and cultures. Ensure that text fits within UI elements without causing layout issues.

13. Error Handling

IMPLEMENT CLEAR ERROR messages and error handling. When players encounter errors or issues, they should receive informative messages that guide them on how to resolve the problem.

14. User Testing

CONDUCT USER TESTING with players who haven't been involved in the development process. Their fresh perspective can reveal usability issues and areas for improvement that you may have missed.

15. A/B Testing

A/B TESTING INVOLVES presenting different versions of your UI to different groups of players to determine which design performs better in terms of user engagement and retention. Use this technique to fine-tune your UI.

Remember that UI/UX design is an ongoing process. As your game evolves, continue to refine and improve your UI based on player feedback and changing design trends. A well-designed UI/UX can significantly enhance your game's appeal and user satisfaction.

Chapter 9: AI and Pathfinding

Section 9.1: Basics of Artificial Intelligence in Games

Artificial Intelligence (AI) plays a crucial role in creating engaging and dynamic gameplay experiences in video games. In this section, we'll explore the basics of AI in games, including its purpose, common AI behaviors, and how AI is implemented in Unity.

The Purpose of AI in Games

AI IN GAMES SERVES several essential purposes:

1. **Opponent and Enemy Behavior:** AI controls non-player characters (NPCs), opponents, and enemies in single-player and multiplayer games. It determines how these entities behave, making them challenging and unpredictable for players.
2. **Companion Behavior:** AI can also be used to control player companions, guiding them to provide assistance or follow specific commands.
3. **Decision Making:** AI makes decisions based on the game's rules, objectives, and player interactions. It can choose strategies, tactics, and actions in response to changing game conditions.
4. **Pathfinding:** AI calculates optimal paths for characters to navigate through game environments, avoiding obstacles and making dynamic decisions.

Common AI Behaviors

AI IN GAMES EXHIBITS various behaviors to create engaging gameplay. Some common AI behaviors include:

1. **Chasing and Fleeing:** AI characters can chase the player, flee from danger, or react to changes in the environment.
2. **Patrolling:** AI characters follow predefined routes or patrol areas, enhancing the realism of game worlds.
3. **Attacking and Defending:** AI-controlled enemies can attack players or defend themselves and their territory.
4. **Communication:** AI characters may communicate with each other, relay information, or engage in dialogues with players.
5. **Decision Trees and Finite State Machines:** AI often uses decision trees or finite state machines to determine actions based on specific conditions and player interactions.

Implementing AI in Unity

UNITY PROVIDES TOOLS and components to implement AI behaviors in games:

1. **NavMesh:** Unity's NavMesh system allows you to create navigation meshes that represent walkable areas in your game world. AI characters can use NavMesh to navigate and avoid obstacles.
2. **NavMesh Agents:** NavMesh Agents are components that you can attach to game objects to make them AI-aware. You can control their movement, set destinations, and define behaviors.
3. **Raycasting:** Raycasting is commonly used for AI perception. AI characters can cast rays to detect the player's presence, obstacles, or other game elements.

4. **Physics Layers:** Unity's layer system allows you to categorize game objects. AI can use layers to filter out irrelevant objects when making decisions.
5. **Scripting:** Custom scripts written in C# or Unity's scripting languages (JavaScript and Boo) enable you to implement complex AI behaviors. You can define AI logic, decision-making processes, and responses to player actions.

Here's a basic example of implementing AI movement using Unity's NavMesh system:

```csharp
using UnityEngine;

using UnityEngine.AI;

public class AIMovement : MonoBehaviour

{

public Transform target; // The target the AI should follow

private NavMeshAgent agent;

void Start()

{

agent = GetComponent<NavMeshAgent>();

}

void Update()

{

if (target != null)

{
```

// Set the destination for the AI to follow the target

```
agent.SetDestination(target.position);

    }

}

}
```

In this script, the AI follows a target using the NavMeshAgent component.

Understanding the basics of AI in games is a crucial foundation for creating complex and engaging AI behaviors. In the following sections, we'll explore more advanced AI techniques, decision-making processes, and pathfinding in Unity games.

Section 9.2: Implementing Simple AI Behaviors

IN THIS SECTION, WE'LL dive into implementing simple AI behaviors in Unity games. Simple AI behaviors are often used for non-player characters (NPCs) or enemies to make them interact with the player or the game world in basic ways.

Patrol and Follow

ONE OF THE MOST COMMON simple AI behaviors is patrol and follow. NPCs or enemies move along predefined paths or waypoints (patrol) and switch to following the player when they detect them. This behavior adds a level of predictability to AI characters' movements while allowing for dynamic interactions with the player.

Implementing Patrol

TO IMPLEMENT A PATROL behavior, you can use waypoints. Create empty GameObjects in your scene to represent waypoints, and then define a sequence of waypoints that an AI character should follow. You can use the NavMeshAgent component to move the character between waypoints.

Here's a basic example of implementing patrol behavior:

```
using UnityEngine;

using UnityEngine.AI;

public class PatrolAI : MonoBehaviour

{

public Transform[] waypoints;

private int currentWaypoint = 0;

private NavMeshAgent agent;

void Start()

{

agent = GetComponent<NavMeshAgent>();

GoToNextWaypoint();

}

void Update()

{
```

```csharp
// Check if the AI has reached the current waypoint

if (!agent.pathPending && agent.remainingDistance < 0.1f)

{

GoToNextWaypoint();

}

}

void GoToNextWaypoint()

{

if (waypoints.Length == 0)

return;

// Set the destination to the next waypoint

agent.destination = waypoints[currentWaypoint].position;

// Move to the next waypoint in a loop

currentWaypoint = (currentWaypoint + 1) % waypoints.Length;

}

}
```

In this script, the AI character follows a sequence of waypoints defined in the waypoints array. When it reaches a waypoint, it moves to the next one in a loop.

Implementing Follow

TO IMPLEMENT FOLLOWING behavior, you can use the same NavMeshAgent component. When the AI detects the player (e.g., through raycasting or triggers), it sets the player's position as the destination for the NavMeshAgent.

Here's a basic example of implementing follow behavior:

```
using UnityEngine;

using UnityEngine.AI;

public class FollowPlayerAI : MonoBehaviour

{

public Transform player;

private NavMeshAgent agent;

void Start()

{

agent = GetComponent<NavMeshAgent>();

}

void Update()

{

// Check if the player is within a certain range (e.g., line of sight)

if (Vector3.Distance(transform.position, player.position) < 10f)

{
```

```
// Set the player's position as the destination

agent.destination = player.position;

    }

  }

}
```

In this script, the AI character follows the player when the player is within a certain range (in this case, 10 units). The NavMeshAgent handles the pathfinding and movement.

Attacking

IMPLEMENTING BASIC attack behavior involves detecting the player's proximity and initiating attacks when they are within the attack range. The attack itself can be implemented in various ways, depending on your game's mechanics.

Here's a simplified example of implementing a basic melee attack:

```csharp
using UnityEngine;

public class MeleeAttackAI : MonoBehaviour

{

public Transform player;

public float attackRange = 2f;

public float attackCooldown = 2f;

private float lastAttackTime;

void Update()
```

```csharp
{
    // Check if the player is within attack range and the attack cooldown has passed
    if (Vector3.Distance(transform.position, player.position) < attackRange && Time.time - lastAttackTime > attackCooldown)
    {
        // Perform the attack (e.g., deal damage to the player)
        Attack();
        lastAttackTime = Time.time;
    }
}

void Attack()
{
    // Implement the attack logic here (e.g., reduce player's health)
    // You can also play attack animations or effects
}
```

In this script, the AI character checks if the player is within the specified attack range and if the attack cooldown has passed. When conditions are met, it calls the Attack method, which you can customize to implement the attack behavior, such as reducing the player's health or triggering animations.

These are basic examples of simple AI behaviors commonly found in games. You can build upon these concepts to create more complex behaviors and interactions for your AI characters. In the next sections, we'll explore advanced AI techniques, decision-making processes, and navigation systems in Unity.

Section 9.3: Advanced AI Techniques and Decision Making

IN THIS SECTION, WE'LL delve into advanced AI techniques and decision-making processes commonly used in Unity game development. These techniques enable AI characters to exhibit more complex and intelligent behaviors, enhancing the overall gameplay experience.

Finite State Machines (FSM)

FINITE STATE MACHINES (FSMs) are a fundamental concept in AI design. They model an AI character's behavior as a finite number of states, where each state represents a specific behavior or action. Transitions between states are triggered by certain conditions or events. FSMs are particularly useful for organizing and managing complex AI behaviors.

Here's a simplified example of implementing an FSM for an AI character in Unity:

```
using UnityEngine;

public enum AIState { Idle, Patrol, Chase, Attack }

public class FSMController : MonoBehaviour
{
```

```
public AIState currentState = AIState.Idle;

void Update()

{

// Perform actions based on the current state

switch (currentState)

{

case AIState.Idle:

// Implement idle behavior

break;

case AIState.Patrol:

// Implement patrol behavior

break;

case AIState.Chase:

// Implement chase behavior

break;

case AIState.Attack:

// Implement attack behavior

break;

}

}
```

```
// Transition to a new state based on conditions

void TransitionToState(AIState newState)

{

currentState = newState;

}

}
```

In this script, the AI character can be in one of four states: Idle, Patrol, Chase, or Attack. Depending on the current state, different behaviors are executed in the Update method. Transitions between states can be triggered by calling the TransitionToState method based on specific conditions.

Behavior Trees

BEHAVIOR TREES ARE another popular approach for modeling AI behaviors. They use a hierarchical structure of nodes to define a sequence of tasks or actions that an AI character should perform. Behavior Trees are versatile and can represent both simple and complex decision-making processes.

A simplified example of a Behavior Tree in Unity might look like this:

```
using UnityEngine;

using BehaviorTree;

public class BehaviorTreeController : MonoBehaviour

{
```

```csharp
private BehaviorTree.BehaviorTree behaviorTree;

void Start()

{

// Create a behavior tree

behaviorTree                        =                        new
BehaviorTree.BehaviorTreeBuilder(gameObject)

.Sequence()

.Selector()

.Condition(() => ShouldPatrol())

.Action(() => Patrol())

.End()

.Selector()

.Condition(() => ShouldChase())

.Action(() => Chase())

.End()

.End()

.Build();

}

void Update()

{

// Update the behavior tree
```

```
behaviorTree.Tick();
}

bool ShouldPatrol()

{

// Implement condition for patrol

return true;

}

void Patrol()

{

// Implement patrol behavior

}

bool ShouldChase()

{

// Implement condition for chase

return true;

}

void Chase()

{

// Implement chase behavior

}
```

```
}
```

In this script, we create a Behavior Tree with sequences and selectors to define the AI character's behavior. Conditions and actions are implemented as methods, allowing for flexibility in behavior design.

Utility AI

UTILITY AI IS A DECISION-making system that assigns utilities (weights) to different actions or behaviors based on their desirability in a given context. The AI character selects the action with the highest utility score. Utility AI is excellent for creating adaptive and context-aware AI behaviors.

Here's a simplified example of Utility AI in Unity:

```csharp
using UnityEngine;

using System.Collections.Generic;

public class UtilityAIController : MonoBehaviour

{

// Define possible actions and their utility functions

private List<UtilityAction> actions = new List<UtilityAction>();

void Start()

{

// Define actions and their utility functions

actions.Add(new UtilityAction("Attack", () => AttackUtility()));

actions.Add(new UtilityAction("Patrol", () => PatrolUtility()));
```

```csharp
}

void Update()

{

// Select the action with the highest utility

UtilityAction selectedAction = SelectBestAction();

// Perform the selected action

selectedAction.Execute();

}

float AttackUtility()

{

// Implement utility calculation for attack

return 0.9f;

}

float PatrolUtility()

{

// Implement utility calculation for patrol

return 0.5f;

}

UtilityAction SelectBestAction()

{
```

```csharp
UtilityAction bestAction = null;

float highestUtility = -1f;

foreach (var action in actions)

{

float utility = action.CalculateUtility();

if (utility > highestUtility)

{

highestUtility = utility;

bestAction = action;

}

}

return bestAction;

}

}
```

In this script, we define possible actions and their utility functions. The AI character selects the action with the highest utility score and executes it. Utility functions determine the desirability of each action based on the current game state.

These advanced AI techniques offer powerful ways to create complex and adaptive AI behaviors in Unity games. Depending on your game's requirements, you can choose the most suitable approach for modeling AI decision-making processes and behaviors.

Section 9.4: Pathfinding and Navigation Systems

PATHFINDING IS A CRUCIAL aspect of AI in game development, enabling characters and entities to navigate through complex game environments intelligently. Unity provides powerful tools and components for implementing pathfinding and navigation systems in your games.

Navigation Mesh (NavMesh)

UNITY'S NAVIGATION Mesh, commonly referred to as NavMesh, is a fundamental component for implementing pathfinding in your games. A NavMesh represents a simplified version of your game's geometry, where walkable surfaces are defined. NavMesh agents can then navigate these surfaces intelligently, avoiding obstacles.

Creating a NavMesh

TO CREATE A NAVMESH, follow these steps:

1. Open the Unity Editor.
2. Select the objects that should be part of the NavMesh (usually the ground and walkable surfaces).
3. In the Inspector window, click on the "Navigation" tab.
4. Click "Bake" to generate the NavMesh.

Using NavMesh Agents

NAVMESH AGENTS ARE components that you can attach to game objects to enable them to navigate the NavMesh. Here's a basic example of setting up a NavMesh agent:

```csharp
using UnityEngine;

using UnityEngine.AI;

public class NavMeshExample : MonoBehaviour

{

public Transform target; // The target the agent should follow

private NavMeshAgent agent;

void Start()

{

agent = GetComponent<NavMeshAgent>();

agent.destination = target.position; // Set the initial destination

}

}
```

In this script, the NavMesh agent is attached to a game object, and its destination is set to the position of the target. The agent will automatically navigate to the target while avoiding obstacles.

Raycasting for Obstacle Avoidance

WHILE NAVMESH PROVIDES an excellent solution for navigation, sometimes you may need to perform more precise obstacle avoidance or detect dynamic obstacles. Raycasting is a technique commonly used for this purpose.

Raycasting involves casting a ray (a straight line) from a point in a specific direction and checking if it intersects with any objects.

This allows you to detect obstacles in real-time and make decisions accordingly.

Here's a simplified example of using raycasting for obstacle avoidance:

```csharp
using UnityEngine;

public class RaycastExample : MonoBehaviour

{

public float raycastDistance = 2f;

private Transform player; // Reference to the player

void Start()

{

player = GameObject.FindWithTag("Player").transform;

}

void Update()

{

// Cast a ray from the AI towards the player

Vector3 direction = player.position - transform.position;

RaycastHit hit;

if (Physics.Raycast(transform.position, direction, out hit, raycastDistance))

{
```

```
// If the ray hits an obstacle, perform avoidance behavior

AvoidObstacle(hit);

}

}

void AvoidObstacle(RaycastHit hit)

{

// Implement obstacle avoidance logic here (e.g., change direction)

}

}
```

In this script, a ray is cast from the AI character toward the player, and if it hits an obstacle, the AvoidObstacle method is called, allowing you to implement avoidance behavior.

Pathfinding Algorithms

UNITY'S NAVMESH SYSTEM uses a variety of pathfinding algorithms under the hood, including A* (A-star) and Dijkstra's algorithm. These algorithms efficiently find the shortest path between two points on the NavMesh while considering obstacle avoidance.

You can also implement custom pathfinding algorithms if your game requires unique navigation behaviors. However, Unity's built-in NavMesh system should suffice for most game scenarios.

Pathfinding and navigation are critical components of AI in Unity game development. Understanding how to create and use NavMesh, utilize raycasting for obstacle avoidance, and work with pathfinding algorithms will empower you to create intelligent and responsive AI characters that can navigate complex game worlds effectively.

Section 9.5: Dynamic AI with Unity's NavMesh

DYNAMIC AI BEHAVIOR is a crucial aspect of many games, where AI characters adapt to changing circumstances, respond to player actions, and make decisions in real-time. Unity's NavMesh system provides features to create dynamic AI that can navigate, follow, and interact with the player and the game environment effectively.

Dynamic Destination Changes

IN MANY GAMES, AI CHARACTERS need to change their destinations dynamically based on changing game conditions. This can be achieved seamlessly using Unity's NavMesh system. Here's a simplified example of how to dynamically change an AI character's destination:

```csharp
using UnityEngine;

using UnityEngine.AI;

public class DynamicDestinationAI : MonoBehaviour

{

private NavMeshAgent agent;

private Transform player; // Reference to the player

void Start()

{
```

```csharp
agent = GetComponent<NavMeshAgent>();

player = GameObject.FindGameObjectWithTag("Player").transform;

// Set an initial destination

SetNewDestination();

}

void Update()

{

// Check if it's time to change the destination

if (Vector3.Distance(transform.position, agent.destination) < 1.0f)

{

SetNewDestination();

}

}

void SetNewDestination()

{

// Calculate a new random destination within a certain range

Vector3 randomDestination = Random.insideUnitSphere * 10.0f;

randomDestination += transform.position;

// Ensure the destination is within the NavMesh bounds

NavMeshHit hit;
```

```
if (NavMesh.SamplePosition(randomDestination, out hit, 10.0f,
NavMesh.AllAreas))
{

// Set the new destination

agent.SetDestination(hit.position);

}

}

}
```

In this script, the AI character initially sets a destination and then continuously checks if it has reached its current destination. When it reaches the destination, it calculates a new random destination within a certain range and ensures it is within the NavMesh bounds using NavMesh.SamplePosition. This allows the AI character to dynamically change its path in response to reaching its current destination.

Dynamic Obstacle Avoidance

DYNAMIC OBSTACLE AVOIDANCE is crucial when AI characters need to navigate around moving obstacles or when new obstacles are introduced into the game world. Unity's NavMesh system provides built-in support for dynamic obstacle avoidance.

To make a game object act as a dynamic obstacle, you can use the NavMeshObstacle component. Here's an example of how to set up a dynamic obstacle:

1. Create a GameObject in your scene and attach a NavMeshObstacle component to it.

2. Configure the NavMeshObstacle component as needed,
    specifying the shape, size, and other properties of the
    obstacle.
3. During gameplay, you can enable or disable the
    NavMeshObstacle component to make the obstacle
    dynamic or static. For example:

```csharp
using UnityEngine;

using UnityEngine.AI;

public class DynamicObstacleController : MonoBehaviour

{

private NavMeshObstacle navMeshObstacle;

void Start()

{

navMeshObstacle = GetComponent<NavMeshObstacle>();

}

void Update()

{

// Enable or disable the NavMeshObstacle dynamically based on game conditions

navMeshObstacle.enabled = ShouldBeDynamic();

}

bool ShouldBeDynamic()
```

```
{

// Implement logic to determine if the obstacle should be dynamic

return true;

}

}
```

In this script, the NavMeshObstacle component is enabled or disabled dynamically based on the logic in the ShouldBeDynamic method. This allows you to control when an obstacle should act as a dynamic obstacle and when it should remain static.

Dynamic AI Behavior

DYNAMIC AI BEHAVIOR often involves responding to player actions, such as chasing the player when detected or fleeing when in danger. Unity's NavMesh system can be combined with other AI techniques and logic to create dynamic behaviors.

For example, you can use raycasting to detect the player and then dynamically set the AI's destination to chase or flee. Here's a simplified example:

```
using UnityEngine;

using UnityEngine.AI;

public class DynamicAIChase : MonoBehaviour

{

private NavMeshAgent agent;

private Transform player; // Reference to the player
```

```csharp
void Start()

{

agent = GetComponent<NavMeshAgent>();

player = GameObject.FindGameObjectWithTag("Player").transform;

}

void Update()

{

// Check if the player is within line of sight

if (CanSeePlayer())

{

// Set the destination to chase the player

agent.SetDestination(player.position);

}

}

bool CanSeePlayer()

{

// Implement raycasting or other detection logic here

return true;

}

}
```

In this script, the AI character checks if it can see the player using the CanSeePlayer method, which can include raycasting or other detection techniques. If the player is detected, the AI character's destination is set to chase the player dynamically.

Dynamic AI behavior is a powerful tool for creating immersive and responsive game experiences. By combining Unity's NavMesh system with dynamic destination changes, dynamic obstacle avoidance, and AI logic, you can create AI characters that adapt to changing game conditions and interact with the player and the game world dynamically.

Chapter 10: Multiplayer and Networking

Section 10.1: Introduction to Multiplayer Game Development

Multiplayer game development is a fascinating and challenging field that allows players to interact with each other in real-time. Whether you're creating competitive shooters, cooperative adventures, or massive online worlds, understanding the fundamentals of multiplayer and networking is essential.

Why Multiplayer Games?

MULTIPLAYER GAMES OFFER a unique and engaging gaming experience. They allow players to:

- Compete against each other in various game modes.

- Collaborate and solve challenges together.

- Create and join communities within the game.

- Enhance the replay value and longevity of a game.

However, developing multiplayer games introduces several complexities that single-player games don't have to deal with, such as network synchronization, latency, and server management.

Networking Models

MULTIPLAYER GAMES CAN use different networking models to connect players and synchronize game state. The two primary models are:

1. **Peer-to-Peer (P2P)**: In a P2P network, each player's device communicates directly with others. This model is suitable for small-scale multiplayer games with a limited number of players.
2. **Client-Server**: In the client-server model, one player's device (the server) acts as the authority for the game state. Other players (clients) send their actions to the server, which then updates the game state and sends it back to all clients. This model is commonly used for larger multiplayer games.

Networking Protocols

NETWORKING PROTOCOLS determine how data is transmitted between players and servers. Some common protocols for multiplayer games include:

• **TCP (Transmission Control Protocol)**: Reliable but slower, ideal for sending important game data that should not be lost.

• **UDP (User Datagram Protocol)**: Faster but less reliable, suitable for real-time game data like player positions.

Choosing the right protocol depends on the type of data you're transmitting and the trade-off between reliability and speed.

Synchronization and Lag

ONE OF THE BIGGEST challenges in multiplayer game development is dealing with network latency, also known as lag. Lag occurs due to the time it takes for data to travel between players and servers. To mitigate lag, developers use techniques like prediction, interpolation, and lag compensation.

Cheat Prevention and Fair Play

IN MULTIPLAYER GAMES, ensuring fair play and preventing cheating is crucial. Developers employ various security measures like server-side validation, anti-cheat software, and monitoring player behavior to maintain a balanced and enjoyable gaming experience.

Scaling and Matchmaking

AS A MULTIPLAYER GAME gains popularity, the player base grows, and the need for scalable server solutions becomes apparent. Scaling involves expanding server capacity to accommodate more players. Matchmaking systems are used to pair players with others of similar skill levels or interests to ensure balanced and enjoyable matches.

Networking APIs and Libraries

UNITY OFFERS NETWORKING solutions like UNet (Unity Networking) and more recently, the Unity Transport package. However, many developers also opt for third-party networking libraries like Photon, Mirror, or Forge Networking Remastered, which provide additional features and flexibility.

In the upcoming sections of this chapter, we'll delve deeper into the specific aspects of multiplayer game development, covering topics like setting up networked games, player synchronization, matchmaking, and optimizing network performance. Building a successful multiplayer game involves mastering these concepts to create a seamless and enjoyable gaming experience for players around the world.

Section 10.2: Setting Up Networked Games in Unity

SETTING UP NETWORKED games in Unity involves several steps to create a foundation for multiplayer gameplay. In this section, we'll explore the essential components and concepts required to get started with networked game development.

Network Identity

IN UNITY'S NETWORKED games, every object that can be networked should have a NetworkIdentity component attached to it. This component serves as a unique identifier for networked objects and helps Unity's networking system recognize and manage them.

To add a NetworkIdentity component to an object:

1. Select the GameObject in the Hierarchy.
2. In the Inspector window, click the "Add Component" button.
3. Search for "NetworkIdentity" and select it to add it to the GameObject.

NetworkManager

THE NetworkManager is a critical component for managing networked games in Unity. It handles various aspects of networking, including spawning players, managing connections, and handling networked objects.

To set up a NetworkManager:

1. Create an empty GameObject in your scene.
2. Attach a NetworkManager component to it. This component allows you to define network settings, such as the maximum number of players, the player prefab, and more.
3. Create a player prefab for your game. This prefab represents the player's character and should include a NetworkIdentity component.
4. In the NetworkManager component, assign the player prefab to the "Player Prefab" field.

Networked Player

TO CREATE A NETWORKED player in Unity, follow these steps:

1. Create a GameObject for the player character in your scene.
2. Attach a NetworkIdentity component to the player GameObject.
3. Write a script to control the player's behavior and movement. Ensure that the script works with both local and remote players. Here's a simplified example:

```csharp
using UnityEngine;

using UnityEngine.Networking;

public class PlayerController : NetworkBehaviour
```

```
{

void Update()

{

if (!isLocalPlayer)

{

return;

}

// Implement player control logic for the local player here

}

}
```

In this script, the isLocalPlayer property ensures that the control logic is executed only for the local player.

1. Attach the PlayerController script to the player GameObject.

NetworkManagerHUD

THE NetworkManagerHUD is a Unity-provided GUI (Graphical User Interface) that simplifies the process of starting and stopping a networked game in the Unity Editor. It allows you to control the network state without writing custom UI code.

To enable the NetworkManagerHUD:

1. In the Unity Editor, select the NetworkManager

GameObject.

2. In the Inspector window, find the "Player Prefab" field and assign your player prefab.

3. Below the "Player Prefab" field, you'll find a section called "Spawn Info." Configure the "Spawn Info" settings as needed for your game.

4. Ensure that the "Show Run Time HUD" checkbox is checked in the NetworkManager component.

5. Play your scene in the Unity Editor. You should see a GUI that allows you to control the network state, such as starting a server, connecting as a client, and stopping the network.

Testing Multiplayer Locally

WHEN DEVELOPING NETWORKED games in Unity, you can test multiplayer functionality locally by running multiple instances of the game in the Unity Editor. Each instance can act as a server or client, allowing you to simulate multiplayer interactions.

To test locally:

1. Launch the Unity Editor.

2. Open your project.

3. Open the scene you want to test.

4. Click the "Play" button in the Unity Editor to start the first instance of the game. This instance will act as the server.

5. In the same Unity Editor, click the "Play" button again to start a second instance of the game. This instance will act as a client.

6. The client instance will automatically attempt to connect to the server. You can see the connection status in the

Unity Editor's console.

By following these steps, you can develop and test networked games within the Unity Editor environment, allowing you to iterate and fine-tune your multiplayer gameplay.

Setting up networked games in Unity is a foundational step in multiplayer game development. Understanding the roles of NetworkIdentity, NetworkManager, and networked player objects, as well as using the NetworkManagerHUD for testing, provides the groundwork for creating engaging and interactive multiplayer experiences in your Unity games. In the following sections, we'll explore more advanced topics related to multiplayer game development, such as player synchronization and network optimization.

Section 10.3: Implementing Player Synchronization

PLAYER SYNCHRONIZATION is a critical aspect of multiplayer game development. It ensures that all players in a networked game have consistent and synchronized experiences. In this section, we'll explore techniques and concepts for implementing player synchronization in Unity.

Network Time

IN A MULTIPLAYER GAME, time synchronization is essential to ensure that all players perceive the game world in a consistent manner. Unity provides the NetworkTime class, which allows you to access synchronized time information across the network. You can use this to:

- Synchronize animations and movements.

- Handle timed events.

- Implement game logic that depends on synchronized time.

Here's an example of how to use NetworkTime to synchronize an animation:

```
using UnityEngine;

using UnityEngine.Networking;

public class SynchronizedAnimation : NetworkBehaviour

{

private Animator animator;

[SyncVar]

private float syncTime;

void Start()

{

animator = GetComponent<Animator>();

}

void Update()

{

if (isLocalPlayer)

{

// Update animation state locally
```

```
float localTime = NetworkTime.time - syncTime;

animator.SetFloat("AnimationTime", localTime);

}

}

[Command]

void CmdSyncTime(float time)

{

// Server receives the client's time and synchronizes it

syncTime = time;

}

}
```

In this script, we use a SyncVar named syncTime to store the synchronized time. The CmdSyncTime method is a command that runs on the server and receives the client's time, synchronizing it across all players. The local player uses NetworkTime.time to calculate the local time based on the synchronized time, which is then used to control the animation.

Player Position Synchronization

SYNCHRONIZING PLAYER positions is vital to ensure that players see each other in the correct locations. Unity's networking system provides built-in player position synchronization using Transform components with SyncVar attributes. Here's an example of how to synchronize player positions:

```csharp
using UnityEngine;

using UnityEngine.Networking;

public class PlayerMovement : NetworkBehaviour

{

[SyncVar]

private Vector3 syncPosition;

[SerializeField]

private Transform playerTransform;

public float lerpRate = 15f;

void Update()

{

TransmitPosition();

LerpPosition();

}

void FixedUpdate()

{

if (isLocalPlayer)

{

// Handle player movement for the local player

// Example: Move the player using input controls
```

```csharp
}

}

[Command]

void CmdProvidePositionToServer(Vector3 position)

{

syncPosition = position;

}

[ClientCallback]

void TransmitPosition()

{

if (isLocalPlayer)

{

CmdProvidePositionToServer(playerTransform.position);

}

}

void LerpPosition()

{

if (!isLocalPlayer)

{

playerTransform.position = Vector3.Lerp(playerTransform.position,
syncPosition, Time.deltaTime * lerpRate);
```

```
}

}

}
```

In this script, we use the SyncVar attribute to synchronize the syncPosition variable across the network. The CmdProvidePositionToServer method runs on the server and receives the client's position, ensuring that it's synchronized across all players. The TransmitPosition method is called by the local player to send their position to the server. Finally, the LerpPosition method smoothly interpolates the position of remote players to create a visually smooth experience.

Remote Procedure Calls (RPCs)

REMOTE PROCEDURE CALLS (RPCs) are a mechanism in Unity's networking system that allows you to invoke methods on remote players or objects. RPCs are useful for triggering actions on remote players or synchronizing events across the network. Here's a basic example:

```csharp
using UnityEngine;

using UnityEngine.Networking;

public class PlayerHealth : NetworkBehaviour

{

[SyncVar(hook = "OnHealthChanged")]

private int health = 100;

void TakeDamage(int damage)
```

```
{

if (!isServer)

return;

health -= damage;

if (health <= 0)

{

// Player is defeated, call an RPC to handle it

RpcDefeated();

}

}

[ClientRpc]

void RpcDefeated()

{

// This method runs on all clients when a player is defeated

// Implement defeat logic here (e.g., show a game over screen)

}

void OnHealthChanged(int newHealth)

{

// This hook is called when the health value changes

// Implement any visual updates or effects here
```

```
}

}
```

In this script, we use SyncVar to synchronize the player's health value across the network. When a player's health reaches zero, we call the RpcDefeated RPC to notify all clients that the player has been defeated. This allows for consistent game behavior across all players.

Player synchronization is a fundamental aspect of multiplayer game development. It ensures that all players experience the game world in a coherent and synchronized manner. By understanding concepts like network time, player position synchronization, and remote procedure calls, you can create multiplayer games that provide a seamless and enjoyable experience for players.

Section 10.4: Building a Simple Matchmaking System

CREATING A MATCHMAKING system is essential for multiplayer games to pair players together based on various criteria such as skill level, geographic location, or game mode preferences. In this section, we'll explore how to build a simple matchmaking system for your Unity multiplayer game.

Matchmaking Components

A BASIC MATCHMAKING system in Unity typically involves the following components:

1. **Player Data**: Each player has associated data that the matchmaking system uses for pairing, such as skill rating, region, and game mode preferences.
2. **Match Queue**: A queue where players wait to be matched

with others. Players enter the queue when they search for a game.

3. **Matchmaking Logic**: Algorithms that determine which players to pair together. This logic considers player data and tries to create balanced matches.
4. **Matchmaking Server**: A server or service responsible for handling matchmaking requests and pairing players.

Player Data

TO IMPLEMENT MATCHMAKING, you need to define player data that can be used for pairing. This data may include:

- Skill rating or rank.

- Geographic region or ping (to ensure low-latency matches).

- Game mode preferences (e.g., casual, competitive).

You should also store this data on the server or a cloud service for easy access during matchmaking.

Match Queue

THE MATCH QUEUE IS where players enter when they want to find a game. When players start searching, they are placed in the queue, and the matchmaking system attempts to find suitable opponents for them.

Here's a simplified example of how to implement a match queue in Unity:

```
using System.Collections.Generic;

public class MatchQueue
```

```csharp
{

private Queue<Player> playersInQueue = new Queue<Player>();

public void AddPlayerToQueue(Player player)

{

playersInQueue.Enqueue(player);

}

public void RemovePlayerFromQueue(Player player)

{

// Remove the player from the queue

// Implement logic to handle removal

}

public bool TryMatchPlayers()

{

if (playersInQueue.Count < 2)

{

// Not enough players for a match

return false;

}

// Implement matchmaking logic to pair players

Player player1 = playersInQueue.Dequeue();
```

```
Player player2 = playersInQueue.Dequeue();

// Create a match with player1 and player2

Match newMatch = new Match(player1, player2);

// Notify players about the match

player1.StartMatch(newMatch);

player2.StartMatch(newMatch);

return true;

    }

}
```

In this simplified example, the MatchQueue class manages players in the queue and attempts to match them when there are at least two players available. The StartMatch method notifies players about their match.

Matchmaking Logic

MATCHMAKING LOGIC IS responsible for pairing players based on their data. The exact algorithms vary depending on the game's requirements, but some common matchmaking algorithms include:

- **Skill-based matchmaking**: Pair players with similar skill ratings to create balanced matches.

- **Region-based matchmaking**: Group players from the same geographic region to reduce latency.

- **Preference-based matchmaking**: Pair players who have similar game mode or map preferences.

You can implement these algorithms in your matchmaking server or service.

Matchmaking Server

THE MATCHMAKING SERVER or service handles matchmaking requests from players. It receives player data, adds players to the match queue, and pairs them when suitable opponents are found. Unity can communicate with the matchmaking server through web requests or custom networking protocols.

A basic matchmaking server in Unity might look like this:

using System.Collections.Generic;

public class MatchmakingServer

{

private MatchQueue matchQueue = **new** MatchQueue();

private List<Player> connectedPlayers = **new** List<Player>();

public void AddPlayer(Player player)

{

// *Add the player to the list of connected players*

connectedPlayers.Add(player);

// *Add the player to the match queue*

matchQueue.AddPlayerToQueue(player);

```
// Attempt to match players

if (matchQueue.TryMatchPlayers())

{

// Players were successfully matched

}

}

public void RemovePlayer(Player player)

{

// Remove the player from the list of connected players

connectedPlayers.Remove(player);

// Remove the player from the match queue

matchQueue.RemovePlayerFromQueue(player);

}

}
```

In this example, the MatchmakingServer class handles player connections, adds them to the match queue, and attempts to match players when the queue has enough players.

Building a matchmaking system is a crucial part of creating a multiplayer game in Unity. While the example provided here is simplified, real-world matchmaking systems can be much more complex, depending on the specific requirements of your game. Implementing a robust matchmaking system ensures that players have enjoyable and balanced multiplayer experiences.

Section 10.5: Handling Network Latency and Optimization

DEALING WITH NETWORK latency and optimizing network performance is crucial for providing a smooth and responsive multiplayer gaming experience. In this section, we'll explore strategies for handling latency and optimizing networking in Unity.

Understanding Network Latency

NETWORK LATENCY, OFTEN referred to as "ping" or "lag," is the delay between sending data from one device to another over a network. In multiplayer games, high network latency can lead to unresponsive controls, delayed actions, and a generally frustrating player experience.

Latency can be caused by various factors, including:

- Geographic distance between players.

- Internet connection quality.

- Server performance.

To address latency issues, consider the following techniques:

Client-Side Prediction

CLIENT-SIDE PREDICTION is a technique used to provide immediate feedback to players while the server processes their actions. Instead of waiting for the server's response, the client predicts the outcome of the action and updates the game state accordingly.

For example, in a first-person shooter, when a player presses the "fire" button, the client can immediately display the gunshot and then reconcile the result with the server's response. This creates the illusion of responsiveness, even in the presence of latency.

Lag Compensation

LAG COMPENSATION AIMS to make games fair for all players, regardless of their network latency. When a player with high latency shoots at a moving target, the server can compensate for the delay by calculating where the target was at the time of the shot, rather than where it is at the moment of impact.

Implementing lag compensation requires careful synchronization between clients and the server to ensure that actions are processed in the correct order and at the right time.

Interpolation and Extrapolation

INTERPOLATION AND EXTRAPOLATION are techniques for smoothing the movement of remote players in a multiplayer game. Interpolation calculates intermediate positions between received updates, while extrapolation predicts future positions based on past data.

By applying these techniques, you can reduce the visual impact of players "teleporting" due to latency or packet loss.

Network Optimization

OPTIMIZING YOUR NETWORKING code is essential to reduce the amount of data sent over the network and minimize network-related issues. Here are some optimization strategies:

- **Minimize Data Sent**: Only send essential data over the network. Avoid sending redundant or unnecessary information.

- **Use Reliable vs. Unreliable Messages**: Use reliable messages (e.g., TCP) for critical data like player positions and unreliable messages (e.g., UDP) for less critical data like non-essential updates.

- **Batching and Compression**: Combine multiple messages into a single batch to reduce overhead. Additionally, consider compressing data to reduce the size of network packets.

- **Client-Side Prediction**: As mentioned earlier, client-side prediction can help reduce the perceived effects of latency.

- **Server-Side Optimization**: Ensure that your server code is optimized to handle a large number of concurrent connections efficiently.

- **Network Monitoring and Debugging**: Implement network monitoring tools to track network performance and identify issues promptly. Debugging tools can help diagnose network-related problems during development.

Networked Physics

IN SOME MULTIPLAYER games, physics simulations can be challenging to synchronize due to latency. Unity's networking system offers solutions like the "NetworkTransform" component, which handles the synchronization of object positions and rotations across the network. Additionally, you can consider implementing custom solutions for complex physics interactions, such as server-authoritative physics.

Bandwidth Considerations

WHEN DESIGNING YOUR game, keep in mind the bandwidth limitations of your target audience. Some players may have limited internet connections, so it's essential to optimize your networking code to be as bandwidth-efficient as possible.

Optimizing network latency and performance in Unity multiplayer games is an ongoing process. By implementing techniques like client-side prediction, lag compensation, interpolation, and extrapolation, you can create a more responsive and enjoyable gaming experience for players, even in the presence of network latency. Regular testing, monitoring, and optimization are key to achieving smooth and lag-free multiplayer gameplay.

Chapter 11: Optimization and Performance

11.1 Analyzing and Improving Game Performance

In this section, we will delve into the crucial aspect of game development: optimizing and improving game performance. Optimizing your game is essential to ensure a smooth and enjoyable player experience. Whether you're targeting high-end gaming PCs or mobile devices, performance optimization is a fundamental concern.

Why Performance Optimization Matters

PERFORMANCE OPTIMIZATION is critical for several reasons:

1. **Player Experience:** A laggy or poorly performing game can frustrate players and lead to negative reviews.
2. **Wider Audience:** Optimized games can run on a broader range of hardware, increasing your potential player base.
3. **Marketplace Visibility:** Many app stores prioritize well-performing games in search results and recommendations.
4. **Energy Efficiency:** On mobile devices, optimizing performance can extend battery life, improving the overall user experience.

Profiling Your Game

BEFORE YOU CAN OPTIMIZE your game, you need to understand where performance bottlenecks exist. Profiling is the process of gathering data about your game's performance, such as CPU and GPU usage, memory consumption, and frame rate.

Unity provides built-in profiling tools that can help you identify performance issues. You can access these tools by going to the "Window" menu, selecting "Analysis," and choosing the profiler.

Here's a basic example of how to use Unity's profiler:

void Update()

{

// Start a profiler sample

Profiler.BeginSample("UpdateLoop");

// Your game logic here

// End the profiler sample

Profiler.EndSample();

}

In the above code, we use Profiler.BeginSample and Profiler.EndSample to create a named sample section in the profiler. This allows you to track the performance of specific parts of your code.

Common Performance Bottlenecks

THERE ARE SEVERAL COMMON performance bottlenecks in Unity games:

1. **Excessive Draw Calls:** Drawing too many objects on the screen can overload the CPU and GPU. Use techniques

like batching and occlusion culling to reduce draw calls.

2. **Inefficient Scripts:** Poorly optimized scripts can consume a significant portion of CPU time. Profile your scripts to identify performance issues and optimize them.

3. **Texture Memory:** Large textures can consume a lot of memory. Use texture compression and mipmaps to reduce memory usage.

4. **Physics Complexity:** Complex physics simulations can be CPU-intensive. Use simplified colliders and physics layers to optimize physics interactions.

Optimization Techniques

ONCE YOU'VE IDENTIFIED performance bottlenecks, you can apply various optimization techniques, including:

- **Object Pooling:** Reusing objects instead of instantiating and destroying them can reduce overhead.

- **Level of Detail (LOD):** Use different levels of detail for distant objects to reduce rendering complexity.

- **Asynchronous Loading:** Load assets and scenes asynchronously to avoid frame rate drops.

- **Code Optimization:** Profile and optimize your scripts, and consider using Unity's job system for multithreaded performance.

- **Shader Optimization:** Optimize shaders to reduce GPU load.

- **UI Optimization:** Simplify and batch UI elements to improve rendering performance.

- **Memory Management:** Minimize memory allocations and use object pooling to reduce garbage collection.

Remember that optimization is an iterative process. Continuously profile and test your game to ensure that your optimizations have the desired impact without introducing new issues.

By carefully analyzing and optimizing your game's performance, you can create a smoother, more enjoyable gaming experience for your players across a variety of platforms and devices.

11.2 Profiling and Debugging Techniques

PROFILING AND DEBUGGING are essential processes in the optimization of a Unity game. Profiling helps you identify performance bottlenecks, while debugging allows you to find and fix errors and issues in your code. In this section, we'll explore various profiling and debugging techniques to help you create a smoother and bug-free gaming experience.

Profiling Your Game

PROFILING IS THE PROCESS of analyzing your game's performance to identify areas that need optimization. Unity provides a built-in profiler that allows you to gather performance data and pinpoint performance bottlenecks. Here's a basic overview of how to use the Unity profiler:

1. **Open the Profiler:** You can access the Unity profiler by going to the "Window" menu, selecting "Analysis," and choosing "Profiler."
2. **Connect to Your Game:** Click the "Connect to Player" button in the profiler window to connect to your running game instance.

3. **Capture Data:** Once connected, you can capture performance data by clicking the "Record" button. Play your game while the profiler is recording.

4. **Analyze Data:** Stop recording, and you'll see a detailed breakdown of CPU, GPU, and memory usage, as well as other performance metrics. You can view this information in various charts and graphs.

5. **Identify Bottlenecks:** Use the profiler to identify areas of your game where performance is suboptimal. Look for functions or code sections that consume a significant amount of CPU time or cause spikes in frame time.

Debugging Your Game

DEBUGGING IS THE PROCESS of finding and fixing errors, bugs, and unexpected behavior in your game's code. Unity provides several tools and techniques to help you debug your game effectively.

Debug.Log Statements

ONE OF THE SIMPLEST debugging techniques is using Debug.Log statements to print information to the Unity console. For example:

```
void Update()

{

int playerHealth = 100;

Debug.Log("Player Health: " + playerHealth);

}
```

This allows you to inspect variable values and see the flow of your code during runtime.

Breakpoints

BREAKPOINTS ARE MARKERS you can place in your code to pause execution and inspect the state of your game. To set a breakpoint, click on the left margin of the code editor window next to the line you want to break on. When the breakpoint is hit, the game will pause, and you can inspect variables and step through code.

Inspector Debugging

UNITY'S INSPECTOR WINDOW is a powerful debugging tool. You can inspect and modify the values of public and serialized fields of components while the game is running. This can help you identify issues with object properties and values.

Visual Studio Debugger (or IDE of Choice)

IF YOU'RE USING AN external code editor like Visual Studio, you can take advantage of its debugging features. You can set breakpoints, step through code, and inspect variables using the debugger.

Debugging Tools

UNITY ALSO OFFERS ADDITIONAL debugging tools, such as the Profiler and the Unity Remote app for mobile debugging. These tools can help you track down performance issues and bugs specific to certain platforms.

Best Practices for Profiling and Debugging

TO EFFECTIVELY PROFILE and debug your game, consider the following best practices:

- **Use Debugging Tools Sparingly:** While debugging tools are valuable, excessive use can impact performance. Remove or disable debugging code in your final build.

- **Reproduce Bugs:** When debugging, try to create a minimal test case that reproduces the issue consistently. This simplifies the debugging process.

- **Version Control:** Use version control systems like Git to track changes in your code. This makes it easier to identify when a bug was introduced.

- **Collaboration:** Collaborate with team members and share debugging information to solve complex issues.

- **Documentation:** Document your code and debugging processes. This helps team members and future developers understand your work.

Effective profiling and debugging are essential skills for game developers. They help you create high-performance and bug-free games that provide an excellent player experience. Utilize these techniques and tools to identify and resolve performance bottlenecks and bugs in your Unity projects.

11.3 Efficient Asset Management

EFFICIENT ASSET MANAGEMENT is a critical aspect of optimizing the performance of your Unity game. Assets include everything from 3D models and textures to audio files and scripts. How you organize, import, and use these assets can significantly impact your game's performance and build times. In this section, we'll explore techniques for efficient asset management in Unity.

Asset Import Settings

UNITY PROVIDES VARIOUS import settings for assets, allowing you to control how they are processed and used in your game. Properly configuring these settings can help reduce memory usage and improve load times.

Texture Compression

WHEN IMPORTING TEXTURES, consider using texture compression to reduce their size. Unity supports several texture compression formats, each with its trade-offs in terms of quality and performance. Choose the compression format that best suits your game's needs.

Texture Size and Format

OPTIMIZE TEXTURE SIZES by using only the necessary resolution for each texture. Additionally, consider the texture format. For example, using compressed formats like DDS or ASTC can save memory compared to uncompressed formats like PNG or TIFF.

Model Polycount

KEEP AN EYE ON THE polygon count of 3D models. High-poly models can significantly impact performance. Use tools like Unity's

LOD (Level of Detail) system to swap out lower-poly versions of models as they move farther from the camera.

Asset Bundles

ASSET BUNDLES ALLOW you to package assets separately from your main game build, enabling dynamic loading and updating of assets. This can be useful for large projects where you want to reduce initial loading times or implement downloadable content (DLC).

To create and manage asset bundles, use Unity's Asset Bundle system. You can build asset bundles from specific assets or entire asset folders and then load them at runtime as needed. This approach reduces the memory footprint of your game and allows for more efficient updates.

Resource Management

CAREFUL MANAGEMENT of resources, such as textures, models, and audio, can help optimize your game's memory usage. Unity's Resources system allows you to load assets dynamically at runtime, reducing the initial memory overhead.

To use the Resources system, move assets you want to load dynamically into a "Resources" folder within your project. Then, you can load these assets using Resources.Load:

```
// Load a prefab named "MyPrefab" from the Resources folder

GameObject prefab = Resources.Load("MyPrefab") as GameObject;

// Instantiate the loaded prefab

Instantiate(prefab);
```

Keep in mind that while Resources can be useful for dynamic loading, it should be used sparingly. Overusing it can make your project harder to maintain and understand.

Scriptable Objects

SCRIPTABLE OBJECTS are a powerful asset management tool in Unity. They allow you to create custom asset types that can be edited in the Unity Inspector. You can use Scriptable Objects to define and manage game data, configuration settings, and more.

For example, you can create a Scriptable Object to store and manage a list of game characters or item data. This data can be easily modified in the Inspector, making it a versatile way to manage game content without writing complex code.

```
[CreateAssetMenu(fileName = "NewCharacterData", menuName = "Game/Character Data")]

public class CharacterData : ScriptableObject

{

public string characterName;

public int health;

public int damage;

}
```

Asset Cleanup

REGULARLY REVIEW AND clean up unused assets in your project. Unity's "Project" window allows you to filter assets by "Unused Assets," making it easier to identify and remove assets that are no longer in use. This helps reduce the size of your project and improves build times.

Efficient asset management is crucial for optimizing your Unity game's performance and memory usage. By using the right import settings, asset bundles, resource management techniques, Scriptable Objects, and asset cleanup practices, you can create a lean and responsive game that provides a seamless player experience.

11.4 Optimizing Graphics and Rendering

OPTIMIZING GRAPHICS and rendering is a critical aspect of improving the performance of your Unity game. Graphics and rendering operations can be resource-intensive, impacting both the frame rate and overall player experience. In this section, we'll explore various techniques to optimize the rendering pipeline and graphics in your Unity project.

Level of Detail (LOD)

LEVEL OF DETAIL (LOD) is a technique used to reduce the detail of 3D models as they move farther away from the camera. This reduces the number of polygons and vertices that need to be rendered, improving performance without sacrificing visual quality.

Unity provides a built-in LOD Group component that you can attach to GameObjects. This component allows you to define multiple levels of detail for a model and specify when each level should be used based on distance from the camera.

// Attach an LOD Group component to a GameObject in the Inspector.

// Add different LOD levels and assign appropriate meshes for each level.

LOD can be applied to terrain, characters, and other complex models. It's a valuable technique for open-world games and scenes with vast landscapes.

Occlusion Culling

OCCLUSION CULLING IS a technique that prevents the rendering of objects that are hidden from the camera's view. Unity's built-in occlusion culling system automatically calculates which objects are visible and hides those that are not.

To enable occlusion culling in your scene, follow these steps:

1. Open the "Window" menu, select "Rendering," and choose "Occlusion Culling" to open the Occlusion Culling window.
2. Bake occlusion data by clicking the "Bake" button in the Occlusion Culling window. Unity will calculate occlusion data for your scene.
3. Assign the "Occlusion Culling" component to your camera in the Inspector.

Occlusion culling can significantly reduce the number of objects that need to be rendered, improving frame rate and performance.

GPU Instancing

GPU INSTANCING IS A rendering technique that allows multiple instances of the same object to be rendered in a single draw call, reducing CPU overhead. It's particularly useful when you have many identical objects in your scene.

To use GPU instancing, you need to enable it for your materials:

1. Create or select a material that you want to use with GPU

instancing.

2. In the material's Inspector, check the "Enable GPU Instancing" checkbox.

3. Assign the material to your GameObjects.

GPU instancing can be especially effective when rendering objects like trees, rocks, or particle systems that appear multiple times in your scene.

Shader Optimization

SHADER OPTIMIZATION is crucial for graphics performance. Shaders control how objects are rendered, and poorly optimized shaders can lead to GPU bottlenecks. Here are some tips for shader optimization:

• Minimize the number of shader passes and complexity.

• Use shader variants only when necessary.

• Avoid expensive calculations in shaders.

• Utilize Unity's Shader LOD feature to automatically adjust shader complexity based on distance.

• Profile your shaders using Unity's built-in shader profiler to identify performance bottlenecks.

Render Texture Optimization

RENDER TEXTURES ARE often used for effects like reflections, shadows, and mirrors. However, they can be resource-intensive. To optimize render textures:

• Use lower resolutions for render textures when possible.

- Limit the number of objects using render textures simultaneously.

- Reduce the size of the render texture's viewport.

Dynamic Batching

UNITY AUTOMATICALLY performs static batching for objects that don't move or change, reducing draw calls. However, for dynamic objects that change position or state frequently, you can use dynamic batching. Unity will attempt to batch together similar dynamic objects to reduce draw calls.

// Ensure that dynamic batching is enabled in the Player Settings.

// Unity will automatically batch dynamic objects when possible.

Dynamic batching is particularly useful for mobile games and scenes with many dynamic GameObjects.

Conclusion

OPTIMIZING GRAPHICS and rendering is essential for maintaining a high frame rate and delivering a smooth gaming experience. By implementing techniques like LOD, occlusion culling, GPU instancing, shader optimization, and efficient use of render textures, you can achieve better graphics performance without compromising on visual quality.

11.5 Handling Large and Complex Scenes

DEALING WITH LARGE and complex scenes is a common challenge in game development. As your Unity project grows, you may encounter performance issues related to scene size, rendering, and resource management. In this section, we'll explore strategies and techniques for effectively handling large and complex scenes in Unity.

Scene Organization

PROPER SCENE ORGANIZATION is crucial for managing large and complex scenes. Here are some tips for organizing your scenes effectively:

- **Modular Design:** Divide your scene into smaller, manageable modules or sections. This makes it easier to work on specific areas and helps maintain a clear hierarchy.

- **Empty GameObjects:** Use empty GameObjects as placeholders to group related objects. This helps maintain a logical structure and simplifies the selection of objects in the Hierarchy window.

- **Scene Folders:** Create folders in the Hierarchy window to group objects by category or function. You can use GameObjects as folders by renaming them with a forward slash (/).

// For example, you can create a folder for lights by renaming an empty GameObject:

// "Lights/"

- **Layer and Tag Usage:** Utilize layers and tags to categorize objects and control their interactions and rendering. This is particularly helpful for managing complex scenes with numerous objects.

Occlusion Culling

OCCLUSION CULLING, as mentioned in the previous section, is essential for optimizing complex scenes. By culling objects that are not visible to the camera, you can significantly reduce rendering overhead.

To maximize the benefits of occlusion culling in complex scenes:

- Ensure that occlusion culling data is correctly baked for your scene.

- Use occlusion areas to fine-tune culling in specific regions of the scene.

- Adjust the camera's near and far clipping planes to reduce the volume that needs to be rendered.

Streaming and Loading

FOR LARGE AND OPEN-world games, streaming and loading techniques are essential to manage scene size and loading times. Unity provides tools for asynchronous scene loading and unloading, allowing you to load portions of the scene as needed.

Here's an example of how to load a scene asynchronously:

```csharp
using UnityEngine;

using UnityEngine.SceneManagement;

public class SceneLoader : MonoBehaviour

{

public string sceneToLoad;
```

```
public void LoadSceneAsync()

{

StartCoroutine(LoadSceneAsyncCoroutine());

}

private IEnumerator LoadSceneAsyncCoroutine()

{

AsyncOperation asyncLoad = SceneManager.LoadSceneAsync(sceneToLoad, LoadSceneMode.Additive);

while (!asyncLoad.isDone)

{

float progress = Mathf.Clamp01(asyncLoad.progress / 0.9f); // Normalize progress

Debug.Log("Loading progress: " + (progress * 100) + "%");

yield return null;

}

}

}
```

Using techniques like scene streaming and asset bundles, you can reduce the initial loading time and memory usage of your game.

LOD and Billboards

AS MENTIONED IN THE previous sections, Level of Detail (LOD) is a valuable technique for managing complex scenes. Implement LOD for objects that are visible at varying distances from the camera. Additionally, consider using billboards for distant objects to improve rendering efficiency.

Billboards are flat, textured planes that always face the camera. They are often used for distant trees, buildings, or other objects. Unity's built-in Tree Creator provides a straightforward way to create billboard-based trees.

Script Optimization

COMPLEX SCENES MAY involve many scripts that interact with numerous objects. Optimize your scripts by:

- **Using Efficient Algorithms:** Choose algorithms and data structures that perform well, especially when dealing with large datasets.

- **Caching Component References:** Avoid frequent calls to GetComponent by caching references during initialization.

- **Minimizing Updates:** Update only the necessary components and objects to reduce CPU load.

- **Pooling Objects:** Implement object pooling for frequently created and destroyed objects to reduce memory allocations.

Conclusion

HANDLING LARGE AND complex scenes in Unity requires careful planning, organization, and optimization. By following best practices for scene organization, utilizing occlusion culling, implementing streaming and loading techniques, using LOD and billboards, optimizing scripts, and applying efficient algorithms, you can create complex and visually impressive games while maintaining optimal performance.

Chapter 12: Mobile Game Development

12.1 Adapting Unity Games for Mobile Platforms

Mobile game development has become a thriving industry, with millions of users playing games on smartphones and tablets. Adapting Unity games for mobile platforms is a common endeavor for game developers. In this section, we will explore the process of optimizing and adapting Unity games for mobile devices.

Understanding Mobile Constraints

MOBILE DEVICES, COMPARED to PCs and consoles, have limited hardware resources. It's crucial to be aware of these constraints when adapting your Unity game for mobile platforms. Key considerations include:

- **Processing Power:** Mobile CPUs are less powerful than those in high-end PCs or consoles. Optimize your game's code and physics calculations to run smoothly on mobile devices.

- **Memory:** Mobile devices have limited RAM. Optimize textures, models, and audio assets to reduce memory usage. Use asset bundles for efficient resource management.

- **Graphics:** Mobile GPUs have less processing power. Adjust graphics settings and implement performance optimizations like LOD and shader simplification.

- **Touch Controls:** Design intuitive touch controls that work well on small touchscreens. Consider how users will interact with your game.

Platform Compatibility

UNITY SUPPORTS A WIDE range of mobile platforms, including iOS and Android. To adapt your game, follow these platform-specific guidelines:

iOS Development

- Install Xcode: Xcode is the integrated development environment for iOS. Install it on your Mac.

- Set Up Provisioning Profiles: Register as an Apple Developer and create provisioning profiles and certificates for iOS development.

- Configure Unity: In Unity, set your build target to iOS and configure player settings, such as bundle identifiers and signing options.

Android Development

- Install Android Studio: Android Studio is the preferred development environment for Android. Install it on your development machine.

• Configure Unity: In Unity, set your build target to Android and configure player settings, such as package names, icons, and permissions.

• APK Splitting: Consider using APK splitting to reduce the initial download size of your game on the Google Play Store.

Performance Optimization

OPTIMIZING PERFORMANCE is critical for mobile games. Here are some performance optimization techniques:

• **Mobile-Friendly UI:** Design user interfaces (UI) that are responsive and touch-friendly. Minimize UI elements that may obstruct gameplay.

• **Texture Compression:** Use texture compression formats suitable for mobile devices to reduce memory usage.

• **Asset Bundles:** Implement asset bundles to load assets dynamically and reduce initial loading times.

• **Shader Optimization:** Simplify shaders and use mobile-friendly shader variants.

• **Frame Rate:** Target a stable frame rate (e.g., 30 or 60 FPS) to ensure a smooth gameplay experience.

Touch and Gyroscope Input

MOBILE DEVICES OFFER unique input methods, including touchscreens and gyroscopes. To utilize these features effectively:

• Implement touch controls that are intuitive and responsive.

• Explore the use of gestures (e.g., swipe, pinch, and multi-touch) to enhance gameplay.

• Consider using the device's gyroscope for motion-based controls or augmented reality features.

Testing and Profiling

THOROUGH TESTING AND profiling are essential to ensure your game performs well on various mobile devices. Use emulators and real devices for testing. Unity provides profiling tools to identify performance bottlenecks.

```
// Example of profiling in Unity

void Update()

{

// Start a profiler sample

Profiler.BeginSample("UpdateLoop");

// Your game logic here

// End the profiler sample

Profiler.EndSample();

}
```

Cross-Platform Development

IF YOU INTEND TO TARGET both iOS and Android, consider using cross-platform development tools and frameworks. Unity is well-suited for this purpose, allowing you to write your game once and deploy it to multiple platforms.

Adapting Unity games for mobile platforms involves optimizing performance, handling touch and gyroscope input, configuring platform-specific settings, and thorough testing. By following these guidelines, you can create engaging and responsive mobile games that run smoothly on a wide range of devices.

12.2 Mobile Input and Touch Controls

MOBILE DEVICES RELY on touchscreens and sensors for user input, making mobile input and touch controls a crucial aspect of mobile game development. In this section, we will explore how to implement responsive and intuitive touch controls for Unity games targeting mobile platforms.

Unity's Input System

UNITY PROVIDES A VERSATILE input system that allows you to handle various types of input, including touch, keyboard, mouse, and game controllers. To start using Unity's Input System for mobile touch controls, follow these steps:

1. **Enable Input System:** In Unity, go to "Edit" > "Project Settings" > "Player," and in the "Other Settings" section, enable the "Active Input Handling" option. Select "Input System Package."
2. **Create Actions:** In the Input System, you define actions for different input types. To create a touch control action,

go to "Window" > "Input Actions" and define a new action map and action.

3. **Bind Controls:** Bind your touch controls to specific actions using the Input System's binding system. You can specify which touch inputs (e.g., tap, swipe, pinch) trigger your actions.

4. **Code Integration:** In your scripts, use the Input System API to check for touch input and trigger actions accordingly.

Here's a simple example of using the Input System to detect a tap or touch on an object:

```csharp
using UnityEngine;

using UnityEngine.InputSystem;

public class TouchInputExample : MonoBehaviour

{

private void OnEnable()

{

// Enable the touch action

TouchControls.TouchAction.Enable();

}

private void OnDisable()

{

// Disable the touch action
```

```csharp
TouchControls.TouchAction.Disable();

}

private void Awake()

{

// Subscribe to the tap event

TouchControls.TouchAction.Tap.started += ctx => OnTap();

}

private void OnTap()

{

// Handle the tap or touch event

Debug.Log("Tap detected!");

}

}
```

Implementing Swipe and Multi-Touch

TO IMPLEMENT MORE COMPLEX touch controls like swipes and multi-touch gestures, you can extend the Input System. For example, to detect swipe gestures, you can calculate the distance and direction between two touch points over time.

```csharp
using UnityEngine;

using UnityEngine.InputSystem;

public class SwipeDetection : MonoBehaviour
```

```csharp
{
    private Vector2 startTouchPosition;

    private Vector2 endTouchPosition;

    private void OnEnable()
    {
        // Enable touch actions

        TouchControls.TouchAction.Enable();
    }

    private void OnDisable()
    {
        // Disable touch actions

        TouchControls.TouchAction.Disable();
    }

    private void Awake()
    {
        // Subscribe to touch events

        TouchControls.TouchAction.Touch.started += ctx => startTouchPosition = ctx.ReadValue<Vector2>();

        TouchControls.TouchAction.Touch.canceled += ctx => DetectSwipe(ctx.ReadValue<Vector2>());
    }
```

```csharp
private void DetectSwipe(Vector2 currentTouchPosition)

{

// Calculate swipe direction

Vector2 swipeDirection = currentTouchPosition - startTouchPosition;

// Determine if it's a horizontal or vertical swipe

if (Mathf.Abs(swipeDirection.x) > Mathf.Abs(swipeDirection.y))

{

// Horizontal swipe

if (swipeDirection.x > 0)

{

Debug.Log("Right Swipe");

}

else

{

Debug.Log("Left Swipe");

}

}

else

{

// Vertical swipe
```

```
if (swipeDirection.y > 0)

{

Debug.Log("Up Swipe");

}

else

{

Debug.Log("Down Swipe");

}

}

}

}
```

For multi-touch gestures like pinching and zooming, you can use the Input System's Gesture Recognizers API to detect and handle such interactions.

Virtual Joysticks and Buttons

MANY MOBILE GAMES USE virtual joysticks and buttons for character movement and actions. You can create these UI elements and map them to in-game actions using Unity's UI system and the Input System. Ensure that these virtual controls are touch-responsive and provide visual feedback to the player.

Testing on Real Devices

TO ENSURE THAT YOUR touch controls work correctly, it's crucial to test your game on real mobile devices. Unity's remote testing feature allows you to connect your device to the Unity editor for real-time testing and debugging.

Responsive and intuitive touch controls are essential for creating a positive player experience in mobile games. By utilizing Unity's Input System and implementing touch gestures, virtual controls, and UI elements effectively, you can design mobile games that are engaging and easy to play on touchscreens.

12.3 Optimization Strategies for Mobile Devices

OPTIMIZING YOUR UNITY game for mobile devices is crucial to ensure smooth performance and a positive player experience. Mobile devices come in various hardware configurations, and optimizing your game allows it to run well across a broad range of smartphones and tablets. In this section, we will explore optimization strategies specifically tailored to mobile platforms.

1. Texture Compression

MOBILE DEVICES OFTEN have limited GPU memory. To conserve memory and improve performance, use texture compression formats suitable for mobile platforms. Unity provides several texture compression options, such as ETC2 for Android and PVRTC for iOS. Additionally, consider using texture atlases to reduce draw calls and memory usage by packing multiple textures into one.

2. LOD (Level of Detail)

IMPLEMENTING LEVEL of Detail (LOD) is crucial for mobile games with 3D graphics. LOD allows you to reduce the level of detail for distant objects, which can significantly improve rendering performance. Unity provides tools to create LOD groups for GameObjects, making it easier to implement this optimization technique.

3. Dynamic Batching

DYNAMIC BATCHING CAN help reduce CPU overhead by batching similar dynamic objects into a single draw call. Unity automatically performs dynamic batching when objects share the same material and meet certain criteria. Ensure that your GameObjects meet the requirements for dynamic batching, such as using the same shader and not exceeding the vertex limit.

4. Static Batching

STATIC BATCHING IS another optimization technique that Unity provides. It combines static GameObjects into a single batch at build time, reducing draw calls during runtime. To benefit from static batching, mark GameObjects as "Static" in their Inspector settings. However, keep in mind that static batching works for GameObjects that don't move or change, so it's suitable for scenery and environment elements.

5. UI Optimization

MOBILE GAME UI SHOULD be designed with efficiency in mind. Use UI components provided by Unity's UI system, as they are optimized for mobile devices. Minimize the use of UI elements with complex graphics or animations that can impact performance. Test your UI on various screen sizes and resolutions to ensure it scales properly.

6. Particle System Optimization

IF YOUR GAME USES PARTICLE systems for effects like explosions or smoke, optimize them for mobile devices. Reduce the number of particles, limit the lifetime of particles, and use simpler shaders for better performance. Consider using Unity's Particle System LOD group to control the level of detail for particle effects.

7. Audio Optimization

MOBILE GAMES OFTEN use audio for immersion and feedback. To optimize audio:

- Use compressed audio formats like AAC or MP3.

- Limit the number of concurrent audio sources to avoid overwhelming the CPU.

- Use 2D audio for non-spatial sounds and 3D audio for sounds that require spatialization.

8. Script Optimization

EFFICIENT SCRIPTING is essential for mobile games. Profile your code to identify performance bottlenecks, and optimize critical code sections. Avoid using heavy computation in Update loops, and use coroutines for asynchronous tasks instead of busy-wait loops.

```
// Example of using a coroutine for asynchronous tasks

IEnumerator MyCoroutine()

{

yield return new WaitForSeconds(1.0f);
```

// Perform an action after waiting

}

9. Memory Management

MOBILE DEVICES HAVE limited RAM, so effective memory management is crucial. Unload unnecessary assets using the Resources.UnloadUnusedAssets() method. Implement object pooling to reduce memory allocation when instantiating and destroying objects frequently.

10. Testing on Real Devices

ALWAYS TEST YOUR GAME on real mobile devices to ensure it performs as expected. Testing on different hardware configurations and screen sizes helps identify potential issues and ensures a smooth player experience.

Optimizing a Unity game for mobile devices is a continuous process that requires a balance between visual quality and performance. By following these optimization strategies and regularly profiling and testing your game, you can create mobile games that run smoothly on a wide range of devices and provide an enjoyable gaming experience for players.

12.4 Publishing and Monetizing Mobile Games

PUBLISHING AND MONETIZING mobile games is a significant aspect of the mobile game development process. Once you've created a compelling game, it's essential to bring it to the market and generate revenue from your hard work. In this section, we'll explore the steps involved in publishing and monetizing your Unity mobile game.

1. Preparing for Publishing

BEFORE YOU CAN PUBLISH your mobile game, there are several preparatory steps to take:

a. App Store Accounts

CREATE DEVELOPER ACCOUNTS on the target app stores, such as the Apple App Store for iOS and Google Play Store for Android. There may be a one-time registration fee for each store.

b. Game Assets and Icons

PREPARE GAME ASSETS, including icons, promotional images, and screenshots. These assets are essential for creating an appealing store listing.

c. Privacy Policy

CREATE A PRIVACY POLICY for your game if it collects any user data. Both Apple and Google require developers to have a privacy policy.

d. Testing and Quality Assurance

THOROUGHLY TEST YOUR game on various devices to ensure it works correctly and is free of critical bugs.

2. Building the Game for Distribution

TO DISTRIBUTE YOUR Unity game on mobile platforms, you need to build it specifically for each target platform:

a. iOS Build

- Configure the iOS build settings in Unity, specifying bundle identifiers, signing certificates, and provisioning profiles.

- Build the game for iOS, producing an Xcode project.

- Open the Xcode project, set the deployment target, and choose a target device (e.g., iPhone, iPad).

- Build and sign the iOS app in Xcode.

b. Android Build

- Configure Android build settings in Unity, specifying package names, icons, and permissions.

- Build the game for Android, producing an APK file.

- Create a digital signing key for your APK using tools like Android Studio.

- Sign the APK with your digital key to prepare it for distribution.

3. Creating Store Listings

a. Apple App Store

- Create a new app listing on the Apple App Store Connect platform.

- Fill in app details, including title, description, keywords, and screenshots.

- Set pricing and availability options.

b. Google Play Store

- Create a new app listing on the Google Play Console.

- Provide app information, including title, description, graphics, and screenshots.

- Set pricing, distribution, and monetization options.

4. Monetization Strategies

THERE ARE VARIOUS MONETIZATION strategies for mobile games, including:

a. In-App Ads

INTEGRATE AD NETWORKS like Google AdMob or Unity Ads to display ads in your game. You can choose between various ad formats, such as banners, interstitials, and rewarded videos.

b. In-App Purchases (IAPs)

OFFER VIRTUAL GOODS, power-ups, or premium features as in-app purchases. Use Unity's IAP services to implement this monetization strategy.

c. Premium/Paid Games

SELL YOUR GAME AS A one-time purchase on the app stores. Ensure your game offers a compelling value proposition to justify the price.

d. Subscriptions

IMPLEMENT SUBSCRIPTION-based monetization models for access to premium content or services within your game.

e. Sponsorships and Partnerships

EXPLORE PARTNERSHIPS with brands or sponsors for promotional opportunities within your game.

5. Promoting Your Game

a. App Store Optimization (ASO)

OPTIMIZE YOUR STORE listings with relevant keywords, eye-catching visuals, and compelling descriptions. ASO helps improve your game's discoverability on app stores.

b. Social Media and Marketing

LEVERAGE SOCIAL MEDIA platforms and marketing campaigns to create buzz and attract players to your game.

c. User Acquisition

USE USER ACQUISITION strategies, including paid advertising and influencer marketing, to drive downloads and installations.

d. Community Building

ENGAGE WITH YOUR PLAYER community through forums, social media, and in-game events. Build a loyal player base and gather feedback for improvements.

6. Post-Launch Support and Updates

CONTINUOUSLY IMPROVE your game by listening to player feedback and releasing updates. Regular updates can maintain player engagement and extend the lifespan of your game.

7. Analytics and Monetization Tracking

IMPLEMENT ANALYTICS tools like Unity Analytics or third-party solutions to track player behavior, in-game monetization, and performance. Analyzing data helps you make informed decisions and refine your monetization strategies.

Publishing and monetizing a mobile game involves careful planning, attention to detail, and ongoing efforts to reach a wider audience and generate revenue. By following the steps outlined above and adapting your strategy based on player feedback and market trends, you can increase the chances of success for your Unity mobile game.

12.5 Case Studies of Successful Unity Mobile Games

EXAMINING CASE STUDIES of successful Unity mobile games can provide valuable insights into the strategies and techniques that have led to their achievements. In this section, we'll explore a few notable examples of Unity-based mobile games that have achieved significant success in terms of downloads, revenue, or player engagement.

1. "Monument Valley" by ustwo Games

"MONUMENT VALLEY" IS a visually stunning puzzle-adventure game developed by ustwo Games. It became a massive success shortly after its release on iOS and Android. Key factors contributing to its success include:

- **Unique Art Style:** The game's beautifully crafted Escher-inspired levels and minimalistic art style set it apart from other mobile games.

- **Engaging Gameplay:** "Monument Valley" offers a blend of innovative puzzles and a captivating narrative, providing players with a memorable gaming experience.

- **Premium Pricing:** Instead of relying on ads or in-app purchases, the game followed a premium pricing model, where players paid upfront for the full game. This approach appealed to users looking for a high-quality gaming experience without interruptions.

- **Awards and Recognition:** The game received critical acclaim and won several awards, generating positive word-of-mouth and media coverage.

2. "Pokémon GO" by Niantic

"POKÉMON GO," DEVELOPED by Niantic in collaboration with The Pokémon Company, took the world by storm upon its release. It is an augmented reality (AR) game that allows players to explore the real world to catch Pokémon. Key success factors include:

- **Augmented Reality:** "Pokémon GO" leveraged AR technology, which was a novel concept at the time, to blend the virtual and real worlds, creating a unique and immersive experience.

- **Franchise Appeal:** The game capitalized on the beloved Pokémon franchise, attracting a massive existing fan base.

- **Community Engagement:** Regular in-game events, social features, and community gatherings kept players engaged and fostered a sense of community.

- **Monetization:** The game utilized various monetization strategies, including in-app purchases for items and a location-based advertising system that encouraged businesses to participate.

3. "Subway Surfers" by SYBO Games

"SUBWAY SURFERS," DEVELOPED by SYBO Games, is an endless runner game that has consistently ranked among the top mobile games in terms of downloads and revenue. Key factors contributing to its success include:

- **Endless Runner Genre:** The endless runner genre has proven to be enduringly popular on mobile platforms, providing simple yet addictive gameplay.

- **Regular Updates:** The game frequently receives updates with new content, challenges, and events, ensuring player retention and engagement.

- **Live Operations:** SYBO Games has a dedicated live operations team that monitors player data and responds with dynamic adjustments to gameplay, rewards, and events.

- **In-App Advertising:** The game effectively incorporates rewarded video ads, which players can voluntarily watch in exchange for in-game rewards, providing a non-intrusive monetization strategy.

4. "Clash Royale" by Supercell

"CLASH ROYALE," DEVELOPED by Supercell, is a real-time multiplayer strategy game that has achieved massive success. Key success factors include:

- **Strategic Gameplay:** The game combines elements of card collection, tower defense, and real-time strategy, offering depth and strategic gameplay.

- **Strong Community:** Supercell actively engages with the player community, listens to feedback, and balances the game regularly to maintain fairness.

- **Monetization Model:** "Clash Royale" utilizes a free-to-play model with in-app purchases for card packs and premium currency. The game's success is attributed to its balanced monetization approach.

- **Esports and Tournaments:** The game has a thriving esports scene with regular tournaments and events, which not only engage the player base but also generate spectator interest.

These case studies demonstrate that successful Unity mobile games can come from various genres and monetization strategies. Key elements such as unique gameplay, engaging art styles, community involvement, and effective monetization models contribute to the success of these games. Learning from these examples can help aspiring mobile game developers create games that resonate with players and achieve their own success in the mobile gaming industry.

Chapter 13: Virtual Reality (VR) and Augmented Reality (AR)

13.1 Introduction to VR and AR in Unity

Virtual Reality (VR) and Augmented Reality (AR) have transformed the way we interact with digital content and the real world. Unity provides robust support for both VR and AR development, making it a versatile platform for creating immersive experiences. In this section, we will introduce the concepts of VR and AR, their differences, and how Unity facilitates their development.

What is Virtual Reality (VR)?

VIRTUAL REALITY (VR) refers to a technology that immerses users in a computer-generated virtual environment. VR typically involves wearing a headset that covers the user's field of vision and often includes motion-tracking sensors for head and hand movements. The primary goal of VR is to create a sense of presence, where users feel like they are inside the virtual world.

Unity supports various VR platforms, including Oculus Rift, HTC Vive, PlayStation VR, and more. To develop VR experiences in Unity, you can use the Unity XR framework, which provides tools and APIs for building VR applications across multiple devices.

What is Augmented Reality (AR)?

AUGMENTED REALITY (AR) overlays digital content onto the real world, enhancing the user's perception of reality. Unlike VR,

AR does not replace the real world but augments it with computer-generated information. AR applications can be experienced through smartphones, tablets, or AR glasses.

Unity's AR Foundation allows developers to create AR applications that run on both iOS and Android devices, as well as AR glasses like Microsoft HoloLens and Magic Leap. AR Foundation abstracts the underlying AR technology, making it easier to develop cross-platform AR experiences.

Key Differences Between VR and AR

- **Immersion Level:** VR aims to completely immerse users in a virtual world, while AR enhances the real world with digital elements.

- **Hardware:** VR often requires specialized headsets with sensors, while AR can be experienced on common devices like smartphones.

- **Use Cases:** VR is commonly used for gaming, training simulations, and virtual tours. AR finds applications in navigation, education, retail, and more.

Unity's Role in VR and AR Development

UNITY PROVIDES A UNIFIED development environment for both VR and AR, allowing developers to create mixed reality experiences. Here are some key features and components in Unity for VR and AR development:

- **Unity XR:** Unity's XR framework allows you to build applications that target multiple VR and AR platforms, providing a single codebase for cross-device compatibility.

- **AR Foundation:** Unity's AR Foundation simplifies AR development, supporting various AR platforms and devices. It includes features for plane detection, object tracking, and face tracking.

- **VR Interaction Toolkit:** Unity offers the VR Interaction Toolkit, a package that streamlines the development of VR interactions like grabbing and throwing objects.

- **Performance Optimization:** Unity provides tools for optimizing VR and AR applications, such as occlusion culling, level of detail (LOD), and frame rate management.

Developers interested in VR and AR can leverage Unity's powerful tools, asset store plugins, and a supportive community to create immersive experiences for a wide range of applications, from gaming to training and beyond. In the following sections, we will delve deeper into VR and AR development in Unity, exploring design principles, development techniques, and best practices for creating compelling VR and AR content.

13.2 Designing Immersive VR Experiences

DESIGNING IMMERSIVE Virtual Reality (VR) experiences is a unique and exciting challenge for developers and designers. Unlike traditional 2D games or applications, VR places users inside a digital environment, which requires careful consideration of various factors to ensure a compelling and comfortable experience. In this section, we will explore key principles and design considerations for creating immersive VR experiences in Unity.

1. Presence and Immersion

THE PRIMARY GOAL OF VR is to create a sense of presence, where users feel like they are truly inside the virtual world. Achieving presence involves:

- **Realistic Graphics:** Utilize high-quality graphics, textures, and lighting to make the virtual environment visually convincing.

- **Smooth Interactions:** Implement realistic interactions, such as grabbing objects, manipulating the environment, or using hand gestures, to enhance immersion.

- **Spatial Audio:** Use spatial audio techniques to create realistic soundscapes that match the visual experience.

2. Comfort and Motion Sickness

VR EXPERIENCES MUST prioritize user comfort to avoid motion sickness. Consider the following guidelines:

- **Smooth Movement:** Implement smooth and natural locomotion methods, like teleportation, to reduce motion sickness.

- **Field of View:** Limit excessive head movement and maintain a stable field of view to prevent disorientation.

- **Frame Rate:** Maintain a consistent high frame rate (e.g., 90 Hz) to ensure smooth visuals and reduce motion-related discomfort.

3. User Interface (UI) Design

DESIGNING UI ELEMENTS in VR requires a user-friendly and intuitive approach:

- **Diegetic UI:** Integrate UI elements into the virtual environment, making them feel like a part of the world rather than overlaid screens.

- **Interaction Methods:** Implement user-friendly interaction methods, such as laser pointers, gaze-based selection, or hand-based interfaces.

- **Readable Text:** Ensure text is legible and appropriately sized for VR, considering the user's proximity to UI elements.

4. Spatial Design

EFFECTIVE SPATIAL DESIGN enhances the sense of immersion:

- **Scale and Proportion:** Pay attention to the scale and proportion of objects to create a sense of realism.

- **Environmental Details:** Add details to the environment to make it visually appealing and engaging.

- **User Movement:** Design environments that encourage users to explore and move naturally.

5. Performance Optimization

OPTIMIZING VR EXPERIENCES for performance is crucial:

- **Low-Poly Models:** Use optimized 3D models with lower polygon counts to maintain a high frame rate.

- **Occlusion Culling:** Implement occlusion culling to avoid rendering objects that are not visible to the user.

- **Level of Detail (LOD):** Use LOD techniques to render high-detail models when they are close to the user and lower-detail models at a distance.

- **Loading Screens:** Minimize loading screens or use creative techniques to hide them to maintain immersion.

6. Testing and Iteration

REGULARLY TEST VR EXPERIENCES on different hardware configurations and gather feedback from users to identify areas for improvement. VR design often involves iteration to fine-tune the user experience.

7. User Comfort and Accessibility

CONSIDER ACCESSIBILITY features for users with different needs, such as seated experiences, adjustable text size, or alternative control methods. Prioritize user comfort and inclusivity in your VR design.

8. Cross-Platform Compatibility

IF YOU INTEND TO RELEASE your VR experience on multiple platforms, ensure that your design and interactions are compatible with various VR hardware and controllers.

Creating immersive VR experiences in Unity is an exciting endeavor, but it comes with unique challenges. By focusing on presence, comfort, user interface design, spatial considerations, performance optimization, testing, accessibility, and cross-platform compatibility, you can craft VR experiences that captivate and engage users while providing a comfortable and enjoyable journey into the virtual world.

13.3 Developing AR Applications with Unity

AUGMENTED REALITY (AR) applications blend digital content with the real world, offering unique and engaging user experiences. Unity provides a robust framework for developing AR applications across various platforms, including iOS, Android, and AR glasses. In this section, we will explore the process of developing AR applications with Unity, covering key concepts and techniques.

AR Foundation: Unity's AR Framework

UNITY'S AR DEVELOPMENT is greatly facilitated by AR Foundation, a framework that abstracts the underlying AR technologies and provides a unified API for building AR applications. AR Foundation supports popular AR platforms, such as ARKit for iOS and ARCore for Android, as well as AR glasses like HoloLens and Magic Leap.

To get started with AR development in Unity, you need to:

1. **Install AR Foundation:** Install the AR Foundation package from the Unity Package Manager.
2. **Choose a Platform:** Select the AR platforms you intend to target. Unity supports multiple platforms, so you can create cross-platform AR applications.
3. **Import AR Subsystems:** Depending on your target platforms, import the AR Subsystems packages (e.g.,

ARKit XR Plugin, ARCore XR Plugin) that correspond to the platforms you want to support.

4. **Implement AR Sessions:** Create an AR session in your scene to manage the AR experience. This session initializes and tracks AR features like the device's position and orientation.

5. **AR Session Origin:** Attach an AR session origin component to a GameObject in your scene. This component serves as the root for all AR content and anchors virtual objects to the real world.

Plane Detection and Tracking

ONE OF THE FUNDAMENTAL aspects of AR is the ability to detect and track surfaces in the real world. AR Foundation provides APIs for plane detection, allowing you to place virtual objects on flat surfaces like tables or floors. To enable plane detection:

```
// Enable plane detection for ARSession

ARSession session = FindObjectOfType<ARSession>();

session.GetComponent<ARPlaneManager>().enabled = true;

// Subscribe to the planeAdded event to handle newly detected planes

ARPlaneManager planeManager = session.GetComponent<ARPlaneManager>();

planeManager.planesChanged += HandlePlanesChanged;

// Implement a method to handle plane detection events

void HandlePlanesChanged(ARPlanesChangedEventArgs args)

{
```

```
foreach (var plane in args.added)

{

// Handle newly detected plane

}

}
```

Object Tracking

AR FOUNDATION ALSO supports object tracking, allowing you to recognize and track specific objects in the real world. This feature is useful for interactive AR applications and games that involve physical objects.

Spatial Anchors

SPATIAL ANCHORS ARE essential for persisting virtual content in the real world. They ensure that virtual objects remain in their specified positions even after the AR session is paused or resumed. You can create and attach spatial anchors to GameObjects in Unity to achieve this behavior.

```
// Create a new spatial anchor at a specific position and attach it to a
GameObject

ARAnchor anchor = ARAnchorManager.AddAnchor(new
Pose(position, rotation));
```

Cross-Platform Development

UNITY'S AR FOUNDATION makes it relatively straightforward to create cross-platform AR applications. By abstracting the underlying AR technologies and providing a unified API, you can develop AR experiences that run on multiple devices with minimal platform-specific code.

However, it's important to consider the differences in hardware capabilities, tracking accuracy, and user interactions across various AR platforms. Testing on different devices and iterating on your AR application is crucial to ensure a consistent and enjoyable user experience.

In summary, Unity's AR Foundation simplifies the development of AR applications by providing a unified framework that supports multiple AR platforms and devices. Whether you're building AR games, educational apps, or industrial solutions, Unity offers the tools and flexibility to create compelling and immersive AR experiences.

13.4 Best Practices for VR/AR User Experience

CREATING A POSITIVE and engaging user experience (UX) in Virtual Reality (VR) and Augmented Reality (AR) applications is essential for the success of your projects. Users expect immersive and comfortable experiences, and adhering to best practices is key to achieving that. In this section, we will discuss some of the best practices for designing user experiences in VR and AR applications developed using Unity.

1. Comfort Is Paramount

COMFORT SHOULD BE THE top priority when designing VR experiences. Motion sickness is a common issue, and it can quickly turn users away from your application. To ensure comfort:

- Implement smooth and gradual movements. Avoid rapid accelerations or sharp turns.

- Offer different locomotion options, such as teleportation or snap-turning, to accommodate users' preferences.

- Provide visual cues or blinkers to reduce motion sickness during movement.

- Use comfortable heights for objects, as users may experience discomfort when bending down too often or reaching too high.

2. Intuitive User Interface (UI)

DESIGN THE USER INTERFACE to be intuitive and user-friendly:

- Keep UI elements simple and easy to understand. Minimize clutter.

- Utilize gaze-based interactions or controllers to select and interact with UI elements.

- Use clear, legible fonts and appropriately sized text for readability.

- Ensure that UI elements are positioned within the user's field of view, making them easily accessible without neck strain.

3. Clear Navigation

NAVIGATION IS CRUCIAL in VR and AR environments:

- Provide clear wayfinding cues or markers to guide users within the virtual space.

- Use teleportation or path visualization to help users navigate smoothly.

- Implement clear exit and return mechanisms to prevent users from feeling trapped in the virtual world.

4. Maintain Realism

MAINTAINING REALISM in VR and AR applications enhances the sense of presence:

- Pay attention to object scale and proportions to match real-world expectations.

- Use realistic physics and interactions for objects.

- Implement convincing lighting and shading to create a more immersive environment.

5. Performance Optimization

OPTIMIZE YOUR VR AND AR applications for performance:

- Maintain a high and consistent frame rate (e.g., 90 Hz) to prevent motion sickness and discomfort.

- Use level of detail (LOD) techniques to optimize the rendering of complex 3D models.

- Implement occlusion culling to reduce unnecessary rendering.

6. Testing and Feedback

REGULARLY TEST YOUR VR and AR applications with users from various backgrounds and levels of experience. Gather feedback and iterate on your design:

- Conduct playtesting to identify any discomfort or usability issues.

- Observe how users interact with your application and adjust the design accordingly.

- Continuously update and improve your application based on user feedback.

7. Accessibility

CONSIDER ACCESSIBILITY features to make your VR and AR experiences inclusive:

- Support seated experiences for users who may have mobility limitations.

- Provide adjustable settings for users to customize comfort settings, such as movement speed or visual effects.

- Ensure that all important information is conveyed through visual and auditory cues to accommodate users with visual or hearing impairments.

8. Cross-Platform Compatibility

IF YOU'RE TARGETING multiple VR or AR platforms, ensure that your application adapts to each platform's hardware capabilities and interaction methods. Tailor the user experience for each device while maintaining a consistent core experience.

9. Documentation and Tutorials

INCLUDE TUTORIALS OR onboarding sequences to help new users become familiar with your VR or AR application. Explain interactions and controls clearly to reduce user confusion.

By following these best practices, you can create VR and AR applications that provide comfortable, immersive, and engaging user experiences. Prioritizing user comfort, usability, and accessibility will not only attract users but also keep them coming back for more immersive adventures in your virtual or augmented worlds.

13.5 Overcoming Challenges in VR/AR Development

VIRTUAL REALITY (VR) and Augmented Reality (AR) development offer exciting opportunities, but they also come with unique challenges. In this section, we'll discuss some common challenges in VR and AR development and strategies to overcome them when working with Unity.

1. Hardware Fragmentation

Challenge:

VR AND AR ECOSYSTEMS encompass a variety of devices, each with different capabilities, sensors, and input methods. Developing for multiple platforms can be challenging.

Solution:

UTILIZE UNITY'S XR framework and AR Foundation to create cross-platform applications. These frameworks abstract the underlying hardware, allowing you to write code that works across various devices.

2. Motion Sickness

Challenge:

MOTION SICKNESS CAN occur in VR applications, especially during movement. It's important to design experiences that minimize discomfort.

Solution:

- Implement comfort options like teleportation.

- Use gradual acceleration and deceleration for motion.

- Offer adjustable settings for comfort.

- Regularly test with users to identify discomfort triggers.

3. Performance Optimization

Challenge:

MAINTAINING A HIGH and consistent frame rate is crucial in VR and AR to prevent motion sickness and ensure a smooth experience.

Solution:

- Profile and optimize your code and assets.

- Implement occlusion culling and level of detail (LOD) techniques.

- Prioritize performance optimizations to ensure a stable frame rate.

4. User Interface (UI) in 3D Space

Challenge:

DESIGNING UI ELEMENTS that are intuitive and user-friendly in 3D space can be challenging.

Solution:

- Use gaze-based interactions or controllers for UI.

- Design UI elements to be easily readable and accessible.

- Create diegetic UI that feels integrated into the virtual environment.

5. Testing and Feedback

Challenge:

GETTING FEEDBACK FROM real users is essential, but it can be challenging to gather meaningful feedback in VR and AR.

Solution:

- Conduct playtesting with users in VR or AR environments.

- Use feedback forms or surveys after playtesting sessions.

- Observe users' behavior and reactions during testing.

6. Content Creation

Challenge:

CREATING HIGH-QUALITY 3D assets and environments for VR and AR can be time-consuming and resource-intensive.

Solution:

- Utilize 3D modeling software and Unity's asset pipeline for efficient asset creation.

- Consider using asset packs from the Unity Asset Store.

- Collaborate with 3D artists and designers to streamline content creation.

7. Accessibility

Challenge:

ENSURING ACCESSIBILITY for all users, including those with disabilities, can be challenging in immersive environments.

Solution:

- Support seated experiences for users with mobility limitations.

- Provide adjustable settings for comfort and accessibility.

- Use alternative sensory cues for information (e.g., audio cues for visually impaired users).

8. Cross-Platform Testing

Challenge:

TESTING YOUR VR OR AR application on multiple devices and platforms can be complex and time-consuming.

Solution:

- Invest in a variety of VR and AR devices for testing.

- Utilize cloud-based testing services for remote testing on multiple devices.

- Prioritize testing on platforms with the largest user base.

9. Content Discovery and Distribution

Challenge:

GETTING YOUR VR OR AR application noticed and distributed to users can be challenging in a competitive market.

Solution:

- Invest in marketing and promotion to increase visibility.

- Publish your application on popular app stores and VR/
AR platforms.

- Consider partnerships with hardware manufacturers or
content distributors.

10. Privacy and Data Security

Challenge:

HANDLING USER DATA and privacy concerns is important but
can be complex in VR and AR applications.

Solution:

- Follow best practices for user data handling and data
security.

- Clearly communicate your privacy policy to users.

- Comply with relevant data protection regulations.

OVERCOMING THESE CHALLENGES in VR and AR
development requires a combination of technical skills, design
expertise, user testing, and a deep understanding of the target
platforms. By addressing these challenges proactively and iteratively,
you can create compelling and comfortable VR and AR experiences
that captivate users and stand out in the immersive technology
landscape.

Chapter 14: Graphics and Rendering Techniques

===

14.1 Advanced Unity Rendering Engines

Rendering is a critical aspect of game development, as it directly impacts the visual quality and performance of your game. Unity provides various rendering engines and techniques to achieve stunning graphics. In this section, we will explore some of the advanced Unity rendering engines that can enhance your game's visuals.

1. Universal Render Pipeline (URP)

THE UNIVERSAL RENDER Pipeline (URP) is a rendering solution optimized for performance and compatibility across a wide range of platforms, including mobile devices and consoles. URP uses a forward rendering approach and offers features like:

- **Shader Graph:** URP includes the Shader Graph, a visual tool for creating shaders without writing code. This allows for highly customizable materials and visual effects.

- **2D Renderer:** URP provides dedicated 2D rendering capabilities, making it ideal for 2D games and applications. It offers optimized sprite rendering, lighting, and post-processing effects.

- **Post-Processing Stack:** URP includes a built-in post-processing stack, which allows you to apply various effects such as bloom, depth of field, and color grading to your scenes.

2. High Definition Render Pipeline (HDRP)

THE HIGH DEFINITION Render Pipeline (HDRP) is designed for creating high-fidelity, visually stunning experiences. It targets platforms with more significant computational power, such as high-end PCs and next-gen consoles. Key features of HDRP include:

- **Physically Based Rendering (PBR):** HDRP employs PBR techniques to achieve realistic lighting, shading, and materials. This results in lifelike visuals with accurate reflections and shadows.

- **Volumetric Lighting:** HDRP supports volumetric lighting, enabling the simulation of realistic light scattering and atmospheric effects.

- **HDRI Sky:** You can use High Dynamic Range (HDR) environment maps for more realistic and dynamic sky and lighting effects.

- **Shader Graph:** Similar to URP, HDRP also supports Shader Graph for creating custom shaders and materials.

3. Custom Shader Development

UNITY ALLOWS YOU TO write custom shaders using ShaderLab and the Shader Graph. This gives you fine-grained control over how your game's graphics are rendered. You can create shaders for various purposes, including:

- **Visual Effects:** Develop shaders for particle systems, trails, and dynamic visual effects.

- **Character Rendering:** Create shaders to achieve unique character appearances, such as stylized or cel-shaded looks.

- **Terrain Shading:** Customize terrain shaders to achieve specific terrain effects, like grass or water rendering.

- **Post-Processing Effects:** Implement custom post-processing effects to enhance the overall visual quality of your game.

4. Lightweight Render Pipeline (LWRP) - Deprecated

NOTE THAT THE LIGHTWEIGHT Render Pipeline (LWRP) has been deprecated in favor of URP. If you were previously using LWRP, it's recommended to migrate your project to URP for ongoing support and improved performance.

5. Graphics Jobs and Burst Compiler

TO OPTIMIZE GRAPHICS performance, Unity introduces Graphics Jobs and the Burst Compiler. These technologies allow for multi-threaded rendering, taking advantage of multi-core CPUs. By optimizing rendering tasks with jobs, you can achieve better performance and frame rate in your games.

6. Ray Tracing

RAY TRACING IS A RENDERING technique that simulates the behavior of light rays to create highly realistic visuals. Unity introduced ray tracing support in HDRP, allowing developers to achieve stunning visuals with real-time ray tracing effects like ray-traced reflections, shadows, and global illumination.

In conclusion, Unity offers a range of rendering engines and techniques to cater to different project requirements, from optimized performance on mobile devices to high-fidelity visuals on powerful hardware. Choosing the right rendering pipeline and techniques depends on your game's target platforms, visual goals, and performance considerations. Experimenting with these rendering options and combining them with custom shaders can lead to visually impressive and captivating game graphics.

14.2 Real-time Lighting and Shadows

REAL-TIME LIGHTING and shadows play a crucial role in creating immersive and visually appealing game environments. Unity provides several techniques and tools to achieve realistic lighting and shadow effects in your games. In this section, we will explore real-time lighting and shadow options and how to implement them effectively.

1. Directional Lighting

DIRECTIONAL LIGHTING simulates the light coming from a distant source, such as the sun. It provides uniform lighting across the entire scene, affecting all objects equally regardless of their position. To set up directional lighting:

```
// Access the Directional Light in Unity

Light directionalLight = RenderSettings.sun;

// Adjust the light properties

directionalLight.intensity = 1.0f;
```

directionalLight.color = Color.white;

Directional lighting is often used for outdoor scenes to create daylight or moonlight effects. It's an efficient way to illuminate large areas and create long shadows.

2. Point and Spot Lights

POINT AND SPOT LIGHTS simulate localized light sources. Point lights emit light in all directions from a specific point in 3D space, while spotlights emit light in a cone shape. These lights are suitable for creating dynamic and detailed lighting effects.

To set up a point light in Unity:

// Create a GameObject and attach a Point Light component

GameObject pointLightObject = **new** GameObject("Point Light");

Light pointLight = pointLightObject.AddComponent<Light>();

// Adjust the light properties

pointLight.type = LightType.Point;

pointLight.intensity = 5.0f;

pointLight.range = 10.0f;

pointLight.color = Color.red;

Spotlights are configured similarly, with additional properties like spot angle and spot exponent to control the shape and intensity of the light cone.

3. Real-time Shadows

SHADOWS ENHANCE THE realism of your game by simulating how objects block light. Unity supports real-time shadow rendering for various light types. To enable real-time shadows for a light:

// Enable real-time shadows for a light

light.shadows = LightShadows.Soft;

Unity offers three types of real-time shadows:

- **Hard Shadows:** These shadows have sharp edges and are ideal for simulating direct sunlight or strong artificial light.

- **Soft Shadows:** Soft shadows have smoother edges and are suitable for simulating diffuse lighting conditions or indirect lighting.

- **Real-time Global Illumination (GI):** Unity's GI system provides real-time indirect lighting and ambient occlusion effects, further enhancing the realism of scenes.

4. Light Probes

LIGHT PROBES ARE A technique used to capture and interpolate lighting information in dynamic scenes. They help maintain consistent lighting on objects that move or change in real-time. Light probes can be placed manually or generated automatically in Unity. To use light probes:

// Attach a Light Probe Group component to a GameObject

LightProbeGroup probeGroup = gameObject.AddComponent<LightProbeGroup>();

// Set the positions and coefficients of the light probes

probeGroup.probePositions = **new** Vector3[] { /* *Array of probe positions* */};

probeGroup.coefficients = **new** SphericalHarmonicsL2[] { /* *Array of coefficients* */};

Light probes are particularly useful for environments with dynamic objects or characters.

5. Global Illumination (GI)

GLOBAL ILLUMINATION is a rendering technique that simulates how light bounces and interacts with surfaces in the environment. Unity's GI system provides real-time GI solutions, including:

- **Real-time Reflection Probes:** These probes capture and update reflections in real-time, making shiny or reflective surfaces appear more realistic.

- **Lightmapping:** Unity's lightmapping system allows you to precompute lighting information for static objects, improving performance while maintaining visual quality.

- **Progressive Lightmapper:** A GPU-based lightmapping solution that provides high-quality results with shorter baking times.

Real-time GI enhances the realism of your scenes by accurately simulating how light behaves in complex environments.

In summary, real-time lighting and shadows are essential components of creating visually stunning and immersive game environments in Unity. By understanding the different types of lights, shadows, and global illumination techniques available, you can choose the right combination to achieve the desired visual effects for your game. Experimenting with these features and fine-tuning their parameters will help you create captivating and realistic lighting in your Unity projects.

14.3 Shader Programming and Material Design

SHADER PROGRAMMING is a powerful tool in Unity that allows you to control how the rendering of objects is handled at a low level. Shaders define the visual appearance of materials and how they interact with light. In this section, we'll explore shader programming and material design in Unity.

1. Shader Basics

A SHADER IS A PROGRAM that runs on the GPU and determines the color and shading of pixels on the screen. In Unity, shaders are written in ShaderLab and a shader language like HLSL (High-Level Shader Language). A basic shader consists of two parts:

- **Vertex Shader:** This stage processes the vertices of 3D objects, transforming them from world space to screen space. It can perform operations like vertex manipulation and texture coordinate calculations.

- **Fragment Shader (Pixel Shader):** The fragment shader is responsible for calculating the final color of each pixel. It can include lighting calculations, texture sampling, and more.

Here's a simple shader example in Unity's ShaderLab:

```
// ShaderLab syntax for a basic shader

Shader "Custom/MyShader"

{

Properties

{

_MainTex ("Texture", 2D) = "white" {}

}

SubShader

{

Tags { "RenderType"="Opaque" }

Pass

{

CGPROGRAM

#pragma vertex vert

#pragma fragment frag

#include "UnityCG.cginc"

struct appdata_t

{

float4 vertex : POSITION;
```

```
float2 uv : TEXCOORD0;

};

struct v2f

{

float2 uv : TEXCOORD0;

float4 vertex : SV_POSITION;

};

sampler2D _MainTex;

v2f vert (appdata_t v)

{

v2f o;

o.vertex = UnityObjectToClipPos(v.vertex);

o.uv = v.uv;

return o;

}

fixed4 frag (v2f i) : SV_Target

{

return tex2D(_MainTex, i.uv);

}

ENDCG
```

```
      }

    }

  }
```

2. Shader Properties

UNITY SHADERS CAN HAVE properties that allow you to expose parameters to the Material Inspector in the Unity Editor. These properties can control aspects like colors, textures, and numerical values, providing flexibility to artists and designers.

In the shader code above, _MainTex is a property that represents a texture. It's defined in the Properties block and can be set in the Unity Editor.

3. Shader Variants

UNITY GENERATES SHADER variants based on the combinations of features used in your scene. These features can include different render pipelines, hardware platforms, and shader keywords. Shader variants are optimized for specific cases, improving runtime performance.

4. Surface Shaders

SURFACE SHADERS IN Unity simplify the process of writing shaders by abstracting some of the low-level details. They automatically handle lighting, shadows, and interaction with Unity's material system. Here's a simple surface shader example:

// Surface shader example

Shader "Custom/SurfaceShaderExample"

```
{

Properties

{

_MainTex ("Texture", 2D) = "white" {}

}

SubShader

{

Tags { "RenderType"="Opaque" }

Pass

{

CGPROGRAM

#pragma surface surf Lambert

struct Input

{

float2 uv_MainTex;

};

sampler2D _MainTex;

void surf (Input IN, inout SurfaceOutput o)

{

o.Albedo = tex2D(_MainTex, IN.uv_MainTex).rgb;
```

```
}

ENDCG

}

}

}
```

Surface shaders abstract the lighting model with a predefined function (Lambert in the example above) and simplify the interaction with textures.

5. Shader Graph

UNITY'S SHADER GRAPH is a visual tool that allows you to create shaders without writing code. It's suitable for artists and designers who want to experiment with shader effects. Shader Graph provides a node-based interface for creating custom shaders and materials, making it more accessible than traditional shader programming.

In conclusion, shader programming and material design are essential aspects of creating visually stunning and unique graphics in Unity. Whether you prefer writing code-based shaders for fine-grained control or using Shader Graph for a visual approach, understanding shaders and materials is crucial for achieving the desired visual style and effects in your Unity projects. Experimenting with shaders and materials can lead to beautiful and captivating visuals that enhance your game's overall appeal.

14.4 Particle Systems and Visual Effects

PARTICLE SYSTEMS ARE a versatile tool for creating a wide range of visual effects in Unity. They allow you to simulate and render thousands of small, individual objects (particles) in real-time. In this section, we'll explore the use of particle systems and how to create various visual effects using Unity's Particle System component.

1. Particle System Basics

A PARTICLE SYSTEM IN Unity is composed of three main components: Emitter, Renderer, and Particle Data. Here's a brief overview of each:

- **Emitter:** This component emits particles into the scene. You can control emission rate, shape, and other parameters to define how and where particles are generated.

- **Renderer:** The renderer component determines how particles are displayed. It includes options for rendering particles as points, billboards, or custom meshes. You can also define materials and textures for particles.

- **Particle Data:** Particle data includes properties like position, velocity, color, size, and lifetime. These properties determine how particles behave and look over their lifespan.

2. Creating Particle Systems

YOU CAN CREATE A PARTICLE System in Unity by selecting GameObject > Effects > Particle System from the Unity Editor menu. This will add a Particle System component to the selected GameObject.

Once you have a Particle System, you can access its settings through the Inspector window. You can adjust parameters such as emission rate, duration, shape, color, size, and more to achieve the desired visual effect.

3. Common Visual Effects

a. Fire and Smoke

TO CREATE A FIRE AND smoke effect, you can adjust the emission rate to create a burst of particles. Use color gradients to transition from red to yellow for flames and from gray to transparent for smoke. Add turbulence to the particle movement to simulate the flickering of flames.

b. Rain or Snow

RAIN OR SNOW EFFECTS can be achieved by emitting small, transparent particles from the sky. Adjust the size and speed of particles to mimic raindrops or snowflakes falling. You can also add a subtle trail or motion blur effect to make it more realistic.

c. Explosions

EXPLOSIONS ARE TYPICALLY created by emitting a large number of particles with high initial velocity. You can use color gradients to create a bright flash at the center of the explosion, followed by fading to transparent particles. Adjust the size and speed variation for a more chaotic explosion effect.

d. Magic Spells or Sparks

FOR MAGIC SPELLS OR sparks, emit small, glowing particles with random velocities. Add a slight color variation to create a magical, sparkling appearance. Adjust the size, speed, and lifetime to control the behavior of the particles.

4. Texture Sheets

TEXTURE SHEETS ARE often used to give particles a more complex appearance. Instead of using a single texture for particles, you can use a sprite sheet containing multiple frames of an animation. Unity's Particle System supports texture sheet animation, allowing you to cycle through frames to create animated effects like fire, smoke, or twinkling stars.

5. Custom Shaders and Materials

YOU CAN FURTHER ENHANCE particle systems by using custom shaders and materials. For example, you can create a shader that distorts particles as they move or one that adds a glow effect. You can also use noise textures to control particle properties dynamically.

6. Scripting

YOU CAN CONTROL AND manipulate particle systems through scripting in Unity. This allows for dynamic effects, such as spawning particles at runtime, changing particle properties, or triggering particle systems in response to gameplay events.

In conclusion, particle systems are a powerful tool for creating a wide range of visual effects in Unity. Whether you want to simulate natural phenomena like fire and rain or create magical and explosive effects, understanding particle systems and their settings is essential. Experimenting with different parameters and combining particle systems with custom shaders and materials can lead to captivating and visually stunning effects in your Unity projects.

14.5 High Definition Render Pipeline (HDRP)

UNITY'S HIGH DEFINITION Render Pipeline (HDRP) is an advanced rendering system designed to achieve high-quality visuals with a focus on high-end platforms such as high-end PCs and next-generation consoles. HDRP provides a range of features and optimizations to create stunning and realistic graphics in your Unity projects. In this section, we'll explore the capabilities and components of HDRP.

1. Physically Based Rendering (PBR)

HDRP LEVERAGES PBR techniques to create realistic and physically accurate materials. PBR allows you to achieve materials with accurate reflections, refractions, and shading. Materials in HDRP are defined using the HDRP Lit Shader, which supports features like subsurface scattering, anisotropic reflections, and clear coat.

2. Volumetric Lighting

HDRP INCLUDES SUPPORT for volumetric lighting effects. This allows you to simulate the scattering of light through the air, creating realistic god rays, light shafts, and atmospheric effects. Volumetric lighting enhances the visual quality of your scenes and adds depth and atmosphere.

3. High-Quality Shadows

HDRP OFFERS HIGH-QUALITY shadow rendering techniques, including contact shadows, shadow mask, and ray traced shadows. These features contribute to more realistic and visually appealing shadows in your scenes. Ray traced shadows, in particular, enable accurate and soft shadowing for dynamic objects.

4. Screen Space Reflections (SSR)

SCREEN SPACE REFLECTIONS in HDRP simulate reflective surfaces by ray tracing reflections in screen space. This creates accurate and dynamic reflections on surfaces, enhancing the realism of materials like water, glass, and polished metals.

5. Decals

HDRP SUPPORTS DECAL rendering, allowing you to project textures onto surfaces in real-time. Decals are useful for adding details like bullet holes, dirt, or graffiti to your game environment. They can also affect lighting and contribute to the overall realism of your scenes.

6. Post-Processing Stack

HDRP INCLUDES A BUILT-in post-processing stack, which provides a wide range of effects like bloom, depth of field, motion blur, and color grading. These effects can be applied to your scenes to enhance the visual quality and create cinematic looks.

7. Shader Graph for HDRP

YOU CAN CREATE CUSTOM shaders for HDRP using the Shader Graph. Shader Graph is a visual tool that allows you to create shaders without writing code. It's compatible with HDRP and provides a user-friendly way to develop complex materials and effects.

8. HDRP Asset

TO USE HDRP, YOU NEED to create an HDRP Asset, which contains global settings and configurations for your project. You can define rendering quality, shadow settings, and other parameters in the HDRP Asset. It provides a central control point for managing the visual quality of your project.

9. Scriptable Render Pipeline (SRP)

HDRP IS BASED ON UNITY'S Scriptable Render Pipeline architecture, which allows you to customize and extend the rendering process. You can create your own custom rendering features, shaders, and optimizations tailored to your project's needs.

10. Performance Optimization

HDRP INCLUDES VARIOUS optimizations to ensure high performance on capable hardware. This includes features like dynamic resolution scaling, which adjusts the rendering resolution based on the GPU's load, and occlusion culling for efficient rendering of only visible objects.

In conclusion, Unity's High Definition Render Pipeline (HDRP) is a powerful rendering system that empowers developers to create high-quality and visually stunning graphics for high-end platforms. By utilizing PBR materials, volumetric lighting, high-quality shadows, and a range of other features, you can achieve realism and cinematic quality in your Unity projects. HDRP is a valuable tool for creating visually impressive games and experiences that push the boundaries of visual fidelity.

Chapter 15: Game Mechanics and Gameplay Design

15.1 Crafting Engaging Game Mechanics

Game mechanics are the core systems and rules that define how a game is played and experienced. Crafting engaging game mechanics is crucial for creating an enjoyable and immersive gaming experience. In this section, we'll explore the principles and techniques behind designing compelling game mechanics.

1. Core Mechanics

CORE MECHANICS ARE the fundamental interactions that drive gameplay. These interactions define the player's goals, actions, and challenges. For example, in a platformer game, core mechanics often involve running, jumping, and collecting items. In a strategy game, core mechanics might include resource management, unit control, and combat.

To create engaging core mechanics:

- **Clarity:** Ensure that core mechanics are easy to understand. Players should grasp the basics quickly, but there can be depth for mastery.

- **Balance:** Fine-tune core mechanics to provide a balanced challenge. Avoid making the game too easy or too difficult.

- **Feedback:** Provide feedback to players when they interact with core mechanics. This can be visual, auditory, or haptic feedback that reinforces their actions.

2. Progression Systems

PROGRESSION SYSTEMS add depth and motivation to gameplay. These systems include elements like leveling up, unlocking new abilities, and achieving goals. Progression systems can keep players engaged and motivated to continue playing.

To design effective progression systems:

- **Goals:** Clearly define goals and rewards. Players should have a sense of what they're working toward and what they'll achieve.

- **Balanced Pacing:** Control the rate of progression to maintain a sense of challenge and achievement. Avoid making progression too slow or too fast.

- **Variety:** Offer a variety of goals and rewards to cater to different player preferences. Some players enjoy collecting items, while others prefer completing challenges.

3. Player Feedback and Rewards

FEEDBACK AND REWARDS play a significant role in player engagement. Positive feedback and rewards for completing actions or achieving goals can create a sense of accomplishment and satisfaction.

Consider the following when designing feedback and rewards:

- **Immediate Feedback:** Provide immediate feedback when players perform actions. For example, when they defeat an enemy, show an explosion effect and play a victory sound.

- **Feedback Loop:** Create a feedback loop that reinforces positive behavior. For example, defeating enemies may grant experience points, which lead to leveling up and unlocking new abilities.

- **Surprise Rewards:** Occasionally surprise players with unexpected rewards or bonuses. This can keep gameplay fresh and exciting.

4. Risk and Reward

INTRODUCING RISK AND reward mechanics can add excitement and tension to gameplay. Players face choices that involve potential gains or losses, making their decisions meaningful.

To implement risk and reward mechanics effectively:

- **Balanced Consequences:** Ensure that the consequences of taking risks or making choices are well-balanced. Players should feel that their decisions matter.

- **Interesting Trade-offs:** Create interesting trade-offs between risk and reward. For example, a player might choose between a high-risk, high-reward strategy and a safer, but less rewarding approach.

- **Player Agency:** Allow players to make meaningful choices. Their decisions should impact the outcome, making them feel in control of their fate.

5. Emergent Gameplay

EMERGENT GAMEPLAY REFERS to unexpected and unscripted interactions that arise from the game's systems and mechanics. It adds depth and replayability to a game by allowing players to discover new strategies and solutions.

To encourage emergent gameplay:

- **Complex Interactions:** Design systems with interlocking and complex interactions. When different mechanics interact, players can discover unique outcomes.

- **Player Creativity:** Allow players to express creativity within the game's mechanics. Provide tools or systems that let them experiment and find novel solutions to challenges.

- **Dynamic Worlds:** Create dynamic and reactive game worlds that respond to player actions. This can lead to unexpected consequences and emergent scenarios.

In conclusion, crafting engaging game mechanics is a critical aspect of game design. It involves creating core mechanics that are easy to grasp but offer depth, designing progression systems that motivate players, providing feedback and rewards, introducing risk and reward mechanics, and allowing for emergent gameplay. By carefully considering these principles and techniques, game designers can

create captivating and immersive gaming experiences that keep
players coming back for more.

15.2 Balancing Gameplay Elements

BALANCING GAMEPLAY elements is a critical aspect of game
design that ensures fairness, challenge, and enjoyment for players.
Game balance involves adjusting various aspects of a game, such as
character abilities, enemy difficulty, resource management, and level
design, to create a satisfying and engaging experience. In this section,
we'll delve into the principles and techniques for balancing gameplay
elements effectively.

1. Player Characters and Abilities

BALANCING PLAYER CHARACTERS and their abilities is
essential to ensure that no character or strategy dominates the game.
Here are some considerations for balancing player characters:

- **Character Roles:** If your game includes multiple
characters or classes, each should have a unique role and
strengths. For example, one character might excel at
dealing damage, while another is better at support or
defense.

- **Ability Costs:** Assign appropriate costs to powerful
abilities or items. This can include resource consumption
(e.g., mana or energy), cooldown periods, or limited usage
per level.

- **Skill Progression:** Design skill or ability progression
to prevent characters from becoming overpowered too
quickly. Gradually increase the power of abilities as
players progress through the game.

2. Enemy Design and Difficulty

BALANCING ENEMY DESIGN and difficulty is crucial to maintaining a challenging but fair gameplay experience. Here's how to approach enemy balancing:

- **Enemy Variety:** Introduce a variety of enemy types with different abilities and behaviors. This keeps gameplay engaging and prevents players from relying on a single strategy.

- **Scaling Difficulty:** Adjust enemy difficulty based on player progress. As players advance, make enemies tougher and introduce new challenges to match their skill level.

- **Boss Battles:** If your game includes boss battles, ensure that these encounters are appropriately challenging and rewarding. Bosses should have unique mechanics and patterns that require players to adapt and strategize.

3. Resource Management

MANY GAMES INVOLVE resource management, such as currency, items, or ammunition. Balancing resource management ensures that players are appropriately rewarded and motivated to make meaningful choices. Consider the following:

- **Economy Balance:** Determine the rate at which players earn and spend resources. Avoid making resources too scarce or too abundant, as this can affect pacing and player motivation.

- **Item Rarity:** If your game has items or equipment, assign rarity levels to them. Rare items should provide significant benefits but be harder to obtain.

- **Resource Progression:** Plan resource progression throughout the game. As players advance, they should gain access to better resources or more efficient ways to gather them.

4. Level and Encounter Design

BALANCING LEVEL AND encounter design is crucial for maintaining a consistent difficulty curve. Here are some principles to follow:

- **Difficulty Spikes:** Avoid sudden and extreme difficulty spikes that can frustrate players. Instead, introduce new challenges gradually and provide opportunities for skill development.

- **Testing and Iteration:** Playtest your levels and encounters extensively to identify balance issues. Make adjustments based on player feedback and observations.

- **Player Agency:** Allow players to approach challenges in different ways. A well-balanced game provides multiple viable strategies for overcoming obstacles.

5. Feedback and Data Analysis

COLLECTING FEEDBACK from players and analyzing gameplay data are invaluable tools for balancing gameplay elements. Here's how to use feedback and data effectively:

- **Player Feedback:** Encourage players to provide feedback through surveys, forums, or social media. Pay attention to their comments and adjust gameplay elements accordingly.

- **Analytics:** Implement analytics tools to track player behavior and progress. Analyze data to identify trends and areas where balancing adjustments may be needed.

- **Regular Updates:** Be prepared to release updates and patches to address balance issues discovered after the game's launch. This shows dedication to maintaining a balanced and enjoyable experience for players.

6. Community Involvement

ENGAGE WITH YOUR GAME'S community to gather input and opinions on gameplay balance. Many successful games involve their player base in the balance process through public testing, forums, and community-driven balance discussions.

In conclusion, balancing gameplay elements is a continuous and iterative process that requires careful consideration of player characters, enemies, resource management, level design, feedback, and data analysis. Achieving the right balance ensures that your game remains enjoyable, challenging, and fair, contributing to a positive player experience and the long-term success of your game.

15.3 Implementing Reward Systems and Progression

REWARD SYSTEMS AND progression mechanics are key elements of game design that can keep players engaged, motivated, and invested in your game. These systems provide incentives for players to continue playing, achieve goals, and explore the game's content. In this section, we'll delve into the principles and techniques for implementing effective reward systems and progression mechanics.

1. Understanding Player Motivation

BEFORE DESIGNING REWARD systems and progression mechanics, it's crucial to understand player motivation. Different players are motivated by various factors, including achievement, competition, exploration, and social interaction. Consider your target audience and what drives them to play your game.

2. Types of Rewards

REWARDS COME IN VARIOUS forms, and each can appeal to different player motivations. Common types of rewards include:

- **In-Game Items:** Items, equipment, or power-ups that enhance a player's abilities or provide new gameplay options.

- **Experience Points (XP):** A resource that represents a player's progress and can be used to unlock new abilities or levels.

- **Currency:** Virtual currency that can be spent on in-game purchases, such as items, skins, or customization options.

- **Achievements:** Milestones or accomplishments that players can earn by completing specific tasks or challenges.

- **Cosmetic Items:** Skins, outfits, or visual customization options that allow players to personalize their characters or items.

- **Story Progress:** Advancing the game's narrative or unlocking new story content as a reward.

3. Balancing Rewards

BALANCING REWARDS IS essential to ensure that they are enticing but not overly disruptive to gameplay. Here are some considerations:

- **Value:** Assign appropriate value to rewards. Powerful rewards should require significant effort or achievement.

- **Pacing:** Control the rate at which rewards are given to maintain a sense of progression. Too many rewards too quickly can diminish their impact.

- **Scaling:** Scale rewards to match player progression. Ensure that rewards remain relevant and appealing as players advance.

4. Progression Mechanics

PROGRESSION MECHANICS are systems that allow players to advance through the game and unlock new content or abilities. Common progression mechanics include:

- **Leveling:** Allowing players to increase their character's level, gaining new abilities or perks as they progress.

- **Skill Trees:** Providing skill trees or talent systems that let players customize their character's abilities.

- **Unlockable Content:** Unlocking new levels, areas, characters, or game modes as players achieve specific milestones.

- **Quests and Objectives:** Offering quests, challenges, or objectives that guide players and reward them for completion.

5. Feedback and Visuals

PROVIDE CLEAR FEEDBACK to players when they earn rewards or progress. This includes visual and auditory cues, such as:

- **Animations:** Use animations to highlight the acquisition of rewards, like item pickups or level-up animations.

- **Sound Effects:** Include sounds that signify achievement, such as a triumphant jingle or fanfare.

- **Visual Effects:** Use particle effects or visual enhancements to draw attention to rewards and progression milestones.

6. Player Choice

ALLOW PLAYERS SOME degree of choice in the rewards they pursue or the paths they take in progression. This fosters a sense of agency and personalization, making the game more engaging. For example, players might choose between different abilities or quests that align with their preferred playstyle.

7. Long-Term Goals

INCLUDE LONG-TERM GOALS and rewards to keep players engaged over an extended period. This might involve rare or epic rewards that require significant dedication and persistence to achieve.

8. Social Interaction

CONSIDER INCORPORATING social features into your reward and progression systems. Players may be motivated by competition, cooperation, or the desire to showcase their achievements to others.

In conclusion, implementing effective reward systems and progression mechanics is essential for creating an engaging and motivating gaming experience. By understanding player motivations, offering diverse and balanced rewards, and designing progression mechanics that cater to different playstyles, you can keep players invested in your game and encourage long-term engagement.

15.4 Puzzle and Level Design Strategies

PUZZLE AND LEVEL DESIGN are critical aspects of game development, particularly in games that involve problem-solving, exploration, and progression. Effective puzzle and level design can provide engaging challenges and memorable experiences for players. In this section, we'll explore strategies and techniques for creating compelling puzzles and well-designed levels.

1. Understanding Player Skill and Progression

BEFORE DESIGNING PUZZLES and levels, it's crucial to understand the skill level of your target audience and the progression of your game. Consider the following:

• **Skill Curve:** Start with relatively simple puzzles or challenges to introduce players to the game's mechanics. Gradually increase the complexity and difficulty as players progress.

• **Player Feedback:** Pay attention to player feedback and iterate on puzzles and levels based on their experiences. A well-balanced difficulty curve ensures that players don't become frustrated.

2. Establish Clear Objectives

EACH PUZZLE OR LEVEL should have clear objectives that players can understand. Whether it's reaching a specific location, solving a riddle, or defeating an enemy, players need to know what's expected of them.

• **Objective Clarity:** Use visual cues, dialogue, or in-game hints to convey objectives without explicitly stating them. Allow players to discover objectives through exploration and observation.

• **Vary Objectives:** Offer a variety of objectives to keep gameplay interesting. Some objectives may require combat skills, while others focus on puzzle-solving or exploration.

3. Consistency in Mechanics

MAINTAIN CONSISTENCY in the game's mechanics and rules. Players should be able to apply what they've learned in previous levels or puzzles to new challenges.

- **Teaching by Doing:** Introduce new mechanics or concepts in a safe environment where players can practice and learn without severe consequences.

- **Combining Mechanics:** Create complex puzzles or challenges by combining multiple mechanics or elements that players have encountered individually.

4. Balance Challenge and Reward

BALANCING CHALLENGE and reward is essential for player engagement. Players should feel a sense of accomplishment and satisfaction when they overcome challenges.

- **Progressive Challenge:** Gradually increase the difficulty of puzzles and levels as players become more skilled. This provides a sense of progression.

- **Rewarding Success:** Reward players for successfully completing puzzles or levels. Rewards can include in-game items, story progression, or access to new areas.

5. Exploration and Discovery

ENCOURAGE EXPLORATION and discovery in your levels. Hidden secrets, optional objectives, and non-linear paths can enhance the player's sense of agency and curiosity.

- **Hidden Secrets:** Include hidden items, shortcuts, or easter eggs that reward observant players.

- **Non-Linear Design:** Allow players to tackle puzzles or levels in different orders or choose between multiple paths. This adds replayability and caters to different playstyles.

6. Testing and Iteration

EXTENSIVE PLAYTESTING and iteration are essential for puzzle and level design. Playtesters can provide valuable feedback on puzzle difficulty, level flow, and potential issues.

- **Iterative Design:** Be prepared to make changes to puzzles and levels based on player feedback. What may seem logical to the designer might not be apparent to players.

- **Accessibility:** Ensure that puzzles and levels are accessible to a wide range of players, including those with varying skill levels and abilities.

7. Story Integration

IF YOUR GAME HAS A narrative, integrate puzzles and level design into the story seamlessly. Make sure that puzzles and challenges make sense within the context of the game world.

- **Motivated Challenges:** Ensure that the challenges players face are motivated by the game's story or objectives. This helps maintain immersion.

8. User-Generated Content

CONSIDER ALLOWING PLAYERS to create their own puzzles or levels in user-generated content (UGC) systems. UGC can extend the longevity of your game and provide unique challenges.

In conclusion, effective puzzle and level design are essential for creating engaging and memorable gaming experiences. By understanding player skill and progression, establishing clear objectives, maintaining consistency in mechanics, balancing challenge and reward, encouraging exploration and discovery, conducting thorough testing, integrating puzzles into the story, and exploring user-generated content, you can create puzzles and levels that captivate players and keep them immersed in your game world.

15.5 Creating Dynamic Game Worlds

DYNAMIC GAME WORLDS are environments that evolve, react, and respond to player actions, creating a sense of immersion and interactivity. Designing dynamic game worlds can greatly enhance the player's experience and make the game world feel alive. In this section, we'll explore strategies and techniques for creating dynamic game worlds.

1. Interactive Objects and Elements

ONE WAY TO MAKE A GAME world dynamic is by incorporating interactive objects and elements. These objects can include levers, switches, movable props, and more. Players can manipulate these objects to affect the environment or trigger events.

- **Physics-Based Interactions:** Implement physics-based interactions to make objects behave realistically. For example, if a player pushes a box, it should slide and react to collisions.

- **Puzzle Elements:** Use interactive objects as components of puzzles or challenges. Players may need to manipulate objects to progress or solve puzzles.

2. Day-Night Cycles and Weather Systems

IMPLEMENTING DAY-NIGHT cycles and weather systems can add depth to your game world. These dynamic systems change the appearance and atmosphere of the environment over time.

- **Aesthetic Changes:** Adjust lighting, shadows, and weather effects to reflect the time of day or weather conditions. This provides a visual cue to players about the passage of time.

- **Gameplay Impact:** Consider how day-night cycles and weather systems affect gameplay. For example, certain creatures or events may only occur at night, or rain might make surfaces slippery.

3. Non-Player Characters (NPCs) and AI

INCORPORATE NPCS AND AI with behaviors that respond to the player's actions and the game world. NPCs can add life and complexity to the environment.

- **NPC Reactions:** Design NPCs to react to the player's actions, decisions, and alignment. NPCs may offer quests, engage in conversation, or become hostile based on the player's choices.

- **Dynamic AI:** Implement dynamic AI routines that adapt to changing circumstances. For example, if the player steals an item, NPCs may become more vigilant.

4. Environmental Changes and Destruction

ALLOW THE GAME WORLD to change over time, especially in response to significant events or player actions. This can include environmental changes or destructible elements.

- **Destructible Objects:** Design elements in the environment that can be destroyed or damaged. This adds realism and interactivity.

- **Environmental Storytelling:** Use environmental changes to tell a story or convey information. For example, a ruined building may hint at a past event.

5. Dynamic Events and Encounters

INTRODUCE DYNAMIC EVENTS and encounters that can occur randomly or in response to player choices. These events keep gameplay fresh and unpredictable.

- **Random Encounters:** Include random events or encounters during exploration. These encounters can offer opportunities for rewards or challenges.

- **Player Choices:** Design events that change based on the player's decisions. Choices made earlier in the game can influence later events and outcomes.

6. Player Influence and Consequences

LET PLAYERS HAVE A meaningful impact on the game world through their choices and actions. This can create a sense of agency and immersion.

• **Choice and Consequence:** Ensure that player choices have consequences, both immediate and long-term. This encourages players to think about their decisions.

• **Multiple Endings:** Consider offering multiple endings based on player choices, providing replay value and a sense of ownership over the game world's fate.

7. Audio and Music

USE DYNAMIC AUDIO AND music to enhance the atmosphere of the game world. Audio cues can signal changes or events.

• **Dynamic Soundscapes:** Implement dynamic soundscapes that change based on the game's events or location. For example, a peaceful forest might have birdsong during the day and eerie silence at night.

• **Music Transitions:** Use music that transitions smoothly to reflect different moods or situations. For example, combat music can start playing when enemies are nearby.

8. Testing and Iteration

DESIGNING DYNAMIC GAME worlds can be complex, so thorough testing and iteration are crucial. Playtest the game to ensure that dynamic elements work as intended and that the world feels cohesive.

• **Player Feedback:** Pay attention to player feedback regarding the game world's dynamic aspects. Players' experiences may reveal issues or opportunities for improvement.

- **Bug Testing:** Test for bugs or unintended interactions related to dynamic elements. Bugs can disrupt immersion and gameplay.

In conclusion, creating dynamic game worlds requires careful planning and consideration of interactive objects, day-night cycles, NPCs and AI, environmental changes, dynamic events, player influence, audio, and thorough testing. When executed effectively, dynamic game worlds can provide players with a rich and immersive gaming experience that feels alive and responsive to their actions.

Chapter 16: Testing and Quality Assurance

Section 16.1: Principles of Game Testing

Game testing is a critical phase in the game development process that ensures your game is free from bugs, runs smoothly, and provides an enjoyable experience for players. In this section, we'll delve into the principles of game testing, highlighting its importance and key practices.

The Role of Testing

TESTING SERVES AS A quality control mechanism, identifying and rectifying issues before they reach players. It involves systematically evaluating various aspects of your game, including functionality, performance, and user experience.

Types of Testing

1. **Functional Testing**: This type focuses on ensuring that all game features work as intended. Testers play through the game, examining mechanics, controls, and interactions.
2. **Regression Testing**: After changes or updates, regression testing ensures that new features or fixes don't introduce new problems or break existing functionality.
3. **Performance Testing**: Performance testing assesses how your game performs under different conditions. It includes load testing to check server capacity for online games and stress testing to see how the game handles extreme scenarios.

4. **Compatibility Testing**: Ensure your game works on various platforms, devices, and operating systems. This is especially crucial for mobile and multi-platform games.
5. **Usability Testing**: Gather feedback from players to assess the game's user interface, controls, and overall user experience. Usability testing helps identify areas where improvements can be made.

Test Planning

EFFECTIVE TESTING STARTS with a well-defined test plan. Consider the following aspects when creating your test plan:

- **Test Objectives**: Clearly define what you aim to achieve through testing, whether it's identifying and fixing specific bugs, optimizing performance, or enhancing user experience.

- **Test Scenarios**: Outline specific scenarios and use cases that testers should explore. These scenarios should cover a wide range of gameplay situations.

- **Test Environment**: Specify the hardware and software configurations that testers should use, including any required test devices or platforms.

- **Test Data**: Prepare test data, including saved game files, player profiles, and any other relevant information, to replicate real-world player experiences.

- **Test Team**: Assign roles and responsibilities within your testing team, including lead testers, automation testers, and beta testers.

Automated Testing

CONSIDER IMPLEMENTING automated testing tools and scripts to streamline repetitive and time-consuming testing tasks. Automation can help with regression testing and ensuring consistent results across different test runs.

```
// Example of a simple automated test script in Unity using the NUnit framework

using UnityEngine;

using NUnit.Framework;

public class GameManagerTest

{

[Test]

public void PlayerScoreIncreases()

{

GameManager gameManager = new GameManager();

int initialScore = gameManager.GetPlayerScore();

gameManager.IncreaseScore(10);

Assert.AreEqual(initialScore + 10, gameManager.GetPlayerScore());

}

}
```

Continuous Testing

INTEGRATE TESTING INTO your development pipeline with continuous integration and continuous deployment (CI/CD) practices. This ensures that tests are run automatically whenever changes are made to the game, helping catch issues early.

Conclusion

TESTING IS A CRUCIAL aspect of game development that should never be underestimated. By following these principles and best practices, you can ensure your game meets the highest quality standards, resulting in a more enjoyable experience for players.

Section 16.2: Setting Up Test Cases and Automation

CREATING EFFECTIVE test cases and implementing test automation are essential components of a robust testing strategy in game development. In this section, we will explore the process of setting up test cases and automation to ensure comprehensive testing of your game.

Test Case Creation

1. **Identify Test Scenarios**: Begin by identifying the various scenarios, features, and functionalities of your game that need testing. Consider both common and edge cases.
2. **Define Test Objectives**: For each scenario, clearly define the objectives of the test. What specific behavior or outcome are you testing for?
3. **Document Test Cases**: Create detailed test cases that include step-by-step instructions for testers to follow. Specify the input conditions, expected results, and any

necessary prerequisites.

4. **Prioritize Test Cases**: Prioritize test cases based on their criticality and potential impact on the player experience. Focus on high-priority tests first.

Test Automation Frameworks

IMPLEMENTING TEST AUTOMATION can significantly speed up the testing process and improve test coverage. Here are some popular test automation frameworks and tools used in game development:

- **Unity Test Framework**: Unity provides its own testing framework that allows you to write and run tests within the Unity Editor. It supports unit tests, integration tests, and play mode tests.

```csharp
// Example of a Unity Test Framework test case

using UnityEngine;

using NUnit.Framework;

public class PlayerTest

{

[Test]

public void PlayerHealthShouldDecreaseOnDamage()

{

Player player = new Player();

int initialHealth = player.GetHealth();
```

```
player.TakeDamage(10);

Assert.Less(player.GetHealth(), initialHealth);

}

}
```

- **Appium**: Appium is an open-source tool for automating mobile app testing. It can be used to automate testing of mobile games on various platforms.

- **Selenium**: While primarily designed for web application testing, Selenium can be adapted for automated testing of browser-based games.

Continuous Integration (CI) and Continuous Deployment (CD)

INTEGRATE YOUR AUTOMATED tests into your CI/CD pipeline. This ensures that tests are run automatically whenever changes are made to the game's codebase. CI/CD tools like Jenkins, Travis CI, or GitHub Actions can automate the entire testing process.

 # Example GitHub Actions workflow for Unity game testing

```
name: Unity Game Testing

on:

push:

branches:

- main
```

```
jobs:

build:

runs-on: ubuntu-latest

steps:

- name: Checkout code

uses: actions/checkout@v2

- name: Set up Unity

uses: game-ci/setup-unity@v2

with:

unity-version: 2021.1.0f1

- name: Build and Test

run: |

unity -projectPath . -runTests -testPlatform editmode
```

Test Data Management

MANAGE TEST DATA EFFECTIVELY, especially for games with complex progression systems. Use test data libraries or scripts to simulate different game states and player profiles for testing.

Test Reporting and Analysis

IMPLEMENT A SYSTEM for reporting and analyzing test results. Test reports should be easily accessible to the development team, highlighting passed and failed tests, along with detailed logs for failed tests.

Conclusion

SETTING UP TEST CASES and automation is crucial for maintaining a high level of game quality and ensuring that your game functions as expected. By following these practices and integrating automation into your development pipeline, you can streamline the testing process and catch issues early in the development cycle, ultimately delivering a more polished and reliable game to your players.

Section 16.3: User Testing and Feedback Loops

USER TESTING IS A CRUCIAL aspect of quality assurance in game development. It involves gathering feedback from actual players to assess the game's usability, playability, and overall user experience. In this section, we'll explore the importance of user testing and how to establish effective feedback loops with your player community.

Why User Testing Matters

USER TESTING PROVIDES invaluable insights into how players interact with your game. It helps identify usability issues, gameplay problems, and areas for improvement that may not be apparent to the development team. Here are some key reasons why user testing is essential:

- **Identifying Usability Issues**: Players can uncover issues related to controls, user interfaces, and overall navigation that may be confusing or frustrating.

- **Balancing Gameplay**: User testing helps assess game balance, difficulty levels, and progression systems, ensuring that the game provides an enjoyable challenge.

- **Finding Bugs and Glitches**: Players often encounter unexpected bugs or glitches that may not have been detected during internal testing.

- **Player Feedback**: Gathering feedback from your target audience helps shape the game based on the preferences and expectations of actual players.

Conducting User Tests

1. **Define Testing Goals**: Clearly define the objectives of your user tests. What aspects of the game are you specifically testing? What feedback are you looking to gather?
2. **Recruit Testers**: Recruit a diverse group of testers who represent your target player demographic. Consider using online platforms or communities dedicated to game testing.
3. **Create Test Scenarios**: Prepare a set of test scenarios or tasks for the testers to complete. These scenarios should cover different aspects of the game.
4. **Gather Data**: During the testing sessions, collect data on player interactions, feedback, and any issues encountered. Encourage testers to think aloud as they play.
5. **Analyze Results**: After the tests, analyze the collected data. Look for common patterns, recurring issues, and areas where players struggled or excelled.

Feedback Loops

ESTABLISHING EFFECTIVE feedback loops is crucial to acting on the insights gained from user testing. Here's how to create feedback loops within your development process:

- **Regular Playtesting**: Schedule regular playtesting sessions throughout development, not just at the end. This allows you to address issues early.

- **Feedback Channels**: Set up dedicated feedback channels such as forums, in-game reporting tools, or surveys to collect ongoing feedback from players.

- **Prioritization**: Prioritize feedback based on severity and impact. Some issues may need immediate attention, while others can be addressed in future updates.

- **Communication**: Maintain open communication with your player community. Acknowledge feedback and keep players informed about updates and changes based on their input.

Post-Launch Feedback

USER TESTING AND FEEDBACK loops should continue even after the game's launch. Monitor player feedback on social media, forums, and review platforms. Use this feedback to plan post-launch updates, bug fixes, and content expansions to keep players engaged.

```
// Example of in-game feedback tool

public class FeedbackSystem : MonoBehaviour

{
```

```
public void CollectPlayerFeedback(string feedback)

{

    // Send player feedback to a dedicated server or database for analysis.

    // You can also include player information to follow up on specific issues.

}

}
```

Conclusion

USER TESTING AND ESTABLISHING feedback loops with your player community are essential components of delivering a successful and player-focused game. By actively involving players in the testing process and continuously listening to their feedback, you can create a more enjoyable and engaging gaming experience while addressing issues and improving your game over time.

Section 16.4: Identifying and Fixing Bugs

IDENTIFYING AND FIXING bugs is an inevitable part of game development. No matter how thoroughly a game is tested, there will always be issues that need to be addressed. In this section, we will explore strategies and best practices for identifying and fixing bugs effectively.

Types of Bugs

BUGS IN GAMES CAN MANIFEST in various ways, from minor inconveniences to game-breaking issues. Understanding the types of bugs you may encounter is essential for effective debugging:

1. **Gameplay Bugs**: These bugs affect the core mechanics and rules of the game. They can include issues with character movement, combat systems, and game progression.
2. **Visual Bugs**: Visual bugs impact the game's graphics and rendering. Examples include texture glitches, graphical artifacts, and rendering errors.
3. **Audio Bugs**: Issues related to sound and music, such as missing audio cues, distorted sounds, or synchronization problems.
4. **Performance Bugs**: Performance-related bugs can lead to frame rate drops, lag, or excessive resource consumption, affecting the game's smoothness and playability.
5. **Multiplayer Bugs**: In online multiplayer games, bugs related to network synchronization, lag compensation, and player interactions can be particularly challenging to identify and fix.

Debugging Tools

GAME ENGINES LIKE UNITY provide a range of debugging tools to help identify and diagnose bugs:

- **Console Logging**: Use Debug.Log statements to print messages to the console, helping you track the flow of execution and variable values.

// Example of using Debug.Log to print a message

```
void Update()

{

float playerSpeed = 10.0f;

Debug.Log("Player speed: " + playerSpeed);
```

}

- **Unity Profiler**: The Unity Profiler allows you to monitor CPU and GPU performance, memory usage, and rendering statistics, helping identify performance-related issues.

- **Inspector**: Use the Unity Inspector to inspect and modify the properties of game objects during runtime, which can be helpful for diagnosing issues related to object states and behaviors.

- **Breakpoints**: Set breakpoints in your code to pause execution at specific points, allowing you to examine variables and step through code step by step.

Reproducing Bugs

TO FIX A BUG, YOU FIRST need to reproduce it consistently. Follow these steps to reproduce bugs effectively:

1. **Identify the Steps**: Document the exact steps or conditions that lead to the bug's occurrence. Be as detailed as possible.
2. **Isolate Variables**: Isolate variables and conditions that may contribute to the bug. This can help narrow down the root cause.
3. **Create a Test Case**: Create a dedicated test case or scenario that reliably reproduces the bug. This will be essential for verifying that the bug is fixed.

Prioritizing and Triaging Bugs

NOT ALL BUGS ARE CREATED equal. Prioritizing and triaging bugs is crucial to ensure that critical issues are addressed promptly while less severe ones can be scheduled for later fixes. Common bug priorities include:

- **Critical**: Bugs that cause crashes, prevent gameplay, or compromise player data integrity.

- **High**: Significant gameplay issues or graphical glitches that severely impact the player experience.

- **Medium**: Non-game-breaking issues that still affect gameplay or aesthetics but may not be critical.

- **Low**: Minor bugs, typos, or cosmetic issues that have minimal impact on gameplay.

Bug Tracking Systems

USE BUG TRACKING SYSTEMS like JIRA, Trello, or GitHub Issues to manage and prioritize bug reports. These systems allow you to assign bugs to specific team members, track their status, and schedule fixes.

Conclusion

IDENTIFYING AND FIXING bugs is an ongoing process in game development. By understanding the types of bugs you may encounter, using debugging tools effectively, reproducing bugs consistently, and prioritizing fixes, you can maintain a stable and enjoyable gaming experience for your players while continuously improving your game.

Section 16.5: Ensuring Game Accessibility and Inclusivity

ENSURING GAME ACCESSIBILITY and inclusivity is not only a moral imperative but also a fundamental aspect of game quality. In this section, we will explore the importance of making games accessible to all players, including those with disabilities, and discuss strategies for achieving inclusivity in game design and development.

Understanding Accessibility

GAME ACCESSIBILITY involves designing and developing games in a way that allows individuals with disabilities to fully enjoy and interact with the game. Disabilities can encompass a wide range of conditions, including visual, auditory, motor, and cognitive impairments. Game accessibility aims to remove barriers and provide alternative ways for players to engage with the game's content.

Legal and Ethical Considerations

MANY COUNTRIES HAVE regulations that require digital content, including games, to be accessible to individuals with disabilities. Compliance with these regulations is not only a legal requirement but also a demonstration of ethical responsibility.

In the United States, for example, the Americans with Disabilities Act (ADA) requires that public accommodations, including digital services, be accessible to individuals with disabilities. Ensuring game accessibility can help game developers avoid legal issues and create a more inclusive gaming community.

Designing for Accessibility

1. **User Interface (UI) Accessibility**: Ensure that your game's

user interface is navigable using keyboard controls and screen readers. Use clear and descriptive labels for UI elements, and provide options to adjust font sizes and colors for readability.

2. **Audio Accessibility**: Provide visual cues or subtitles for important audio information, such as dialogues, sound effects, and music. Allow players to adjust volume levels and provide alternatives for players with hearing impairments.

3. **Visual Accessibility**: Implement features such as high-contrast modes, colorblind-friendly palettes, and adjustable screen brightness. Avoid relying solely on color coding to convey information.

4. **Motor Accessibility**: Design controls and gameplay mechanics to accommodate players with motor disabilities. Offer customizable controls and support for alternative input devices like adaptive controllers.

Playtesting with Diverse Audiences

INCLUDE PLAYERS WITH disabilities in your playtesting sessions to gather valuable feedback on accessibility issues. These players can provide insights into areas where improvements are needed and help you fine-tune your game's accessibility features.

Accessibility Guidelines and Resources

FAMILIARIZE YOURSELF with accessibility guidelines and best practices, such as the Web Content Accessibility Guidelines (WCAG) and the Game Accessibility Guidelines (GAAD). These resources offer detailed recommendations and techniques for making games accessible.

<!—Example of providing alt text for images in Unity UI—>

<Button>

<Image src="button_icon.png" alt="Play Button">

</Button>

Ongoing Commitment

ACCESSIBILITY IS NOT a one-time effort but an ongoing commitment. As you update and expand your game, continue to assess and improve its accessibility features. Engage with the accessibility community and gather feedback to ensure that your game remains inclusive.

Conclusion

ENSURING GAME ACCESSIBILITY and inclusivity is a vital aspect of game development that benefits both players and developers. By designing with accessibility in mind, following legal and ethical considerations, playtesting with diverse audiences, and staying informed about accessibility guidelines, you can create games that are enjoyed by a broader and more inclusive player base while upholding the principles of equality and accessibility.

Chapter 17: Launching and Marketing Your Game

Section 17.1: Preparing for Game Launch

Preparing for the launch of your game is a crucial step that can significantly impact its success. In this section, we will explore the essential tasks and considerations when getting ready to launch your game.

Define Your Launch Goals

BEFORE LAUNCHING YOUR game, it's essential to have clear goals in mind. What are you trying to achieve with the launch? Goals can include:

- **Building Hype**: Generating excitement and anticipation among your target audience.

- **Acquiring Players**: Getting as many players as possible to try your game.

- **Monetization**: Earning revenue through game sales, in-app purchases, or ads.

- **Community Building**: Growing a dedicated player community around your game.

Create a Launch Plan

A WELL-THOUGHT-OUT launch plan is essential for a successful release. Here are key elements to consider:

- **Launch Date**: Choose a launch date that aligns with your goals and avoids clashes with other major game releases.

- **Marketing Materials**: Prepare promotional materials such as trailers, screenshots, and press releases to showcase your game.

- **Storefront Optimization**: Optimize your game's store page on platforms like Steam, the App Store, or Google Play. Use eye-catching visuals and compelling descriptions.

- **Community Engagement**: Engage with your player community through social media, forums, and newsletters. Build excitement and anticipation.

- **Review Campaigns**: Send review copies of your game to gaming journalists, influencers, and YouTubers for early reviews and coverage.

- **Launch Events**: Consider organizing launch events, livestreams, or giveaways to celebrate the release.

Quality Assurance

ENSURE THAT YOUR GAME is thoroughly tested and free from critical bugs before launch. Consider running a closed beta test to gather feedback from a select group of players and make necessary improvements.

Distribution Platforms

CHOOSE THE DISTRIBUTION platforms that align with your game and target audience. Popular options include Steam, Epic Games Store, PlayStation Network, Xbox Live, the App Store, and Google Play. Each platform has its submission and review process, so plan ahead.

Pricing and Monetization

DETERMINE YOUR GAME'S pricing strategy and monetization model. Options include free-to-play with in-app purchases, one-time purchase, subscription, or ad-supported. Ensure your pricing aligns with your game's value and target audience.

Marketing and Promotion

EFFECTIVE MARKETING and promotion are critical for a successful launch. Consider the following marketing strategies:

- **Press Releases**: Write and distribute press releases to gaming news outlets.

- **Social Media**: Utilize social media platforms to create buzz and engage with your community.

- **Influencer Marketing**: Partner with gaming influencers to review and promote your game.

- **Email Marketing**: Use newsletters to keep your audience informed about the launch.

- **Storefront Features**: Leverage featured placements and discounts on the distribution platforms.

Post-Launch Support

PLAN FOR POST-LAUNCH support, including bug fixes, updates, and additional content. Ongoing support can help maintain player interest and retention.

Conclusion

PREPARING FOR YOUR game launch is a complex but essential process. By defining your launch goals, creating a detailed launch plan, ensuring quality, choosing the right distribution platforms, setting appropriate pricing and monetization strategies, and executing effective marketing and promotion, you can maximize the chances of a successful launch and set your game on a path to success in the competitive gaming industry.

Section 17.2: Effective Marketing Strategies for Indie Developers

EFFECTIVE MARKETING is crucial for indie developers to compete in the crowded game market. In this section, we will explore marketing strategies tailored to indie game developers, helping you promote your game and reach your target audience.

Building Your Brand

ESTABLISHING A STRONG brand identity is the foundation of effective marketing. Your brand encompasses your game's personality, values, and visual identity. Here are key elements to consider:

- **Logo and Visual Identity**: Create a memorable logo and visual assets that represent your game's theme and style.

- **Consistent Messaging**: Maintain consistent messaging across all marketing materials and channels.

- **Unique Selling Proposition (USP)**: Identify what makes your game unique and communicate it clearly to your audience.

Website and Landing Page

CREATE A PROFESSIONAL website or landing page for your game. This is where players and potential customers can learn more about your game, view trailers, and access press kits. Ensure your website is mobile-friendly and optimized for search engines (SEO).

Social Media Presence

UTILIZE SOCIAL MEDIA platforms to connect with your audience and build a community around your game. Here's how:

- **Choose the Right Platforms**: Identify the social media platforms that are most relevant to your target audience. For example, Twitter and Instagram are popular choices for game promotion.

- **Consistent Posting**: Maintain a regular posting schedule to keep your audience engaged. Share updates, behind-the-scenes content, and teasers.

- **Engage with Followers**: Respond to comments, answer questions, and actively engage with your followers. Building a personal connection can foster a dedicated fanbase.

Influencer Marketing

PARTNERING WITH GAMING influencers and YouTubers can help expose your game to a wider audience. When working with influencers:

- **Research and Outreach**: Identify influencers who align with your game's genre and style. Reach out to them with a compelling pitch.

- **Provide Review Copies**: Offer early access or review copies to influencers, allowing them to create content about your game.

- **Disclosure**: Ensure influencers disclose their partnership and any compensation in accordance with relevant regulations.

Press and Media Coverage

BUILD RELATIONSHIPS with gaming journalists and bloggers. Create press releases and reach out to gaming news outlets for coverage. A well-crafted press kit with high-quality assets can make it easier for journalists to write about your game.

Community Engagement

INTERACT WITH YOUR player community on forums, social media, and your website. Show appreciation for fan art, fan fiction, and other contributions. Encourage discussions and feedback to keep your community active and engaged.

Crowdfunding and Early Access

CONSIDER CROWDFUNDING platforms like Kickstarter or early access on platforms like Steam. These approaches can provide funding and valuable player feedback while generating buzz for your game.

Email Marketing

COLLECT EMAIL ADDRESSES from interested players and fans. Send regular newsletters with updates, exclusive content, and special offers to keep your audience informed and engaged.

```
<!—Example of an email signup form on your game's website—>

<form action="/subscribe" method="post">

<input type="email" name="email" placeholder="Enter your email">

<button type="submit">Subscribe</button>

</form>
```

Analytics and Iteration

USE ANALYTICS TOOLS to track the performance of your marketing efforts. Analyze which strategies are most effective in driving engagement and conversions. Adjust your marketing plan based on these insights.

Conclusion

EFFECTIVE MARKETING is a vital aspect of game promotion for indie developers. By building a strong brand, creating a compelling online presence, engaging with your community, and utilizing a mix of marketing strategies tailored to your game and target audience, you can increase the visibility and success of your indie game in a competitive market.

Section 17.3: Building a Community Around Your Game

BUILDING A COMMUNITY of dedicated players and fans is a powerful way to promote your game, gather feedback, and ensure its long-term success. In this section, we will explore strategies for nurturing a vibrant and engaged player community around your game.

Why Community Building Matters

A STRONG PLAYER COMMUNITY can provide numerous benefits to indie developers:

- **Loyal Fanbase**: Engaged players are more likely to support your game, recommend it to others, and stay with you for future projects.

- **Feedback and Testing**: Your community can serve as a valuable source of feedback during development, helping you identify and fix issues.

- **Word of Mouth**: Enthusiastic players can become ambassadors for your game, spreading the word through reviews, social media, and recommendations to friends.

- **Monetization Opportunities**: A dedicated community can contribute to your game's revenue through purchases, donations, or participation in crowdfunding campaigns.

Early Community Engagement

START BUILDING YOUR community as early as possible in the development process. Even before your game is complete, you can engage potential players by:

- **Launching a Website**: Create a website or landing page for your game, where visitors can sign up for newsletters and follow development updates.

- **Social Media Presence**: Establish a presence on social media platforms relevant to your target audience. Share concept art, development progress, and engage with followers.

- **Developer Diaries**: Share behind-the-scenes developer diaries or video blogs (vlogs) to give players insight into your creative process.

Interact and Listen

ENGAGE WITH YOUR COMMUNITY actively and genuinely. Listen to their feedback, answer questions, and acknowledge their contributions. Here's how:

- **Forums and Social Groups**: Create official forums, subreddits, or Discord servers where players can discuss the game and provide feedback.

- **Feedback Surveys**: Conduct surveys to gather opinions on gameplay, features, and improvements.

- **Developer Q&A**: Host live Q&A sessions where players can ask questions and get direct answers from the development team.

> **Player123**: Will there be a multiplayer mode?

>

> **Developer**: Yes, we're actively working on implementing multiplayer. It's a top priority for us!

Exclusive Content

REWARD YOUR MOST DEDICATED fans with exclusive content or early access. For example:

- **Closed Beta Testing**: Invite a select group of players to participate in closed beta testing, providing them with a sneak peek and the opportunity to contribute to the game's development.

- **Exclusive Merchandise**: Offer exclusive in-game items or physical merchandise to early supporters.

Transparency

BE TRANSPARENT ABOUT the development process, progress, and challenges you face. Transparency builds trust and shows players that you value their input and opinions.

- **Development Roadmap**: Share a development roadmap outlining planned features and updates.

- **Bugs and Fixes**: Acknowledge and communicate the status of reported bugs and the timeline for fixes.

In-Game Community Features

INCORPORATE COMMUNITY-building features directly into your game:

- **Player-Created Content**: Allow players to create and share custom content, such as mods, levels, or skins.

- **Leaderboards and Competitions**: Foster competition by implementing leaderboards and hosting in-game competitions with rewards.

Events and Livestreams

HOST EVENTS, LIVESTREAMS, or in-game gatherings to bring your community together:

- **Livestream Playthroughs**: Stream yourself playing the game and interacting with the community.

- **Fan Art Contests**: Organize fan art or fan fiction contests with prizes.

Moderation and Guidelines

ESTABLISH CLEAR COMMUNITY guidelines and appoint moderators to ensure a positive and respectful environment. Address toxic behavior promptly to maintain a welcoming community.

Conclusion

BUILDING A DEDICATED player community around your game takes time and effort but can be immensely rewarding. By engaging early, interacting genuinely, offering exclusive content, and fostering a sense of belonging and participation, you can create a thriving community that not only supports your current game but also becomes a valuable asset for future projects.

Section 17.4: Navigating Game Distribution

Platforms

GAME DISTRIBUTION PLATFORMS play a pivotal role in reaching your target audience and monetizing your game. In this section, we will explore the key aspects of navigating these platforms effectively.

Choosing the Right Platforms

SELECTING THE MOST suitable distribution platforms for your game is a crucial decision. Here are some considerations:

- **Audience**: Identify where your target audience is most active. PC gamers may prefer platforms like Steam, while mobile gamers use app stores like Google Play and the App Store.

- **Revenue Models**: Different platforms support various revenue models, such as one-time purchases, free-to-play with in-app purchases, or subscription services. Choose the model that aligns with your game's monetization strategy.

- **Platform Requirements**: Be aware of each platform's technical and content requirements. These may include system specifications, content guidelines, and submission processes.

Steam

STEAM IS ONE OF THE most prominent PC gaming platforms. To release your game on Steam:

1. **Steamworks SDK**: Integrate the Steamworks SDK into

your game to access features like multiplayer, achievements, and Steam Cloud.

2. **Greenlight or Steam Direct**: Submit your game through Steam Greenlight (for community voting) or Steam Direct (a direct submission process).
3. **Store Page**: Create an enticing store page with high-quality visuals, gameplay videos, and a compelling game description.
4. **Pricing and Discounts**: Set your game's price and consider running promotional discounts during sales events.

<!—Example of a Steam store page trailer embed code—>

```
<iframe src="https://store.steampowered.com/widget/123456" width="400" height="200" frameborder="0"></iframe>
```

App Stores (Google Play, App Store)

FOR MOBILE GAME DISTRIBUTION on platforms like Google Play and the App Store:

1. **Developer Accounts**: Create developer accounts on the respective platforms.
2. **App Store Optimization (ASO)**: Optimize your app store listing with relevant keywords, screenshots, and a compelling app description.
3. **In-App Purchases**: Implement in-app purchase systems if your game uses them.
4. **User Reviews and Ratings**: Encourage players to leave reviews and ratings, as these can influence visibility in app stores.

Console Platforms (PlayStation, Xbox)

RELEASING GAMES ON console platforms involves specific requirements and processes:

1. **Developer Accounts**: Register as a developer with the respective console manufacturer (e.g., Sony or Microsoft).
2. **Development Kits**: Acquire the necessary development kits to create and test your game on the console.
3. **Certification**: Your game must pass certification by the platform holder before release.
4. **Marketing and Promotion**: Collaborate with the platform holder to promote your game through their channels.

Game Distribution Aggregators

CONSIDER USING GAME distribution aggregators like itch.io or Game Jolt, especially for indie developers. These platforms offer more flexibility and control over your game's distribution.

Monetization and Revenue Sharing

UNDERSTAND THE REVENUE sharing model of each platform. Platforms typically take a percentage of your game's sales or in-app purchases. Familiarize yourself with these fees to make informed pricing decisions.

Post-Launch Support

AFTER YOUR GAME IS live, continue to provide support, updates, and bug fixes. Engage with your player community and address their feedback promptly.

Conclusion

NAVIGATING GAME DISTRIBUTION platforms effectively is essential for reaching your target audience and maximizing the success of your game. By choosing the right platforms, meeting their requirements, optimizing your store pages, and understanding monetization models, you can increase your game's visibility and enhance its chances of commercial success.

Section 17.5: Post-Launch Support and Updates

YOUR RESPONSIBILITIES as a game developer don't end with the game's launch; they continue through post-launch support and updates. In this section, we will explore the importance of post-launch support and strategies for keeping your game fresh and engaging for players.

Why Post-Launch Support Matters

POST-LAUNCH SUPPORT is vital for several reasons:

- **Bug Fixes**: Despite thorough testing, bugs may still exist at launch. Timely bug fixes ensure a smoother player experience.

- **Player Retention**: Continuously updating your game keeps players engaged and encourages them to return.

- **Community Engagement**: Post-launch support fosters a sense of community by showing players that you are committed to improving the game based on their feedback.

- **Monetization**: Updates can introduce new content or features, creating opportunities for monetization through DLCs, expansions, or microtransactions.

Bug Fixes and Quality Assurance

AFTER YOUR GAME'S RELEASE, prioritize identifying and fixing bugs. Implement a system for players to report issues, and provide regular updates to address them. Quality assurance is an ongoing process that ensures your game remains stable and enjoyable.

```
// Example of a bug fix in Unity

void FixedUpdate()

{

if (playerHealth <= 0)

{

// Fix the issue of negative player health

playerHealth = 0;

}

}
```

Content Updates

CONTENT UPDATES ARE an effective way to keep players engaged. Consider adding:

- **New Levels**: Expand the game world with additional levels or areas.

- **Characters and Skins**: Introduce new playable characters or cosmetic items.

- **Game Modes**: Add new game modes or challenges to provide fresh experiences.

- **Story Expansions**: Extend the game's narrative with downloadable story content.

Balancing and Tweaking

CONTINUOUSLY MONITOR gameplay data and player feedback to make balance adjustments. Address overpowered or underpowered elements to maintain fair and competitive gameplay.

—Example of balancing adjustments in a Lua script

```lua
function AdjustWeaponDamage(weapon)

if weapon.damage > 100 then

weapon.damage = 100

end

end
```

Community Feedback

ENGAGE WITH YOUR PLAYER community and actively seek their feedback. Use forums, social media, and in-game surveys to gather opinions and suggestions. Show that you value player input by implementing popular ideas and addressing concerns.

Transparency

MAINTAIN TRANSPARENCY with your community by sharing your post-launch plans and update schedules. Keep players informed about what to expect and when to expect it.

> **Player321**: When can we expect the next update?

>

> **Developer**: We're planning to release the next update in early September. It will include new levels and bug fixes. Stay tuned for more details!

Live Events

HOST LIVE EVENTS WITHIN your game, such as holiday-themed events, challenges, or in-game celebrations. These events can encourage player engagement and offer exclusive rewards.

Monetization Opportunities

EXPLORE MONETIZATION opportunities through post-launch content, such as downloadable expansions, in-game purchases, or subscription models. Ensure that monetization is balanced and fair to players.

Player Feedback Loop

ESTABLISH A FEEDBACK loop with your player community. Acknowledge and thank players for their contributions, whether it's bug reports, suggestions, or fan-created content.

Conclusion

POST-LAUNCH SUPPORT and updates are crucial for maintaining the success and longevity of your game. By addressing bugs promptly, adding new content, balancing gameplay, engaging with your community, and offering transparent communication, you can create a dynamic and thriving gaming experience that keeps players coming back for more.

Chapter 18: Advanced Scripting and Custom Tools

Section 18.1: Writing Advanced Scripts in C

In the world of game development, scripting plays a pivotal role in defining game behavior, interactions, and mechanics. In this section, we will delve into the realm of advanced scripting in C# for Unity, providing insights and techniques for creating powerful and flexible game systems.

The Power of Advanced Scripting

ADVANCED SCRIPTING enables you to go beyond the basics and create complex and dynamic game elements. Whether you're developing intricate AI behaviors, crafting interactive environments, or implementing sophisticated gameplay systems, advanced scripting skills are invaluable.

Object-Oriented Programming (OOP)

UNITY'S SCRIPTING ENVIRONMENT is built upon C#, an object-oriented programming (OOP) language. Understanding OOP principles is essential for writing advanced scripts. Key concepts include:

- **Classes and Objects**: Classes define the blueprint for objects, while objects are instances of classes.

- **Inheritance**: Inheritance allows you to create new classes based on existing ones, inheriting their properties and methods.

- **Polymorphism**: Polymorphism enables different objects to respond to the same method or function in unique ways.

```csharp
// Example of a base class and a derived class

public class Animal

{

public void Speak()

{

Debug.Log("Animal makes a sound");

}

}

public class Dog : Animal

{

public void Bark()

{

Debug.Log("Dog barks");

}

}
```

Custom Data Structures

ADVANCED SCRIPTS OFTEN require custom data structures to manage complex game data efficiently. You can create custom classes and data containers tailored to your game's needs.

```
// Example of a custom data structure

public class InventoryItem

{

public string itemName;

public int quantity;

}
```

Delegates and Events

DELEGATES AND EVENTS are essential tools for implementing callback systems and event-driven behaviors in your game. They allow you to create flexible and responsive scripts.

```
// Example of using delegates and events

public class PlayerHealth

{

public delegate void HealthChangedDelegate(int newHealth);

public event HealthChangedDelegate OnHealthChanged;

private int health;

public void TakeDamage(int damage)

{
```

```csharp
health -= damage;

OnHealthChanged?.Invoke(health);

}

}
```

Coroutine-Based Scripting

UNITY'S COROUTINE SYSTEM allows you to write scripts with asynchronous behaviors, such as animations, timed events, and state machines. Coroutines are a powerful tool for advanced scripting.

```csharp
// Example of using a coroutine for animation

private IEnumerator ShakeCamera(float duration, float intensity)

{

Vector3 originalPosition = transform.position;

float elapsedTime = 0f;

while (elapsedTime < duration)

{

transform.position = originalPosition + Random.insideUnitSphere * intensity;

elapsedTime += Time.deltaTime;

yield return null;

}

transform.position = originalPosition;
```

}

ScriptableObjects

SCRIPTABLEOBJECTS ARE asset types that allow you to store data and create custom assets within Unity's editor. They are useful for creating custom tools, game data, and editor extensions.

// Example of a ScriptableObject for storing game data

[CreateAssetMenu(fileName = "New Item", menuName = "Game/Item")]

public class ItemData : ScriptableObject

{

public string itemName;

public int itemValue;

}

Conclusion

ADVANCED SCRIPTING in C# for Unity opens up a world of possibilities for game developers. By mastering OOP principles, custom data structures, delegates and events, coroutines, and ScriptableObjects, you can create complex and interactive game systems that set your game apart and provide a rich and engaging player experience.

Section 18.2: Creating Custom Editor Tools

CUSTOM EDITOR TOOLS are an essential part of the game development process in Unity. They can streamline workflows, enhance productivity, and simplify complex tasks. In this section, we'll explore the creation of custom editor tools to enhance your Unity development experience.

Why Custom Editor Tools?

UNITY'S DEFAULT EDITOR provides a range of features, but it may not always align with your specific project requirements. Custom editor tools allow you to:

- **Automate Repetitive Tasks**: Simplify repetitive tasks, such as generating level layouts, setting up character controllers, or managing assets.

- **Visualize Data**: Create custom inspectors to visualize complex data structures or game objects in a more intuitive way.

- **Debugging and Profiling**: Develop tools for debugging and profiling to identify and resolve issues efficiently.

Unity's Custom Editors

UNITY ALLOWS YOU TO create custom editors for your scripts using C#. By inheriting from Unity's Editor class, you can define how your script's properties are displayed in the Unity Inspector.

```
using UnityEngine;

using UnityEditor;

[CustomEditor(typeof(MyScript))]
public class MyScriptEditor : Editor
{
```

```
public override void OnInspectorGUI()

{

MyScript myScript = (MyScript)target;

// Custom Inspector GUI code here

EditorGUILayout.LabelField("Custom Editor for MyScript");

myScript.myProperty = EditorGUILayout.IntField("My Property",
myScript.myProperty);

if (GUILayout.Button("Custom Button"))

{

myScript.CustomMethod();

}

}

}
```

Custom Editor Windows

IN ADDITION TO CUSTOMIZING script inspectors, Unity allows you to create entirely custom editor windows. These windows can host various tools, including level editors, asset management, and more.

```
using UnityEditor;

using UnityEngine;

public class MyCustomWindow : EditorWindow

{
```

```csharp
[MenuItem("Window/My Custom Window")]
public static void ShowWindow()
{
GetWindow<MyCustomWindow>("My Window");
}
private void OnGUI()
{
// Custom window GUI code here
GUILayout.Label("This is a custom editor window.");
if (GUILayout.Button("Click Me"))
{
// Handle button click
}
}
}
```

Editor Coroutines

YOU CAN USE COROUTINES in custom editor tools to create interactive and responsive interfaces. Editor coroutines run in the Unity Editor and can be used for tasks such as animations or procedural content generation within the editor.

```csharp
using UnityEditor;
```

```csharp
using UnityEngine;

public class MyEditorCoroutineExample : EditorWindow

{

private float progress = 0f;

[MenuItem("Window/Coroutine Example")]

public static void ShowWindow()

{

GetWindow<MyEditorCoroutineExample>("Coroutine
Example");

}

private void OnGUI()

{

if (GUILayout.Button("Start Coroutine"))

{

EditorCoroutineUtility.StartCoroutine(ProgressCoroutine(), this);

}

EditorGUI.ProgressBar(new Rect(10, 70, position.width - 20, 20),
progress, "Progress");

}

private IEnumerator ProgressCoroutine()

{
```

```
for (float i = 0; i <= 1; i += 0.01f)

{

progress = i;

yield return new WaitForSeconds(0.02f);

}

progress = 1f;

}

}
```

Asset Customization

CUSTOM EDITOR TOOLS can also be used to create custom asset inspectors and property drawers. This allows you to visualize and modify asset properties in a tailored way.

Conclusion

CUSTOM EDITOR TOOLS are a valuable addition to your Unity development toolkit. By creating custom inspectors, editor windows, and utilizing editor coroutines, you can streamline your workflow, visualize data more effectively, and enhance your game development process. These tools empower you to tackle complex tasks with ease and create a more efficient and enjoyable game development experience.

Section 18.3: Extending Unity with Plugins

UNITY'S EXTENSIBILITY allows developers to enhance the engine's capabilities by creating and integrating custom plugins. In this section, we will explore the concept of creating and utilizing plugins to extend Unity's functionality.

What Are Unity Plugins?

UNITY PLUGINS, ALSO known as native plugins, are dynamic libraries (DLLs or .so files) written in languages like C++ or C#. These libraries can be loaded into Unity to provide additional functionality or access to external systems, libraries, or hardware.

When to Use Plugins

PLUGINS ARE USEFUL in various scenarios:

- **Performance Optimization**: When you need to optimize performance-critical code, such as physics simulations or rendering algorithms, by implementing them in native code.

- **Integration with External Libraries**: To connect Unity with external libraries, APIs, or hardware devices that require low-level access.

- **Cross-Platform Development**: When you want to reuse code across different platforms, as native plugins can be platform-specific.

Creating Native Plugins

CREATING A NATIVE PLUGIN involves several steps:

1. **Create the Plugin**: Write the plugin code in a compatible language (C++ or C#) and compile it into a dynamic library (DLL or .so file).
2. **Import the Plugin**: Place the compiled library in the

appropriate folder within your Unity project.

3. **Accessing the Plugin in Unity**: Use PInvoke (for C++) or Unity's DllImport attribute (for C#) to access the functions and classes defined in your plugin.

```csharp
// Example of importing a C++ plugin function in C#

using System.Runtime.InteropServices;

public class MyScript : MonoBehaviour

{

[DllImport("MyPlugin")]

private static extern int MyPluginFunction(int param);

private void Start()

{

int result = MyPluginFunction(42);

Debug.Log("Plugin result: " + result);

}

}
```

Managed Plugins (Assembly Definition Files)

MANAGED PLUGINS ALLOW you to create reusable code libraries in C# that can be used across multiple Unity projects. By creating assembly definition files for your managed plugins, you can organize your code into separate namespaces and enforce modularity.

Unity Package Manager (UPM)

UNITY PACKAGE MANAGER (UPM) simplifies the distribution and installation of plugins within Unity. You can create custom packages to share your plugins with others, making it easier to manage dependencies and updates.

Plugin Security

WHEN USING NATIVE PLUGINS, be mindful of security concerns. Ensure that the plugins you use or develop do not pose security risks, especially if they have access to sensitive data or system functions.

Platform-Specific Plugins

KEEP IN MIND THAT NATIVE plugins are platform-specific. You may need to develop and maintain separate plugins for different target platforms (e.g., Windows, macOS, iOS, Android).

Conclusion

UNITY'S EXTENSIBILITY through plugins empowers developers to optimize performance, integrate with external libraries, and extend the engine's capabilities. Whether you are creating native plugins, managed plugins, or utilizing Unity Package Manager, understanding how to create and use plugins is a valuable skill for expanding Unity's functionality to suit your specific project needs.

Section 18.4: Automation and Workflow Enhancements

AUTOMATION AND WORKFLOW enhancements are essential aspects of game development, particularly when working on large projects with complex tasks and repetitive processes. In this section, we will explore strategies and techniques to automate tasks, improve workflow efficiency, and boost productivity in Unity.

The Need for Automation

GAME DEVELOPMENT INVOLVES various repetitive tasks, such as building asset bundles, generating player character animations, or exporting content for different platforms. Automating these processes can save time, reduce human error, and ensure consistency.

Unity Editor Scripting

UNITY OFFERS POWERFUL scripting capabilities within the editor, allowing you to create custom tools and scripts to automate tasks. You can use C# to develop editor scripts that streamline workflows.

```csharp
using UnityEditor;

using UnityEngine;

public class MyEditorScript : EditorWindow

{

[MenuItem("MyTools/Custom Task")]

public static void CustomTask()
```

```csharp
{

// Your custom task code here

Debug.Log("Custom task executed.");

}

}
```

Asset Pipelines and Build Automation

ASSET PIPELINES ARE crucial for organizing, managing, and automating asset-related tasks. Unity's Asset Post-Processing Pipeline (A2P2) and Asset Import Pipeline (AIP) allow you to create custom importers and processors to automate asset import and manipulation tasks.

```csharp
using UnityEngine;

using UnityEditor;

public class MyAssetPostProcessor : AssetPostprocessor

{

void OnPostprocessModel(GameObject model)

{

// Manipulate imported 3D models

Debug.Log("Model imported: " + model.name);

}

}
```

Version Control and Continuous Integration (CI)

IMPLEMENT VERSION CONTROL systems like Git to track changes and collaborate with team members efficiently. Integrate your project with continuous integration (CI) tools like Jenkins or Travis CI to automate builds, tests, and deployment processes.

Editor Window Customization

CUSTOMIZING UNITY'S editor windows allows you to create tailored workspaces for specific tasks. You can develop editor windows for level design, scene management, asset organization, and more.

```csharp
using UnityEditor;

using UnityEngine;

public class MyCustomEditorWindow : EditorWindow

{

[MenuItem("Window/My Custom Window")]

public static void ShowWindow()

{

GetWindow<MyCustomEditorWindow>("My Custom Window");

}

void OnGUI()

{

// Custom editor window GUI here
```

```
GUILayout.Label("Custom Editor Window Content");

}

}
```

Asset Bundles

ASSET BUNDLES ARE CRUCIAL for optimizing game performance and managing assets efficiently. You can automate the creation of asset bundles to ensure assets are correctly bundled and loaded at runtime.

Build Pipelines

UNITY'S BUILD PIPELINE system allows you to define custom build processes, automate build configurations for different platforms, and manage build targets and settings programmatically.

```csharp
using UnityEditor;

public class MyBuildScript

{

[MenuItem("Build/Build Game")]

public static void BuildGame()

{

// Define build settings and process here

BuildPipeline.BuildPlayer(

new string[] { "Assets/Scenes/Level1.unity" },

"Builds/MyGame.exe",
```

```
BuildTarget.StandaloneWindows,

BuildOptions.None

);

}

}
```

Scriptable Build Pipelines

UNITY'S SCRIPTABLE Build Pipeline (SBP) allows for more advanced automation and customization of the build process. It lets you define custom build steps, dependencies, and parallel processing.

Conclusion

AUTOMATION AND WORKFLOW enhancements are essential for efficient game development. Whether you're creating custom editor tools, optimizing asset pipelines, implementing version control and CI, or automating build processes, these strategies and techniques will help you streamline your workflow, reduce errors, and focus more on the creative aspects of game development. By embracing automation, you can enhance productivity and create high-quality games more effectively.

Section 18.5: Integrating Third-Party Services and APIs

INTEGRATING THIRD-PARTY services and APIs is a common practice in game development to enhance functionality, analytics, monetization, and user engagement. In this section, we will explore the process of integrating external services into Unity games.

Benefits of Third-Party Integration

INTEGRATING THIRD-PARTY services and APIs can provide various benefits:

- **Monetization**: Incorporate ad networks, in-app purchase systems, or affiliate programs to generate revenue from your game.

- **Analytics**: Gather valuable data on player behavior, user retention, and game performance to make informed decisions and optimize your game.

- **Social Features**: Implement social media sharing, leaderboards, and multiplayer functionalities to enhance the social aspect of your game.

- **Authentication**: Enable user account management, login, and player profiles using third-party authentication services.

- **Cloud Services**: Utilize cloud services for data storage, synchronization, and multiplayer gameplay.

Popular Third-Party Services

THERE IS A WIDE RANGE of third-party services available for game developers. Some popular categories and examples include:

- **Ad Networks**: AdMob, Unity Ads, Chartboost.

- **Analytics**: Google Analytics, Flurry, GameAnalytics.

- **Monetization**: Unity IAP, AdColony, IronSource.

- **Authentication**: Facebook Login, Google Sign-In, Apple Sign-In.

- **Cloud Services**: Amazon Web Services (AWS), Firebase, PlayFab.

Integration Process

INTEGRATING THIRD-PARTY services and APIs typically involves the following steps:

1. **Registration**: Sign up for an account with the third-party service provider and create a project or application.
2. **Access Credentials**: Obtain the necessary access credentials (e.g., API keys, client IDs) from the service provider.
3. **SDK Integration**: Import and integrate the SDK or plugin provided by the service into your Unity project. This may involve adding scripts, configuring settings, and handling callbacks.
4. **Initialization**: Initialize the service within your game, usually in a central location such as the game's main menu or initialization script.

```
// Example of initializing a third-party service in Unity

void Start()

{

ThirdPartyService.Initialize("API_KEY");

}
```

1. **API Calls**: Use the provided API methods and functions

to interact with the third-party service. This may include showing ads, tracking events, or retrieving data.

2. **Error Handling**: Implement error handling to manage situations where the service is unavailable or encounters issues.

3. **Testing**: Test the integration thoroughly to ensure that it works as expected in various scenarios.

4. **Privacy Compliance**: Be aware of privacy regulations, such as GDPR, and ensure that you handle user data and permissions appropriately.

Handling Callbacks

MANY THIRD-PARTY SERVICES utilize callbacks or event-based systems to notify your game of specific events or actions. You need to implement callback functions to respond to these events effectively.

```
// Example of handling a callback from a third-party service

ThirdPartyService.OnAdCompleted += HandleAdCompleted;

void HandleAdCompleted()

{

// Reward the player for watching the ad

player.AddCoins(10);

}
```

Documentation and Support

CONSULT THE SERVICE provider's documentation for detailed integration instructions, code samples, and troubleshooting guides.

Many providers also offer support forums or customer support channels to help with integration issues.

Conclusion

INTEGRATING THIRD-PARTY services and APIs can enhance your game's functionality, monetization, and user experience. By following the integration process, handling callbacks, and referring to documentation and support resources, you can successfully integrate external services into your Unity game and unlock a range of features to improve your game's performance and engagement.

Chapter 19: Legal and Ethical Considerations

Section 19.1: Intellectual Property Rights in Game Development

Intellectual property (IP) rights are a crucial aspect of game development, governing the legal protection and ownership of creative assets. In this section, we will delve into the realm of IP rights and their significance in the game development industry.

Understanding Intellectual Property

INTELLECTUAL PROPERTY refers to legal rights granted to creators and owners of intellectual and creative works. In game development, various types of IP are involved:

- **Copyright**: Copyright protects original creative works, such as game code, graphics, music, and storylines. It grants exclusive rights to the creator, preventing others from copying or using their work without permission.

- **Trademarks**: Trademarks protect brand names, logos, and symbols associated with a game or game studio. Trademarks distinguish one product or brand from another, preventing consumer confusion.

- **Patents**: Although less common in game development, patents can protect unique gameplay mechanics or technical innovations. Patent rights provide exclusivity for a defined period.

Copyright in Game Development

COPYRIGHT IS PARTICULARLY relevant in game development. As soon as you create an original game, it is automatically protected by copyright. This protection extends to source code, game art, music, and any other creative content.

// Example of copyright notice in source code

*/**

Copyright (c) [Year] [Your Name]

Permission is hereby granted, free of charge, to any person obtaining a copy of this software and associated documentation files (the "Software"), to deal in the Software without restriction, including without limitation the rights to use, copy, modify, merge, publish, distribute, sublicense, and/or sell copies of the Software, and to permit persons to whom the Software is furnished to do so, subject to the following conditions:

The above copyright notice and this permission notice shall be included in all copies or substantial portions of the Software.

THE SOFTWARE IS PROVIDED "AS IS," WITHOUT WARRANTY OF ANY KIND, EXPRESS OR IMPLIED, INCLUDING BUT NOT LIMITED TO THE WARRANTIES OF MERCHANTABILITY, FITNESS FOR A PARTICULAR PURPOSE AND NONINFRINGEMENT. IN NO EVENT SHALL THE AUTHORS OR COPYRIGHT HOLDERS BE LIABLE FOR ANY CLAIM, DAMAGES OR OTHER LIABILITY, WHETHER IN AN ACTION OF CONTRACT, TORT OR OTHERWISE, ARISING FROM, OUT OF OR IN CONNECTION WITH THE SOFTWARE OR THE USE OR OTHER DEALINGS IN THE SOFTWARE.

*/

Licensing and Permissions

WHEN USING ASSETS CREATED by others, including music, sound effects, or artwork, it's essential to obtain the appropriate licenses or permissions. Many assets are available under various licenses, such as Creative Commons, which have specific terms regarding usage and attribution.

Fair Use

FAIR USE IS A LEGAL doctrine that allows limited use of copyrighted material without permission from or payment to the copyright holder. However, it is a complex and context-dependent concept, and its application in game development can be challenging.

Protecting Your IP

TO PROTECT YOUR GAME'S intellectual property:

- **Register Copyright**: Consider registering your game's copyright with relevant authorities, such as the U.S. Copyright Office. Registration provides additional legal protections.

- **Use Contracts**: When collaborating with others or hiring freelancers, use contracts that clearly define ownership and licensing of intellectual property.

- **Trademark Your Brand**: If you have a unique game title or brand, consider registering it as a trademark to protect it from unauthorized use.

Conclusion

INTELLECTUAL PROPERTY rights are fundamental in game development. Understanding copyright, trademarks, patents, and licensing is crucial for protecting your creative work and respecting the IP rights of others. Complying with legal and ethical considerations ensures a fair and lawful game development process.

Section 19.2: Navigating Licensing and Copyright Issues

NAVIGATING LICENSING and copyright issues is a critical aspect of game development, ensuring that you respect the intellectual property rights of others and protect your own creative work. In this section, we will explore the complexities of licensing, copyright infringement, and how to address these challenges in game development.

Licensing Models

WHEN DEALING WITH ASSETS, including software libraries, art, music, and more, it's essential to understand the licensing models that govern their usage:

- **Open Source**: Open-source licenses grant users the right to use, modify, and distribute the source code. Examples include MIT, Apache, and GNU General Public License (GPL).

- **Proprietary**: Proprietary licenses restrict certain rights and may limit usage, modification, or distribution. These licenses often apply to commercial software and proprietary assets.

- **Creative Commons**: Creative Commons licenses offer a range of permissions, allowing creators to specify how others can use their work. Options include attribution, non-commercial use, and share-alike.

Asset Licensing

IN GAME DEVELOPMENT, you may acquire assets, such as 3D models, textures, or sound effects, from various sources. Understanding the licenses associated with these assets is crucial. Some common scenarios include:

- **Royalty-Free**: Royalty-free assets can be used without recurring payments, but you may still need to purchase the asset initially.

- **Attribution**: Some licenses require attribution, meaning you must credit the original creator when using the asset.

- **Non-Commercial Use**: Some assets are only licensed for non-commercial projects, restricting use in commercial games.

Code Licensing

WHEN USING CODE LIBRARIES, engines, or frameworks in your game development, it's vital to review their licenses. Many popular game engines, like Unity and Unreal Engine, have specific licensing terms that may affect your project's distribution and revenue sharing.

```
// Example of Unity Asset Store asset license in code

/*
```

© *[Year] [Asset Creator]*

Licensed under Unity Asset Store Terms of Service.

*/

Copyright Infringement

COPYRIGHT INFRINGEMENT occurs when you use someone else's creative work without permission or in violation of their license terms. It can lead to legal consequences, including cease-and-desist orders, fines, and lawsuits. To avoid copyright infringement:

- **Read License Terms**: Carefully read and understand the license terms associated with any assets or code you use.

- **Attribute Properly**: If required by the license, provide proper attribution to the original creators.

- **Obtain Permissions**: Seek explicit permissions or licenses for any usage that is not covered by open-source or public domain terms.

Protecting Your Work

TO PROTECT YOUR OWN game's intellectual property:

- **Register Copyright**: Consider registering your game's copyright to strengthen legal protections.

- **Use Licensing**: Clearly define how others can use your assets or code through licenses. Consider open-source licenses if applicable.

• **Monitor Usage**: Regularly check for unauthorized use of your assets or code and take appropriate action when infringement is identified.

Conclusion

LICENSING AND COPYRIGHT issues are integral aspects of game development. It's crucial to navigate these issues diligently, respecting the rights of creators, and ensuring that your own work is protected. By understanding licensing models, adhering to license terms, and taking proactive measures to address copyright concerns, you can create a legal and ethical foundation for your game development endeavors.

Section 19.3: Ethical Considerations in Game Design

ETHICAL CONSIDERATIONS in game design are essential to ensure that games are enjoyable, respectful, and responsible. In this section, we will explore various ethical aspects that game developers should keep in mind when creating games.

Player Well-being

1. **Player Safety**: Prioritize the safety and well-being of players. Implement measures to prevent harassment, bullying, and toxic behavior in multiplayer and online games.
2. **Mental Health**: Be aware of the potential impact of game mechanics on players' mental health. Avoid excessive grind, pay-to-win mechanics, or other elements that can lead to addiction or negative emotional states.
3. **Accessibility**: Design games with accessibility in mind,

making them inclusive for players with disabilities. Consider options like customizable controls, subtitles, and colorblind-friendly visuals.

Content and Themes

1. **Age-Appropriateness**: Clearly label and restrict games with mature or explicit content to ensure they are not accessible to underage players.
2. **Cultural Sensitivity**: Be culturally sensitive and avoid perpetuating stereotypes or offensive content. Consider seeking advice from experts when portraying cultures, traditions, or historical events.
3. **Representation**: Strive for diverse and inclusive representation in characters, stories, and settings. Avoid harmful stereotypes and promote positive diversity.

Monetization and Microtransactions

1. **Transparency**: Provide clear information about in-game purchases and microtransactions. Avoid manipulative tactics to encourage spending, especially among younger players.
2. **Loot Boxes**: Exercise caution with loot box mechanics, which can be perceived as a form of gambling. Some jurisdictions have regulations regarding loot boxes.
3. **Pay-to-Win**: Avoid making gameplay advantages available only through purchases, as this can create an unfair experience for players who don't spend money.

Data Privacy

1. **User Data**: Handle user data responsibly and transparently.

Clearly communicate data collection and usage practices
and comply with data protection regulations.

2. **Consent**: Obtain informed consent for data collection,
especially from minors. Ensure that players understand
what data is being collected and why.

Social Impact

1. **Impact on Society**: Consider the broader social impact of
your game. Games can influence behavior, attitudes, and
opinions, so be mindful of the messages your game
conveys.
2. **Education and Positive Influence**: Use games as a tool for
education, positive social change, and addressing real-
world issues.

Community and Moderation

1. **Community Guidelines**: Establish and enforce
community guidelines to maintain a respectful and
welcoming player community.
2. **Moderation**: Implement moderation tools to handle
inappropriate content and behavior within the game's
community.

Fairness and Balance

1. **Game Balance**: Ensure that your game is balanced and fair
to all players. Avoid favoring paying players over non-
paying ones.
2. **Cheating**: Take measures to prevent cheating and hacking,
as it can ruin the experience for legitimate players.

Ethical Design Principles

1. **Informed Choice**: Allow players to make informed choices within the game. Avoid manipulative or predatory design tactics.
2. **Respect for Playtime**: Respect players' time and commitment by providing meaningful rewards and experiences.
3. **Long-Term Engagement**: Aim for long-term player engagement without exploiting addictive behaviors.

ETHICAL CONSIDERATIONS in game design are essential to create enjoyable and responsible gaming experiences. By prioritizing player well-being, content sensitivity, responsible monetization, data privacy, positive social impact, fair play, and ethical design principles, game developers can contribute to a more ethical and enjoyable gaming ecosystem.

Section 19.4: Community Guidelines and Player Safety

COMMUNITY GUIDELINES and player safety are crucial aspects of maintaining a healthy and welcoming gaming environment. In this section, we will explore the importance of establishing clear community guidelines and implementing measures to ensure the safety and well-being of players in online games.

Setting Community Guidelines

1. **Clear Rules**: Create clear and concise community guidelines that outline expected behavior within the game's community. Include guidelines regarding respectful communication, harassment, hate speech, and cheating.

2. **Transparency**: Make the guidelines easily accessible to all players, both within the game and on external platforms if applicable (e.g., website, forums).

3. **Consistency**: Apply guidelines consistently to all players, regardless of their status or in-game achievements.

4. **Enforcement**: Implement mechanisms for enforcing community guidelines. This may include reporting systems, moderation tools, and penalties for rule violations.

5. **Appeals Process**: Provide a way for players to appeal decisions made by moderators or automated systems. Ensure transparency in the appeals process.

Promoting Player Safety

1. **User Reporting**: Allow players to report inappropriate behavior, harassment, or offensive content. Take reports seriously and investigate them promptly.

2. **Moderation Team**: Assemble a team of trained moderators to monitor in-game chat, forums, and social media channels associated with the game.

3. **Real-Name Policies**: Consider implementing real-name policies to discourage toxic behavior by linking player actions to their real identities.

4. **Age Verification**: For games with age restrictions, implement age verification mechanisms to prevent underage players from accessing inappropriate content.

Hate Speech and Harassment

1. **Zero Tolerance**: Adopt a zero-tolerance policy for hate speech, discrimination, and harassment. Make it clear that such behavior will result in severe consequences.

2. **Safe Reporting**: Ensure that reporting systems for hate

speech and harassment are straightforward and easy to use. Protect the anonymity of those making reports if requested.

3. **Educational Initiatives**: Run educational campaigns within the game community to promote tolerance, diversity, and inclusivity.

Anti-Cheating Measures

1. **Anti-Cheat Systems**: Implement robust anti-cheat systems to maintain fair gameplay. Regularly update these systems to adapt to new cheating techniques.
2. **Fair Play**: Communicate the importance of fair play to the community and encourage players to report suspected cheaters.
3. **Consequences for Cheating**: Clearly outline consequences for cheating in the community guidelines, including temporary or permanent bans.

Privacy and Data Protection

1. **Privacy Policy**: Maintain a transparent privacy policy that explains what data is collected, how it is used, and how player privacy is protected.
2. **Data Security**: Prioritize data security to prevent data breaches and protect player information.

Regular Communication

1. **Community Engagement**: Engage with the player community regularly through official channels. Address concerns, share updates, and foster a sense of community.
2. **Feedback Loops**: Use player feedback to make continuous

improvements to the game and community management.

3. **Education**: Educate players about the importance of community guidelines and safety measures through in-game messages, newsletters, and tutorials.

COMMUNITY GUIDELINES and player safety initiatives are essential for creating a positive gaming experience. By establishing clear rules, enforcing guidelines consistently, promoting player safety, addressing hate speech and harassment, implementing anti-cheating measures, ensuring privacy and data protection, and maintaining open communication, game developers can foster a welcoming and enjoyable gaming community while minimizing toxic behavior and maintaining fair play.

Section 19.5: The Importance of Inclusive Game Design

INCLUSIVE GAME DESIGN is a crucial aspect of modern game development, aiming to create games that can be enjoyed by a wide and diverse audience. In this section, we will explore why inclusive game design matters and how game developers can embrace it.

Broadening the Player Base

1. **Diverse Player Demographics**: The gaming audience is incredibly diverse in terms of age, gender, abilities, and backgrounds. Inclusive game design acknowledges this diversity and seeks to cater to a broader range of players.

2. **Expanding Accessibility**: By making games more inclusive, developers can ensure that players with disabilities can enjoy their creations. This includes providing options for different control schemes, subtitles, and colorblind-friendly visuals.

3. **Reaching New Markets**: Inclusive game design can open doors to new markets and player segments that might have been underserved in the past.

Representing Diversity

1. **Diverse Characters**: Inclusive games feature characters of various genders, ethnicities, and backgrounds, promoting representation and allowing players to see themselves in the game world.
2. **Avoiding Stereotypes**: Game developers should strive to avoid perpetuating stereotypes and biases, ensuring that characters and narratives are respectful and authentic.

Gameplay Options

1. **Customization**: Inclusive games often allow players to customize their gameplay experience. This can include difficulty settings, control options, and personalization features.
2. **Difficulty Levels**: Offering multiple difficulty levels ensures that both casual and hardcore gamers can enjoy a game at their own pace.
3. **Multiple Playstyles**: Designing games that accommodate different playstyles, such as exploration, combat, or puzzle-solving, appeals to a broader audience.

Positive Social Impact

1. **Promoting Inclusivity**: Inclusive game design can contribute to social change by promoting inclusivity, empathy, and understanding among players.
2. **Empowerment**: Games can empower players by offering

them agency and representation, helping them feel more connected to the game world.

Avoiding Exclusivity

1. **Exclusivity Limitations**: Exclusive or restrictive design choices can alienate potential players. Inclusive design aims to minimize such limitations.
2. **Fostering a Welcoming Environment**: Inclusive games often foster more welcoming communities, where players from diverse backgrounds feel valued and respected.

Legal and Ethical Considerations

1. **Legal Obligations**: In some regions, there may be legal obligations to make games accessible to individuals with disabilities.
2. **Ethical Responsibility**: Game developers have an ethical responsibility to create experiences that are respectful and considerate of all players.

The Role of Playtesting

1. **Diverse Playtesters**: Inclusive game design is enhanced by involving a diverse group of playtesters who can provide valuable feedback from various perspectives.
2. **Iterative Process**: Iterative design and continuous playtesting help identify and address accessibility and inclusivity issues throughout the development cycle.

Conclusion

INCLUSIVE GAME DESIGN is not only about reaching a wider audience but also about creating experiences that respect and celebrate the diversity of players. It involves representing diversity in characters and narratives, providing gameplay options, and fostering a welcoming environment. By embracing inclusive game design, developers can create games that are not only enjoyable but also socially responsible and respectful of all players.

Chapter 20: Continuing Your Game Development Journey

Section 20.1: Staying Current with Unity and Industry Trends

Staying current with the ever-evolving world of game development and Unity is essential for maintaining a successful career in this dynamic field. In this section, we will explore strategies for staying updated on Unity and industry trends and furthering your game development journey.

The Importance of Continuous Learning

1. **Dynamic Industry**: The game development industry is constantly changing, with new technologies, tools, and trends emerging regularly. Continuous learning is crucial to keep up with these developments.
2. **Unity Updates**: Unity, as a game engine, undergoes frequent updates and improvements. Staying informed about these updates can help you leverage new features and optimizations.

Online Resources

1. **Official Documentation**: Unity's official documentation is a valuable resource. Regularly refer to it to learn about new features and best practices.
2. **Tutorials and Courses**: There are numerous online tutorials and courses available, covering various aspects of

Unity and game development. Platforms like Udemy, Coursera, and Pluralsight offer many relevant courses.

3. **YouTube and Blogs**: Game developers and Unity experts often share their knowledge through YouTube channels, blogs, and podcasts. Subscribe to these channels and follow industry blogs to stay updated.

Forums and Communities

1. **Unity Forums**: Unity has an active community on its official forums. Engage with other developers, ask questions, and participate in discussions to learn from your peers.
2. **Reddit and Social Media**: Platforms like Reddit (r/Unity3D) and Twitter have active game development communities. Follow relevant subreddits and Twitter accounts to stay informed about trends and news.

Conferences and Events

1. **Game Development Conferences**: Attend game development conferences and events, such as GDC (Game Developers Conference) and Unite. These events provide opportunities to network and learn about industry trends.
2. **Local Meetups**: Look for local game development meetups or Unity user groups in your area. These gatherings offer a chance to connect with fellow developers and share knowledge.

Game Jams and Side Projects

1. **Game Jams**: Participate in game jams to challenge yourself and experiment with new ideas. These events can boost

your creativity and keep your skills sharp.

2. **Personal Projects**: Work on personal game projects to explore new concepts and technologies. Building games in your free time can be both educational and fulfilling.

Collaborative Learning

1. **Collaborative Projects**: Collaborate with other developers on projects. Joining a development team or contributing to open-source projects can provide valuable experience and insights.

Industry Publications

1. **Industry Magazines**: Subscribe to industry publications like Game Informer or Develop to stay informed about the latest industry news and trends.

Experimentation and Innovation

1. **Experimental Projects**: Don't be afraid to experiment with new technologies or game genres. Innovation often arises from taking risks and exploring uncharted territories.

Conclusion

CONTINUING YOUR GAME development journey requires dedication to learning, staying connected with the community, and embracing innovation. By regularly accessing online resources, engaging with forums and communities, attending conferences, and pursuing personal and collaborative projects, you can ensure that you remain up-to-date with Unity and industry trends. This commitment to growth and adaptation will contribute to your success as a game developer in an ever-evolving field.

Section 20.2: Joining Game Development Communities

JOINING GAME DEVELOPMENT communities is a valuable step in furthering your career and knowledge in the field. These communities provide a platform for learning, networking, collaboration, and staying updated with the latest industry trends. In this section, we'll explore the benefits of joining game development communities and how to get involved.

The Value of Game Development Communities

1. **Networking**: Game development communities offer opportunities to connect with fellow developers, industry professionals, and enthusiasts. Networking can lead to collaborations, job opportunities, and mentorship.

2. **Learning Opportunities**: Engaging with a community exposes you to a wide range of experiences and knowledge. You can learn from others' successes and failures, gaining insights into best practices and innovative approaches.

3. **Feedback and Support**: Communities provide a platform for seeking feedback on your projects, whether it's a game prototype, artwork, or code. Constructive criticism can help you improve your work.

4. **Collaboration**: Game development often involves multidisciplinary teams. Communities allow you to find potential collaborators with different skills and expertise.

5. **Stay Informed**: Being part of a community ensures you stay informed about industry news, emerging technologies, and the latest trends. This knowledge is valuable for your career growth.

How to Join Game Development Communities

1. **Online Forums**: Many game development communities have dedicated online forums where members discuss various topics. Examples include the Unity forums, IndieDB, and TIGSource.
2. **Social Media**: Platforms like Twitter, Reddit, and Discord host active game development communities. You can follow relevant hashtags, subreddits, or join Discord servers to engage in discussions.
3. **Game Jams**: Participating in game jams, which often have community aspects, is an excellent way to connect with like-minded developers.
4. **Local Meetups**: Check if there are game development meetups or events in your area. Local communities provide a chance to meet developers face-to-face.
5. **Online Courses**: Enroll in online courses or workshops related to game development. These courses often have a community aspect where you can interact with instructors and peers.

Active Participation

1. **Contribute Constructively**: When participating in discussions or forums, contribute constructively. Provide helpful feedback and share your knowledge to foster a positive community atmosphere.
2. **Share Your Work**: Don't hesitate to share your game projects, art, or code for feedback and discussion. Sharing your work is an excellent way to showcase your skills and get valuable insights.
3. **Attend Events**: If possible, attend game development conferences, expos, and meetups. These events offer

unparalleled networking opportunities.

4. **Mentorship and Mentorship**: Consider mentoring less experienced developers or seeking mentorship from experienced professionals within the community.

Building Your Online Presence

1. **Portfolio and Website**: Create a professional portfolio and personal website to showcase your work and provide a way for others to learn more about you.

2. **Blogging and Content Creation**: Start a game development blog, YouTube channel, or social media presence to share your experiences and insights.

Conclusion

JOINING GAME DEVELOPMENT communities is a proactive step in advancing your career and enhancing your skills as a game developer. The benefits include networking, learning opportunities, feedback, collaboration, and staying informed about industry trends. Whether you're engaging in online forums, social media, local meetups, or attending events, active participation and contribution to these communities can be a significant asset in your game development journey.

Section 20.3: Further Learning Resources and Courses

CONTINUOUS LEARNING is a fundamental aspect of a successful game development career. As the industry evolves, staying updated with the latest tools, technologies, and techniques is essential. In this section, we will explore additional learning resources and courses that can help you advance your game development skills.

Online Learning Platforms

1. **Udemy**: Udemy offers a vast library of game development courses covering various engines, programming languages, and topics. Courses are often created by industry experts.
2. **Coursera**: Coursera partners with universities and institutions to provide game development courses. These courses offer a structured curriculum and often come with certifications.
3. **edX**: Similar to Coursera, edX offers courses from universities and organizations worldwide. Game development courses cover both technical and design aspects.

Specialized Game Development Schools

1. **Game Development Institutes**: Consider enrolling in specialized game development schools or programs such as DigiPen Institute of Technology, Full Sail University, or the National Academy of Video Game Trade Reviewers (NAVGTR) Institute.

Online Game Development Communities

1. **Unity Learn**: Unity offers a wide range of tutorials, projects, and courses through Unity Learn. These resources cover everything from beginner to advanced topics.
2. **Unreal Engine Online Learning**: Unreal Engine provides free courses and tutorials for users of its engine. Topics include game design, programming, and art creation.

3. **Game Development Subreddits**: Subreddits like r/gamedev and r/learnprogramming often feature valuable resources, including courses and tutorials recommended by the community.

Game Development Books

1. **"The Art of Game Design" by Jesse Schell**: This book explores game design principles and provides a solid foundation for aspiring game designers.
2. **"Game Programming Patterns" by Robert Nystrom**: It delves into programming techniques and design patterns specifically tailored for game development.
3. **"Unity in Action" by Joe Hocking**: This book is an excellent resource for learning Unity and C# game development.

YouTube Tutorials

1. **Brackeys**: The Brackeys YouTube channel offers a wide range of Unity tutorials, including beginner-friendly content and more advanced topics.
2. **The Cherno**: Known for in-depth game development tutorials, The Cherno covers C++ and graphics programming concepts.

Online Coding Platforms

1. **Codecademy**: While not game development-specific, Codecademy offers courses on programming languages commonly used in game development, such as Python and JavaScript.
2. **HackerRank**: HackerRank provides coding challenges and

competitions, which can help you improve your problem-solving and programming skills.

Industry-Specific Courses

1. **Game Design and Development Degrees**: Many universities and colleges offer specialized degrees in game design and development. These programs cover a wide range of topics.

Game Development Conferences

1. **GDC Vault**: The Game Developers Conference (GDC) offers a vault of recorded talks and presentations from industry professionals. These sessions provide valuable insights into game development trends and best practices.
2. **Other Conferences**: Look for conferences specific to your area of interest, whether it's indie game development, virtual reality, or esports, as they often feature educational sessions.

Conclusion

THE GAME DEVELOPMENT industry is dynamic and continually evolving. To excel in this field, it's essential to embrace lifelong learning. The resources mentioned above, including online learning platforms, specialized schools, online communities, books, YouTube tutorials, coding platforms, and industry-specific courses, provide a wealth of opportunities to expand your knowledge and skills. By taking advantage of these resources, you can stay at the forefront of game development and achieve your career goals in this exciting industry.

Section 20.4: Expanding into Other Game Genres and Platforms

EXPANDING YOUR HORIZONS in game development often involves exploring different game genres and platforms. In this section, we will discuss the importance of diversifying your skill set and how you can transition into new genres and platforms.

The Value of Diversification

1. **Skill Versatility**: Learning to develop games in various genres and for different platforms enhances your skill versatility. It allows you to tackle a broader range of projects and job opportunities.
2. **Market Opportunities**: Different game genres and platforms cater to diverse audiences. Expanding your repertoire can open doors to new market opportunities and player demographics.
3. **Creative Growth**: Exploring different genres can stimulate your creativity and provide fresh perspectives on game design and storytelling.
4. **Risk Mitigation**: Diversifying your portfolio reduces the risk associated with focusing solely on one genre or platform. A diversified skill set can better withstand shifts in industry trends.

Transitioning into New Genres

1. **Research and Study**: Begin by researching the genre you want to explore. Play games within that genre to understand its mechanics, design principles, and player expectations.
2. **Analyze Successful Games**: Analyze successful games in

the chosen genre to identify what makes them appealing and why players enjoy them.

3. **Practice and Experimentation**: Start small by creating prototypes or small projects within the new genre. Experiment with mechanics and gameplay elements to gain experience.

4. **Seek Feedback**: Share your work with peers or mentors for feedback. Constructive criticism can help you refine your skills.

Platforms and Technology

1. **Platform-specific Learning**: Each platform (e.g., PC, console, mobile, VR) has its unique requirements and challenges. Invest time in learning the technical aspects and limitations of the platforms you intend to target.

2. **Adaptation**: Be prepared to adapt your development processes and design choices to suit the chosen platform. Optimization is crucial for delivering a smooth player experience.

3. **Tools and Engines**: Familiarize yourself with the game engines and tools commonly used for the target platform. Unity and Unreal Engine, for example, offer versatile options for multiple platforms.

Building a Portfolio

1. **Portfolio Projects**: Create portfolio projects that showcase your proficiency in the new genre or platform. A well-executed portfolio is your best calling card when seeking opportunities in the industry.

2. **Collaboration**: Collaborate with other developers who have expertise in the genre or platform you're targeting.

Team projects can provide valuable learning experiences.

Research the Market

1. **Market Analysis**: Research the market to understand the demand for the genre or platform you're interested in. Identify potential niches and trends.
2. **Player Feedback**: Engage with players to gather feedback on your projects and understand their preferences. Player insights can guide your development decisions.

Leveraging Existing Skills

1. **Transferable Skills**: Identify skills from your current expertise that can be applied to the new genre or platform. For example, strong coding skills are transferable across genres.
2. **UI/UX Design**: UI/UX design principles are valuable across various platforms and genres. Developing user-friendly interfaces is a skill in high demand.

Conclusion

EXPANDING INTO DIFFERENT game genres and platforms is a strategic move for game developers looking to grow their careers and adapt to industry changes. Diversification enhances your skill set, provides access to new markets, fuels creativity, and mitigates risks. Whether you're transitioning into a new genre, exploring different platforms, or a combination of both, the key is continuous learning, adaptation, and building a strong portfolio that demonstrates your proficiency in these areas.

Section 20.5: Building a Career in Game

Development

BUILDING A SUCCESSFUL career in game development requires more than technical skills—it demands strategic planning, networking, and a strong understanding of the industry. In this section, we will explore how to establish and grow your career in this competitive field.

Define Your Goals

1. **Career Objectives**: Begin by defining your career objectives. Do you want to become a game designer, programmer, artist, or work in another role? Knowing your goals will help you chart a clear path.
2. **Short-Term and Long-Term Goals**: Set both short-term and long-term goals. Short-term goals may include learning specific skills, while long-term goals could involve becoming a lead developer or starting your game studio.

Skill Development

1. **Continuous Learning**: The game development industry is ever-evolving. Commit to continuous learning and improving your skills to stay relevant.
2. **Master Your Craft**: Focus on mastering one area while developing a good understanding of related disciplines. Being exceptional at one thing can make you a valuable asset.

Building a Portfolio

1. **Quality Over Quantity**: Create a portfolio showcasing your best work. Quality matters more than quantity.

Highlight projects that align with your career goals.

2. **Variety**: Include a variety of projects in your portfolio to demonstrate your versatility. Showcase different genres, styles, or platforms you've worked on.
3. **Personal Projects**: Don't wait for professional opportunities to build your portfolio. Work on personal projects to showcase your passion and creativity.

Networking and Collaboration

1. **Networking**: Attend industry events, conferences, and local meetups to network with professionals. Establishing connections can lead to job opportunities and collaborations.
2. **Collaborate**: Collaborate with other developers on projects. Teamwork skills are highly valued in the industry.
3. **Online Presence**: Maintain an online presence through social media, a personal website, or a blog. Sharing your knowledge and work can attract potential employers or clients.

Job Search and Interviews

1. **Job Search**: Use industry-specific job boards, company websites, and networking contacts to find job openings.
2. **Tailor Your Resume**: Customize your resume and cover letter for each application, highlighting relevant skills and experiences.
3. **Interview Preparation**: Prepare for interviews by researching the company, practicing common interview questions, and showcasing your enthusiasm for the role.

Freelancing and Contracts

1. **Freelance Opportunities**: Consider freelancing or contract work to gain experience and build your portfolio. Freelancers often work on a variety of projects.
2. **Networking for Contracts**: Networking can also lead to freelance opportunities. Building a reputation in the industry can attract clients.

Starting Your Studio

1. **Entrepreneurship**: If you aspire to start your game development studio, research the business aspects, including funding, marketing, and team management.
2. **Indie Development**: Independent game development allows for creative freedom but requires a strong entrepreneurial spirit and the ability to wear multiple hats.

Industry Trends

1. **Stay Informed**: Keep an eye on industry trends, emerging technologies, and market shifts. Adapting to changing landscapes is essential for long-term success.

Persistence and Resilience

1. **Rejection and Challenges**: Be prepared for rejection and challenges. The game industry can be competitive, but persistence and resilience are key to overcoming setbacks.

Mentorship and Learning from Others

1. **Mentorship**: Seek mentorship from experienced professionals in your chosen field. Learning from their

experiences can accelerate your career growth.

Conclusion

BUILDING A CAREER IN game development is a journey that requires dedication, skill development, networking, and adaptability. Defining clear goals, building a strong portfolio, and continuously improving your skills are fundamental steps. Whether you're aiming to work for established game studios, pursue freelance opportunities, or start your studio, remember that persistence, resilience, and a passion for games are your most valuable assets in this exciting and competitive field.